8/05

D0117511

STREETWISE

GET YOUR BUSINESS ONLINE

Carnegie Public Library
202 N. Animas St.
Trinidad, CO 81082-2643

Books in the Streetwise series include:

STREETWISE

GET YOUR BUSINESS ONLINE

How to Conceptualize, Design and Build an Effective Business Web Site in Less than 30 Days

Robert T. Gorman

Carnegie Public Library
202 N. Animas St.
Trinidad, CO 81082-2643

Adams Media Corporation
Holbrook, Massachusetts

Copyright ©2000, Robert T. Gorman. All rights reserved.
This book, or parts thereof, may not be reproduced
in any form without permission from the publisher; exceptions are made
for brief excerpts used in published reviews.

Published by Adams Media Corporation
260 Center Street, Holbrook, MA 02343. U.S.A.
www.adamsmedia.com

ISBN: 1-58062-368-9

Printed in the United States of America.

J I H G F E D C B A

Library of Congress Cataloging-in-Publication data
available upon request from publisher.

This publication is designed to provide accurate and authoritative information with regard to the subject matter covered. It is sold with the understanding that the publisher is not engaged in rendering legal, accounting, or other professional advice. If legal advice or other expert assistance is required, the services of a competent professional person should be sought.
 — From a *Declaration of Principles* jointly adopted by a Committee of the American Bar Association and a Committee of Publishers and Associations

Many of the designations used by manufacturers and sellers to distinguish their products are claimed as trademarks. Where those designations appear in this book and Adams Media was aware of a trademark claim, the designations have been printed in initial capital letters.

Cover illustration by Eric Mueller.

8-20-05

This book is available at quantity discounts for bulk purchases.
For information, call 1-800-872-5627.

Visit our exciting small business Web site: www.businesstown.com

Dedication

To my sons, Ian and Ryan, who checked off the chapters one by one.

To Beth for helping me through this project with her loving encouragement.

To my mother and late father for all of their support.

Acknowledgments

Thank you to Mike Snell for making this project a reality and for helping me to solve a difficult problem. Thank you also to Jere Calmes and the rest of the hard-working staff at Adams Media for getting this work into print.

CONTENTS

PART I: DEVELOPING A PLAN TO START OR MOVE YOUR BUSINESS ONLINE

PART II: EVALUATING THE TECHNICAL CONSIDERATIONS OF GOING ONLINE

CONTENTS

PART III: PUTTING YOUR BUSINESS UP ON THE WEB FOR EVERYONE TO SEE

PART IV: MARKETING YOUR ONLINE BUSINESS WITH NEW AND TRADITIONAL ADVERTISING STRATEGIES

PART IV: MARKETING YOUR ONLINE BUSINESS WITH NEW AND TRADITIONAL ADVERTISING STRATEGIES

Introduction

> The number of users who make purchases over the Web will
> jump from 31 million in 1998 to more than 183 million in 2003.
>
> INTERNATIONAL DATA CORPORATION (IDC), *WWW.IDC.COM*

Welcome to *Get Your Business Online.* No matter whether you're an
entrepreneur or small business owner, you don't have to be told how
the Internet is changing the business world. You've heard the stories
of how small upstart businesses, like Amazon.com, have achieved
sales of over a billion dollars a year by setting up an online business.
What you probably don't know is that getting your business online is
a relatively easy process that can be achieved in a matter of weeks—
all for less than the cost of your monthly phone bill! Using prepackaged software and widely available Web hosting services, you can get
your business online right away.

This book is about doing things fast. It's about using off-the-
shelf software and commonly available services to create and market
your Web site. This book is not about raising millions of dollars from
a venture capitalist to create the next Yahoo! or Amazon.com; it's not
about buying special computer equipment and hiring outside consultants to build your Web site; and it's certainly not about programming languages with acronyms like HTML, ActiveX controls, and
JPEG files. It's about doing things yourself to take advantage of an
opportunity that you will never have again.

If you don't take the necessary steps to get your business online,
someone else will come along and start stealing your customers, just
as Amazon.com has shown the larger book retailers. At a minimum, a
competitor might uncover a whole segment of prospects that you
never even knew existed and capture them as its own customers.

The question is not whether you need to get your business
online but how fast can you do it. *Get Your Business Online* gives
you the answers.

> Getting your business
> online is a relatively easy
> process that can be achieved
> in a matter of weeks.

What's the Big Deal?

Many business owners and executives throughout the world are still asking themselves, "What's the big deal about the Internet?" They don't comprehend its importance and the opportunity it gives them to build relationships with the millions of other individuals and businesses that are now online. If you are one of those business owners or executives, then perhaps a couple of examples will help you to understand what the big deal is!

Making Sales Online

There is no doubt that the main reason why the World Wide Web has generated so much enthusiasm is the new opportunity it gives a business to make sales online. It has opened up a whole new channel of distribution (the Web) from which nearly every business can benefit. Now, instead of being limited geographically, or by normal business hours, you can sell online all the time to anyone in the world.

If you have never bought anything online, or don't know what e-commerce means, take a look at what some businesses are selling online today: You can buy pharmaceuticals from Drugstore.com; purchase toys from Etoys.com; order custom stationery from Iprint.com; choose office supplies from OfficeMax.com; get a mortgage from Quicken.com; and open a bank account with Wingspan.com.

These e-businesses provide just a sampling of what is being sold online today. If you search hard enough, you can probably buy just about anything online today that you might otherwise buy offline through traditional outlets. In fact, the Association of National Advertisers reports that in 1999, "Forty-four percent of U.S. companies are selling online; 36% more say they will do so by the end of the year."

Saving Money Online

Although many entrepreneurs approach the Internet as the next great way to make a lot of sales, the reality for most businesses is that many traditional functions can be done less expensively online. For example:

> The Web has enabled a whole new channel of distribution from which every business can benefit.

> Many traditional functions can be done less expensively online.

- You can publish your sales brochure to reduce your printing expenses.
- You can take orders online to reduce your customer service expenses.
- You can answer questions online to reduce your telephone support expenses.
- You can sell over a wide geographic area to reduce your real estate expenses.

The World Wide Web is making businesses more efficient, and partly helps to explain why there has been such an improvement in U.S. productivity over the past few years. Things that used to take a lot of time and resources, like building relationships via telephones and regular mail ("snail mail"), can now be done using a Web site and e-mail.

Getting the Most Out of This Book

This book was written for new businesses that are planning to set up shop online, and for existing offline businesses that want to find new customers online. It goes deeper than the many books that merely show you how to create a business Web page, or the others that are primarily written to help you market a Web site. It covers everything you need to get your business online, including: creating a business plan; identifying online prospects and customers; choosing the best name for your online business; designing your Web site; picking the right software and services to publish your site; and advertising to a worldwide audience.

Wherever possible, this book includes multiple references to online resources where you can go for more information. Although it is not meant as an explicit recommendation of these online resources, I have tried to stick with resources that have been around for a while and have a reputable track record. Unfortunately, even as this book goes to print, some of the online resources mentioned here undoubtedly will fold up or change their Web address (URL). Therefore, please accept my apologies in advance if you look for a Web site and find that it has moved or no longer exists.

Things that used to take a lot of time and resources, like building relationships via telephones and regular mail ("snail mail"), can now be done using a Web site and e-mail.

Every chapter in this book has a brief section on the OfficeLinks.com Web site, which I created in January, 1999, using Microsoft FrontPage and MindSpring Web hosting services. It is not the most elaborate site on the Web, but I have received enough positive comments and lucrative offers to realize that it is a respectable online business. If you have any questions regarding its content or construction, feel free to e-mail me at: RTGorman@OfficeLinks.com.

You will get the most out of this book if you think of it as the beginning of your journey, rather than a roadmap to your final destination. The Internet changes so rapidly that you need to stay abreast of the latest developments. For instance, today you have to pay for dial-up access, while tomorrow you may not. Today you can get a sophisticated e-commerce service for free, while tomorrow you might have to pay for it. Today, most people cannot take advantage of the multimedia capabilities inherent in the Web because they have slow 56K connections, while tomorrow everyone might have faster connections.

> You will get the most out of this book if you think of it as the beginning of your journey, rather than a roadmap to your final destination.

What You'll Need to Know and Have to Get Your Business Online

You don't need to know much in order to get your business online. As long as you know how to surf the World Wide Web using your mouse and Web browser, you will have little difficulty in setting up your online business. THERE IS NO PROGRAMMING REQUIRED. As you will see, most of the software tools and technologies required to build a Web site use drag-and-drop technology and are designed to make the process as easy as possible. You don't need to know HTML, JavaScript, Visual Basic, or any of those other scary computer terms in order to get your business online!

In order to use this book, you do need to be connected to the Internet via a personal computer and have a newer Web browser, like Microsoft Internet Explorer or Netscape Navigator. There is a whole chapter devoted to selecting the right computer and dial-up service (Chapter 5), but you can skip it if you already have a Pentium Class computer and an Internet connection such as America Online (AOL). A reliable Internet connection is not only essential for building your Web site but also for visiting many of the online resources that are highlighted throughout this book.

If you are planning to start an online business at home and use the family's computer or one that is shared with someone else, you should seriously consider getting a new machine just for the business. This will keep others from thinking you have become a "computer hog." Also, you will probably be able to "write off" the new computer on your Federal tax return as a business expense (just make sure to check with your accountant first).

As you get further along in this book, you will learn that you might need to get a Web hosting service and buy a software package to create your Web site, but these are not requirements. There are many free Web hosting services and software development tools available to build your online business. Your decision will ultimately come down to the amount of flexibility you require, and whether you want to have your own domain name (www.yourbiz.com).

Today, there are essentially two types of software tools, sometimes called templates, for creating an online business. There are software tools that Web hosting services provide online to their subscribers at no additional charge. In most cases, these are fill-in-the-blank forms that allow you to set up your Web site very quickly, and no additional software is required.

There are also off-the-shelf software packages, like Microsoft FrontPage, that offer a little more flexibility than the tools provided by a Web host. These packages are easy to use and include fill-in-the-blank forms or templates, so that you can get your business online quickly. If you decide to take this route, then you will have to purchase an additional software package that costs between $75 and $300.

> There are many free Web hosting services and software development tools available to build your online business.

Organization of this Book

This book is organized into four parts, each covering the different aspects of setting up an online business. Every part is further divided into chapters to make it as easy as possible to find what you're looking for. Although you will probably want to skip around some, depending on your knowledge of the World Wide Web and different Web site technologies, you should definitely develop a business plan before you begin the process of creating and marketing your online business.

Finally, I would like you to know that I tried to write this book the way I read other "how-to" books; meaning that I tend to read a chapter and then experiment with the different technologies and concepts that are described in the chapter, rather than reading the whole book and then getting to work.

In order to accomplish this, I have repeated some relevant concepts and material in different parts of the book to make the chapters more complete. For instance, Chapter 4, "Getting Your Business Online in Less Than 30 Days," should be viewed as a book within a book, or a synopsis of things that can be done to get online in less than 30 days. So if you get a feeling like "haven't I read this before" at some point, this was done intentionally to reinforce important concepts.

Developing a Plan to Start or Move Your Business Online

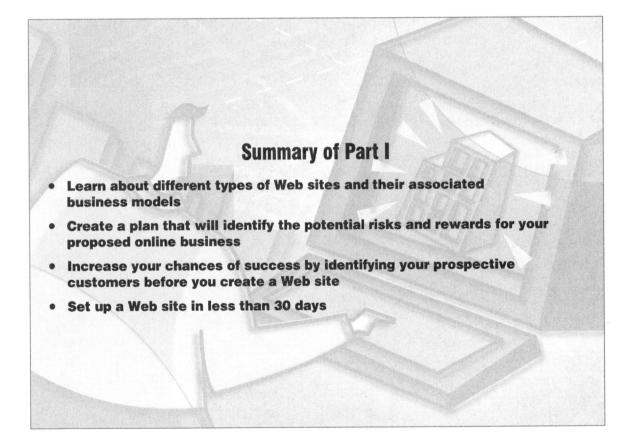

Summary of Part I

- Learn about different types of Web sites and their associated business models

- Create a plan that will identify the potential risks and rewards for your proposed online business

- Increase your chances of success by identifying your prospective customers before you create a Web site

- Set up a Web site in less than 30 days

Chapter 1

Understanding the Different Types of Online Businesses

Topics covered in this chapter

- Categorizing the different types of online businesses
- Reviewing the business models of the "four horsemen"
- Exploring the Web for other business models
- Moving your offline business online

[There are] sites that sell stuff (called "transaction sites") and information/entertainment destinations (called "content" sites) in addition to business-to-business sales and paid subscription sites.

JACLYN EASTON, *WWW.STRIKINGITRICH.COM*

Before you can begin the process of creating a Web site, you need to ask yourself, "What need is it going to fulfill?" For instance, if you are a small store owner, then you might decide that it will be more convenient for some of your customers to buy online, rather than having to travel a great distance to your store or to shop at your location during regular store hours. In this instance, you are making your store more accessible to a wider variety of customers and fulfilling their need to have an easier shopping experience.

In the past couple of years, companies doing business on the Internet have begun to separate themselves by meeting the needs of different online market segments. For instance, there are content Web sites, like Yahoo!, that provide information to a very large and general online audience, and others, like Dr. Koop, that focus on a particular *niche* of the online population. As time progresses, and additional market needs are identified, you can expect to see more and more online businesses focusing on narrower segments of the online market.

If you are new to the Internet, or haven't really decided how your online business is going to operate, then you should study what types of businesses are operating on the Internet today. As you begin this study, you will find it useful to categorize Web sites according to the functions they perform. One good classification comes from Jaclyn Easton, author of *StrikingItRich.com* (CommercenNet Press, 1999). She identifies Web sites as content sites, paid subscription sites, or transaction sites. Once you can categorize different Web sites, then you will have a better understanding of their business models and how they make money.

Another way to categorize Web sites is to look at the business models of America Online (AOL), Yahoo!, eBay, and Amazon.com. CBS MarketWatch.com (*www.cbs.marketwatch.com*) and other financial press outlets have called these online businesses the "four

---

> As time progresses, and additional market needs are identified, you can expect to see more and more online businesses focusing on narrower segments of the online market.

Web sites fall into different categories, including content sites, paid subscription sites, and transaction sites.

horsemen" of the Internet because they are leading the *charge* of businesses getting online. Each of these companies has a different business model that meets the needs of its online audience.

In addition to Jaclyn Easton's classification, or the models of the *four horsemen*, there are many other ways to categorize and evaluate online businesses. For instance, using studies from 100hot.com or Media Metrix you can look at their growth rates or the number of unique visitors they attract each month. Alternatively, you might want to check the rankings published by *Inc. Technology* magazine, which classifies the best small business Web sites. If you already have an offline business, you may want to research what businesses that started offline are now doing online. No matter what method you choose to categorize your Web site, you need to understand what type of online business you are planning to start and how it is going to make money.

Categorizing the Different Types of Online Businesses

As mentioned earlier, Jaclyn Easton in her book *StrikingItRich.com* classifies Web sites according to three major categories: content sites; paid subscription sites, and transaction (e-commerce) sites. For instance, Yahoo! (*www.yahoo.com*) is a content site; the Wall Street Journal (*www.wsj.com*) is a paid subscription site; and Amazon.com (*www.amazon.com*) is a transaction site. Still, she says most Web sites typically fall into at least two of the three categories.

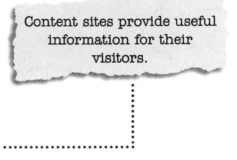

Content sites provide useful information for their visitors.

Content Sites

Content sites provide useful information for their visitors and are commonly separated into two categories: *general* and *niche* content sites. General content sites are designed to appeal to as wide an online audience as possible and provide a lot of information (content) on many subjects. Niche content sites, on the other hand, are designed for a specific group, or segment, of the online audience and limit their content to a single subject area.

General content sites are much like the large broadcast television networks, such as ABC, NBC, and CBS, because they provide a variety of content (programming) that appeals to many different viewers. For instance, large content sites like Yahoo! (*www.yahoo.com*) and Excite (*www.excite.com)* have the latest news stories, online interviews with rock bands, chat rooms, stock quotes, auctions, and other information that is of interest to the general online audience.

General content sites are much like the large broadcast television networks, such as ABC, NBC, and CBS, because they provide a variety of content (programming) that appeals to many different viewers.

GENERAL CONTENT SITES	WEB ADDRESS
Yahoo!	*www.yahoo.com*
America Online (AOL)	*www.aol.com*
Excite	*www.excite.com*
Ask Jeeves	*www.askjeeves.com*
Lycos	*www.lycos.com*

Niche content sites are more similar to some of the cable TV stations, like the History Channel or the Food Network, since they only provide useful information for a single group, or segment, of the online audience. For instance, Dr. Koop's Web site (*www.drkoop.com*) has only medical content, iVillage (*www.ivillage.com*) provides content for women, and CBS MarketWatch.com (*www.cbs.marketwatch.com*) provides up-to-date financial news.

NICHE CONTENT SITES	WEB ADDRESS	TYPE OF CONTENT
EarthWeb	*www.earthweb.com*	Information technology
CareerBuilder	*www.careerbuilder.com*	Recruiting and hiring
Autobytel.com	*www.autobytel.com*	Automobile services
Alloy	*www.alloy.com*	Interests for Generation Y
Dr. Koop	*www.drkoop.com*	Medical advice

The other main similarity that you can draw between content sites and television stations is that they are *free* to watch (understanding of course that you have to pay for cable service). In order to read and see any of the content on the sites discussed above, you don't need to pay or subscribe, you only need a Web browser and access to the Internet. Just like the television networks, these content sites make their money from advertising.

Paid Subscription Sites

Think of paid subscription sites as being analogous to magazines that you buy in the offline world. For the most part, paid subscription sites like TheStreet.com (*www.thestreet.com*) and The Wall Street Journal (*www.wsj.com*) provide narrowly focused content (news and advice, for instance) for a fee.

Paid subscription sites also share other characteristics with their offline counterparts. For instance, many offline magazines will normally offer a couple of free issues in order to get you to subscribe. In the online world, some paid subscription sites will let you access a portion of their content for free but require a payment if you want to see it all. In other instances, you get a free trial membership by using a temporary password that allows you to access the entire Web site for a set period of time. Then you either have to pay, or your password expires and you can no longer access the site.

Transaction or E-Commerce Sites

Transaction sites also have real world counterparts: mail order catalogs and retail outlets. Today, probably the most famous online transaction site is Amazon.com. Visitors to Amazon.com can browse through its merchandise-filled Web pages for books, music, electronics, and more, then make a purchase online using their credit cards. This is similar to the way you might look through a mail order catalog of merchandise, and then call an 800-number to make your purchase by credit card. The main difference is that you actually speak to a customer service representative from the mail order catalog, while at Amazon.com you fill out an order form online.

One rapidly expanding trend is for traditional retail outlets to extend their business online. This trend is commonly called "clicks and mortar," since consumers can buy online with a "click" of a

Paid subscription sites have a similar business model to magazines and newspapers.

Today, probably the most famous online transaction site is Amazon.com.

mouse, or offline at a store made out of "bricks and mortar."
In fact, it is not uncommon for many traditional retailers to employ all three channels of distribution: retail outlets, online sales, and mail order catalogs.

Breaking Down the Walls Between the Web Site Categories

As Jaclyn Easton points out, most Web sites typically fall into at least two of the three main categories. For instance, while Yahoo! is typically considered a content site, it also has online stores and auctions that are characteristic of transaction sites. However, what separates Yahoo! from Amazon.com, is that Yahoo! does not have warehouses full of merchandise like Amazon.com. Instead, Yahoo! acts as a middleman (or storefront) for its merchants.

Also, with the advent of affiliate programs, every content and paid subscription Web site has the ability to sell merchandise without having a warehouse full of inventory. In their simplest form, affiliate programs give Web site owners the ability to sell the products and services of other merchants for a commission, or flat fee, by placing links to these merchants on their own Web sites. If you would like to learn more about affiliate programs, read Chapter 16, "Making Your Web Site Pay for Itself Through Affiliate Programs."

Other Categories of Web Sites

Besides content, paid subscription, and transaction Web sites, there are many other ways to categorize Web sites. For instance, Microsoft, in its FrontPage Web site development software, allows you to choose from templates for the following types of Web sites:

- Corporate presence
- Customer support
- Discussion group
- Project site

The corporate presence Web site is very popular among many traditional offline businesses, and it usually represents their first

> Most Web sites typically fall into at least two of the three main categories.

attempt at getting their business online. For the most part, corporate presence sites display content that provides more information about a business, such as the names of the owners, directions to its different locations, phone numbers for customer service, and descriptions of its products and services.

A couple of other terms that you have probably heard to describe a Web site are *search engine* and *portal*. Yahoo!, described earlier as primarily a content site, began its early days as a directory that helped users search the Internet for a wide variety of information. Now, in addition to including a "Search box" prominently on its home page, Yahoo! also provides numerous links and services for its user population, including chat rooms, stock quotes, retailing locations, travel services, and much more. It has become a portal, or gateway, for Internet users.

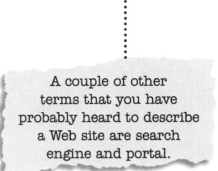

A couple of other terms that you have probably heard to describe a Web site are search engine and portal.

Reviewing the Business Models of the "Four Horsemen"

The financial press has begun referring to America Online (AOL), Yahoo!, eBay, and Amazon.com as the "four horsemen" of the Internet because they are leading the *charge* of businesses getting online. These pioneering companies of online business have found success by satisfying the needs of consumers through different business models. For instance, eBay unites buyers and sellers online through its auction model, and Amazon.com has become the largest seller online by employing a retail oriented model.

America Online (AOL), Yahoo!, eBay, and Amazon.com are the "four horsemen" of the Internet.

Think of a business model as the way a business operates to make money. For instance, Dell Computer and Compaq Computer both manufacture and sell computers but have different business models. Dell builds computers and sells them directly to customers from orders it receives over the phone or online. Compaq, on the other hand, builds computers and then sells them to customers through third-party outlets, such as distributors and retail stores. The difference in these business models—selling direct or through a third party—has led to the recent success of Dell Computer and disappointment at Compaq.

By studying the business models of the "four horsemen," you will learn what works today in the online world and be able to design your own business model accordingly. Although it is unlikely that you will be able to duplicate the success of these "four horsemen" by simply copying their current business models, familiarizing yourself with how they operate and make money will improve your chances for success.

> AOL generates three main types of revenues: subscription services, advertising and commerce, and enterprise solutions revenues.

America Online (AOL) *www.aol.com*

To many people, AOL *is* the Internet. However, in a filing with the Securities and Exchange Commission (SEC), AOL describes itself as "the world's leader in interactive services, Web brands, Internet technologies, and electronic commerce services." Unfortunately, this general description doesn't tell you much about its business model. It's only until you dig deeper into the same SEC filing (available at *www.biz.yahoo.com/e/l/a/aol.html*) that you begin to learn the business model of AOL and how it makes money.

According to the filing, AOL generates three main types of revenues: subscription services, advertising and commerce, and enterprise solutions revenues. Its subscription revenues are generated from customers subscribing to its AOL and CompuServe services. Advertising, commerce, and other revenues mainly include advertising and related revenues, fees associated with electronic commerce, and the sale of merchandise. Enterprise solutions revenues principally come from product licensing fees and fees from technical support, consulting, and training services."

Currently, AOL's main source of revenue is from its subscription services—its business of being an Internet service provider (ISP). This is perhaps why many people think AOL is the Internet; over 20 million people access the Internet through its subscription services. However, this portion of its business model (getting people online through their PCs and dial-up connections) separates AOL from the businesses of Yahoo!, eBay, and Amazon.com.

Yahoo! *www.yahoo.com*

Yahoo! is more like AOL than eBay or Amazon.com because it generates most of its revenue from advertising. The Yahoo! business model relies on selling advertising to other businesses that want to promote their products and services to the Yahoo! user base. In fact, it operates much like a television network, where advertisers pay to run commercials of their products and services for the network's viewers.

An SEC filing describes Yahoo! Inc. as a "global Internet media company that offers a branded network of comprehensive information, communication, and shopping services to millions of users daily. As the first online navigational guide to the World Wide Web (the 'Web'), www.yahoo.com is a leading guide in terms of traffic, advertising, household and business user reach, and is one of the most recognized brands associated with the Internet."

In most surveys Yahoo! is usually recognized as the number one site on the Internet in terms of visitors or page views. Yahoo!'s popularity can be attributed to its engaging content and ease of use. In simple terms, Yahoo! attracts a lot of "eyeballs" and can therefore charge hefty premiums for businesses that want to advertise on its site.

> The Yahoo! business model relies on selling advertising to other businesses that want to promote their products and services.

eBay *www.ebay.com*

eBay has become synonymous with online auctions. In its words, "eBay pioneered online person-to-person trading by developing a Web-based community in which buyers and sellers are brought together in an efficient and entertaining auction format to buy and sell personal items such as antiques, coins, collectibles, computers, memorabilia, stamps and toys."

In the eBay business model, revenue is generated from auction-related services. Sellers pay eBay a fee to list their products on the auction Web site, and also a percentage of any sales that are made. Since eBay does not actually sell the items that are listed (the sellers do), it does not have any of the procurement, inventory, or shipping expenses that are associated with other online auctioneers or e-commerce businesses.

You should be aware that both Yahoo! and Amazon.com now also provide online auction services. However, auctions are only a small portion of their total business models, and have yet to be as successful as eBay's primary business model.

Amazon.com *www.amazon.com*

Amazon.com became one of the "four horsemen" after being one of the first commercial ventures to successfully initiate the retail model online. Initially it was "earth's biggest bookstore," but it has broadened its offerings to now include music, auctions, toys, electronics, and more. The Amazon.com model is all about selling products over the Internet. It maintains warehouses of merchandise that its customers can buy through its Web site.

Additionally, according to an SEC filing, "Amazon.com provides a community of online shoppers an easy and safe way to purchase and sell a large selection of products through Amazon.com Auctions. Amazon.com is a proven technology leader; the Company developed electronic commerce innovations such as 1-Click ordering, personalized shopping services and easy-to-use search and browse features."

The Amazon.com model is one of the most popular ones imitated today by traditional offline retailers. These offline retailers are becoming known as "click and mortar" stores as they move their businesses online.

Exploring the Web for Other Business Models

As you begin to form a picture in your mind of what your online business is going to look like, it is important that you explore the Web for models that are similar to yours. Today there are probably many other Internet businesses and Web sites that exhibit at least some of the characteristics of your proposed online venture. Your job is to find them.

Some of the best places to begin your research include the portals Yahoo!, AltaVista, Excite, and Netscape Netcenter. Not only can you do keyword searches by product and business type at these portal sites, but they also include *hyperlinked* directories of many online

> The Amazon.com model is all about selling products over the Internet.

businesses. Let's say, for example, that you were thinking of selling a wide variety of air filters through your online business. The following are some ideas for how to locate other Web sites that sell or contain information about air filters.

- Do a keyword search on the large portals like Yahoo! (*www.yahoo.com*), AltaVista (*www.altavista.com*), Excite (*www.excite.com*), and Netcenter (*www.netcenter.com*). You should not only search for the keywords "air filters" but also for manufacturers, such as 3M, and for other keyword combinations, such as "furnace air filters" and "lawnmower air filters."
- Next, look under the directory headings on these portals to see if you can locate any other businesses or information about air filters.
- Finally, check other online directories and publications that might have more information about air filters. A good starting place is the National Directory of Magazines (*www.mediafinder.com*), which provides a catalog of over 100,000 publications.

Just a few hours of research through the portals and other online publications should give you a good idea about the types of businesses that sell air filters online. One thing that you should do right from the beginning of your search is to "mark," or record, the different domain names ("www.theirbiz.com") of the sites most applicable to your online business. You can do this by using the "Favorites" menu option with Microsoft Internet Explorer, "Bookmarks" with Netscape, or your personal directory with AOL.

> You should conduct a thorough search of the Internet to find other businesses like your proposed venture.

Finding the Most Popular Web Sites

There are many online surveys to help locate the most popular Web sites on the Internet. Sites are usually ranked according to the most page views or the most unique visitors during a specific time period, like a month or a quarter. Some good places to learn about the most popular sites are shown in the following table.

RANKING SERVICE	WEB ADDRESS	DESCRIPTION
100hot.com	*www.100hot.com*	Ranks top 100 Web sites
CyberAtlas	*www.cyberatlas.com*	Ranks top 25 and many others
Media Metrix	*www.mediametrix.com*	Ranks 500 Web sites

> After you have found Web sites that are most similar to your proposed online business, study them for their features and functionality.

After you have found Web sites that are most similar to your proposed online business, study them for their features and functionality. For example, if you are going to be selling a product online (and thus be a transaction Web site), locate and study other transaction sites to see how they operate. What are their terms and conditions? What is their return policy? What types of credit cards do they accept? Do they take phone calls? What delivery options do they offer? Do they offer any guarantees?

Inc. magazine, in its November 15, 1999, technology issue, published an article called "The Best of the Small Business Web: You don't have to be a 'dot-com' to thrive online." The article identified 20 companies (out of 400 entries) that have succeeded online and ranked them according to return on investment (ROI), utility, innovation, design, and local sites. The 20 winners are shown in the following table.

TOP SMALL ONLINE BUSINESSES	WEB ADDRESS	TYPE
Advanced Radiant Technology	*www.advancedradiant.com*	HVAC advice
ArtSource	*www.artsourceonline.com*	Art galleries
Atkinson-Baker, Inc.	*www.depo.com*	Legal services
Business Response, Inc.	*www.regcen.com*	Product recalls
Clif Bar, Inc.	*www.clifbar.com*	Food products
Compaero, Inc.	*www.compaero.com*	Electronic connectors
CRI	*www.crisj.com*	Office furniture
Daddy's Junky Music, Inc.	*www.rockauction.com*	Musical instrument auction
Ex Officio, Inc.	*www.exofficio.com*	Travel apparel
Lakeside Development Co.	*www.lakesidedevelopment.com*	Home builder
Livingston & Haven Industrial	*www.lhtech.com*	Industrial products
On Air Digital Audio	*www.onair.ca*	Audio services
Pinnacle Building Systems	*www.modguys.com*	Modular homes

TOP SMALL ONLINE BUSINESSES	WEB ADDRESS	TYPE
Pinnacle Decision Systems	*www.pinndec.com*	Employee training
Prairie Frontier	*www.prairiefrontier.com*	Flower seeds
Quality Transmission Service	*www.quality-trans.com*	Auto repair
ReloNetworks	*www.relonetworks.com*	Relocation services
Results Accountants' Systems	*www.ras-net.com*	Accounting training
US Sports Camps, Inc.	*www.ecamps.com*	Sports camps
Watermark Group, Inc.	*www.atmmagazine.com*	ATM supplies

Many of the sites on the *Inc.* technology list were started for less than $10,000, and some now have revenues in excess of $2 million a year.

Moving Your Offline Business Online

If you already own an offline business, then you should consider at least getting some of it online. As mentioned previously, there is a growing trend in the retail industry that is commonly referred to as a "clicks and mortar" strategy. Traditional offline retailers are opening online stores to reach a larger geographic region and to capture a new segment of customers. Offline retailers have been successful using the Internet to move their selling process online for many reasons, including:

- Merchandise can easily be displayed on Web pages
- Payments can be done via credit cards
- Delivery can be arranged through a variety of shipping services
- Consumers are familiar with this type of model in the form of mail-order catalogs

Although many traditional offline businesses lend themselves well to the Internet (retail stores, for example), others need a different approach to do business online. For instance, if you own a restaurant or a hair salon, making use of the Internet may not seem practical because you cannot move your "sales function" online.

> Many of the sites on the *Inc.* technology list were started for less than $10,000.

However, this does not mean that you should not be online; it only means that you cannot use the Internet to serve food or cut hair! Many functions in your offline business can be moved online to save you money or promote your business, including:

- Taking reservations
- Answering customer inquiries
- Displaying product literature or catalogs
- Maintaining customer service relationships

One of the most practical functions that any offline business can move online is customer service. If you or employees are constantly answering the phone to field questions from your prospects and customers, then you should evaluate whether some of these inquiries couldn't be handled more efficiently online. For instance, you might consider using the Internet to take reservations for your restaurant, or to display driving directions to your hair salon. This way you will save money by eliminating, or at least reducing, the amount of costly phone support needed to help your customers.

The Internet is also being used successfully to market many offline businesses. Many businesses simply publish their brochures and product descriptions online, and then handle the rest of the selling process through traditional methods. For instance, if you run a hotel or a real estate agency, you can quickly set up a Web site to promote your business. This works especially well when you get a lot of business from customers who are not familiar with your geographic area. Prospective online customers will find your business by entering the type of business they are looking for, and its associated town, in one of the large search engines, such as Yahoo! or Excite.

As you consider moving some your offline business functions online, you should be aware that building and maintaining a Web site is not a requirement. Some functions, like customer inquiries, can be handled simply through e-mail, while others, like promoting your business, may involve no more that getting listed in an online directory. Still, building a Web site of your own will give your offline business more visibility and provide you with a greater opportunity to display your product and service benefits.

> The Internet is also being used successfully to market many offline businesses.

Creating the Online Business Model for OfficeLinks.com

Q: How would you describe the business model for OfficeLinks.com?

A: OfficeLinks.com is primarily a *niche* portal, or content site, that provides information and services for small business.

Q: What do you mean by a *niche* portal?

A: By niche, I mean that I focus only on serving the needs of small businesses. All of the content on OfficeLinks.com is designed to be of value for small businesses. Also, all of the advertising that I do is geared toward the small business market.

Q: Why aren't you trying to reach a larger market?

A: The market for small business in the United States is huge and growing very fast, especially online. There is ample opportunity in this market for OfficeLinks.com.

Q: How does OfficeLinks.com make money?

A: Essentially there are two sources of revenue for the Web site. The first is from merchants that want to advertise to the small business market on OfficeLinks.com, and the second is through affiliate relationships with similar types of companies.

Q: What is an affiliate relationship?

A: Affiliate programs give me an opportunity to earn a commission every time I refer a prospect to another Web site from OfficeLinks.com. If they make a purchase on one of those other Web sites, I earn a commission.

Q: Is your business model similar to any of the "four horsemen"?

A: Yes. If you want to make a comparison to eBay, Amazon.com, Yahoo! or AOL, then you could say that my business model is most similar to Yahoo!.

Q: What are the similarities between your site and Yahoo!?

A: Well, both sites are portals, or content sites, and both generate money from advertisers.

Q: What are the differences between your site and Yahoo!?

A: The major difference, other than size, is that Yahoo! is a general purpose portal that appeals to a much larger online audience. OfficeLinks.com is a specialized site designed to appeal to a smaller segment of the online market. However, you should be aware that Yahoo! also has an entire portion of its Web site devoted to the needs of small businesses.

Q: Does your site have any offline applications?

A: Not yet. However, I am thinking about using it to promote an offline venture. For instance, I think that I will be able to create an advertising campaign online faster than I can do it offline. It only takes a couple of days to start an online banner ad campaign, whereas offline this can take a couple of months.

Online Business Model Resources

100hot.com (*www.100hot.com*)

The Hot 100, a Go2Net Web site, provides a list of the most popular, or visited, Web sites on the Internet. Additionally, you can find out the popularity of Web sites in different categories, including technology, entertainment, shopping, sports, news, gaming, lifestyles, education, and business.

CyberAtlas (*www.cyberatlas.com*)

CyberAtlas is now part of the Internet.com portal, and includes a lot of good marketing segmentation articles and data. For instance, there is *The CyberAtlas Statistics Toolbox*, which is a "resource that allows CyberAtlas visitors to easily find statistics, numbers, and tables that have run on the site."

Inc./Cisco Growing with Technology Awards (*www.inc.com/custom_publishing/cisco/*)

Inc. magazine and Cisco Systems hand out awards to small and midsize companies (less than 500 employees) that "demonstrate how innovative use of networking and the Internet can increase profits and provide the ultimate competitive edge." The above Web site provides links to all of the award-winning companies.

Media Metrix (*www.mediametrix.com*)

According to their home page, Media Metrix is "the pioneer and leader in the field of Internet and digital media measurement services." From their home page, you can access listings of the most popular Web sites on the Internet.

StrikingItRich.com (*www.strikingitrich.com*)

Although Jaclyn Easton's Web site is designed primarily to promote her book of the same name, she does include links to "Profiles of 23 Incredibly Successful Websites You've Probably Never Heard Of." If you want to learn more about different business models and smaller Web sites, definitely start here.

Yahoo! Publicly Traded Content Web Sites (*biz.yahoo.com/research/indgrp/internet_contnt.html*)

In its stock quoting section, Yahoo! provides a list of Internet content sites that you might want to review. From this URL, you can access a host of information, including the home pages of over forty publicly traded content Web sites.

Summary

In this chapter you've learned that there are many ways to categorize the different types of Web sites that can be found online today. No matter whether you are going to create a content site, a paid-subscription site, or a transaction (e-commerce) site, you must have a clear understanding of your business model and how you are going to make money.

One of the best ways to learn about successful business models is to study the "four horsemen" of the Internet: Yahoo!, AOL, Amazon.com, and eBay. Each of these has become an online leader by being first to market with products and services that appeal to a large audience. In addition to these leaders, you should also familiarize yourself with some other categories of Web sites, like those ranked by popularity according to MediaMetrix or those reviewed by *Inc.* Magazine.

For more information on this topic, visit our Web site at www.businesstown.com

Preparing a Business Plan to Get Online

Topics covered in this chapter

- Identifying the key elements of your online business plan
- Putting it all together with your business plan outline
- Setting goals and objectives for your online business
- Measuring your operational and financial results

> While every business plan is unique to the business, there are certain goals and certain content that every plan should have.
>
> BUSINESS PLANNING RESOURCE CENTER,
> *WWW.BPLANS.COM/BPLANS.HTM*

Your business plan should include goals and objectives based on your anticipated growth rate.

Starting a business without a plan is like taking a road trip without a map! Creating a plan for your online business is particularly important because you will be dealing not only with traditional aspects of a business, like marketing, finance, and management, but also many new technologies, like computers, software, Web hosting, and telecommunications. Your business plan will address how you are going to combine the traditional elements with the new technologies to create a successful online enterprise.

Whether you already have an ongoing business, or are just starting out, you need to have a plan to get your business online.

Whether you already have an ongoing business, or are just starting out, you need to have a plan to get your business online. Your plan must address how you are going to get your business online, how it is going to work once it gets there, and (most importantly) how your customers are going to benefit from your online business. While the bulk of this book is concerned with how to get your business online and how it will work once it gets online, this chapter provides solid planning advice that you will find invaluable once you get to work.

As noted earlier, every business plan should cover certain aspects of the proposed venture, including a description of the business, a marketing strategy, a financial budget, and a staffing plan. However, the format, content, and length of your plan will primarily be determined by your target audience. For instance, a business plan that you are creating just for yourself will be different from one you are creating to get a bank loan or raise venture capital. For yourself, a simple two- or three-page document covering the key aspects of the business should suffice; for banks and investors, on the other hand, your plan will have to be much more detailed and cover most of the items shown in the "SBA Elements of a Business Plan" presented in this chapter.

In the plan for your online business, you should also establish goals and objectives that can be accomplished in the next few years.

Your goals will be more general targets (for example, being the most visited Web site in your market) that are backed up with specific objectives (like getting 10,000 page views a month in the first year of operation). You should also set sales and profitability goals for your online business that will be determined by your projected growth rate and levels of funding.

Finally, once you develop your business plan and set it into motion, you will need operational and financial systems to measure your results. It is important to measure your results. Beyond using them to see where your online business is today, they will be invaluable in projecting where your business will be in the coming months and years. Additionally, if you foresee seeking outside financing someday for your online business, you will need to have financial and operational systems in place to show your investors how it is doing.

Identifying the Key Elements of Your Online Business Plan

Although some business plans are highly detailed documents that describe every aspect of a newly formed business, and others are simply brief descriptions of a proposed venture, they all must cover certain key elements of the business. According to the U.S. Small Business Administration (*www.sba.gov*), a business plan should include four distinct elements, as shown in the following description.

The amount of detail that you provide in a business plan depends in large part on its intended audience. For instance, if this is just a planning document for yourself, details can be kept to a minimum. On the other hand, if your business plan is going to be used to raise venture capital or get a business loan, you will need to more fully describe every aspect of your proposed business.

Describing Your Online Business

The description section of your plan should "paint the entire picture" of your proposed online business. It should give enough information for readers to know what your online business is and

The Business Plan— What It Includes

"What goes in a business plan? This is an excellent question. And, it is one that many new and potential small business owners should ask, but oftentimes don't ask. The body of the business plan can be divided into four distinct sections: 1) the description of the business, 2) the marketing plan, 3) the financial management plan, and 4) the management plan. Addenda to the business plan should include the executive summary, supporting documents, and financial projections."
U.S. Small Business Administration,
www.sba.gov/starting/ indexbusplans.html

The content of your business plan will be determined by your audience.

what it is going to do. Your description will be supported by the other sections of your business plan, and readers can turn to those if they want more information.

The description section of a business plan is not only important for planning purposes, but much of it can be used for your Web site. Portions of a well-written description can be cut and pasted into your "Home" and "About" pages of your Web site. The same information can be used again when you submit your site to search engines and online directories.

Some of the questions that your business description should answer include:

- What is your online business? A transaction site? Content site? Paid subscription site?
- What is the name of your online business? The domain name ("www.yourbiz.com")?
- When did you start your online business?
- What products and services are you selling online? What are their benefits?
- What is your business model? How are you going to make money?
- How fast is your online business going to grow? In revenue? In profits?
- What are your financial and operational goals and objectives?

A good starting place to learn more about writing business plan descriptions, and business plans in general, can be found online in the documents that publicly traded companies are required to file with the Securities and Exchange Commission (SEC). For instance, the following description of Zany Brainy (a toy retailer that recently announced an online presence) was included in its SEC S-1 Filing.

You can find SEC business documents for any publicly traded company at Yahoo! Finance (*www.finance.yahoo.com*), Hoover's Online (*www.hoovers.com*), or at EDGAR Online (*www.edgar-*

The description section of a business plan is not only important for planning purposes, but much of it can be used for your Web site.

online.com). To find business descriptions that are applicable to your online business, simply go to one of these sites and search for your competitors or other businesses that are in a similar industry as yours.

Marketing Your Online Business

One reason why so many online businesses are unprofitable is the enormous amount of money they spend on marketing and advertising. It is not unusual for big companies like Amazon.com to spend up to $50 to acquire a new customer for their Web site. If that customer's initial purchase is only a $15 book, you can see that the sale results in a $35 loss for the company. However, over time, as this customer returns to the Amazon.com site to buy again, the incremental advertising expense declines and profits will increase (at least that's the plan).

> It is not unusual for big companies like Amazon.com to spend up to $50 to acquire a new customer for their Web site.

Sample Business Description—from Zany Brainy

"Zany Brainy is a leading and rapidly growing specialty retailer of high quality toys, games, books and multimedia products for kids. We are a different kind of toy store with a unique product mission and a passionate commitment to our customers. We believe that learning should be fun. We sell over 15,000 products that entertain, educate and spark the imaginations of children up to 12 years of age. Zany Brainy combines this distinctive merchandise offering with superior customer service and daily in-store events to create an interactive, "kid-friendly" and exciting shopping experience for children and adults. We opened our first store in Pennsylvania in 1991 and, as of March 15, 1999, we operated 77 stores in 19 states. We opened 23 new stores last year and plan to add approximately 25 stores in 1999, two of which we have already opened, and 25 stores in 2000. Our sales grew 36.6% in 1998 to $168.5 million and we experienced comparable store sales growth of 9.1% in 1997 and 9.9% in 1998."

SEC documents in Yahoo! Finance,
www.biz.yahoo.com/e/990319/zany.html

The marketing section of your business plan must address how you are going to market your online business. Traditional marketing addresses the four "Ps" of a business: product, promotion, price, and place. Additionally, you can include detailed sales forecasts according to product and demographic statistics in this section.

The Marketing Section of a Business Plan

MARKETING VARIABLE	DESCRIPTION
Product	The most important thing you can tell your prospects about your products is their "benefits." Product benefits satisfy a user's needs by being more entertaining, less expensive, faster, or better.
Promotion	Describe how you will advertise your online business, both online and offline. Online advertising includes search engine listings, banner ads, link exchanges, and affiliate programs. Offline advertising includes business cards, and print, radio, and even television commercials.
Price	Determine how you are going to price your products and services. Are your prices going to be above, the same, or below the competition? Keep in mind that using the "lowest priced" strategy is usually an unprofitable strategy, especially on the Internet where all prices can be compared relatively easily by consumers.
Place	Since you are starting an online business, your "place" marketing variable is already predetermined. However, you might want to include your Web hosting service and e-commerce features in this section.

Make sure to identify your online target market in your business plan.

In addition to the four "Ps" of your marketing strategy outlined above, you will need to identify your online target market. This information will help you to identify your potential customer base and how fast the market for your products and services is growing. Market segmentation and target marketing are more fully explained in the next chapter.

Financing Your Online Business

The rapid expansion of the Internet has often been called a "gold rush" by the financial press. However, it's not because online businesses are making such huge profits. Rather, it's the ease with which they have been able to raise start-up funds, or seed money, for their new ventures. You don't need to look any further than the *Wall Street Journal* to read about another "dot-com" that just went public through an initial public offering (IPO) and raised millions of dollars for its investors.

All of these IPOs are backed up by a set of financial statements that include an *income statement, balance sheet,* and *statement of cash flow.* For the purposes of your online business plan, you will need to at least create a cash flow statement to estimate your sales and expenses for the next three years. Normally you will want to present this monthly for your first full year of operation, and then quarterly thereafter.

Some questions that your financial statements will help answer include the following:

- Is your online business profitable? If not, how soon is it going to be profitable?
- How fast are your online sales and profits going to grow during the next three years?
- Is your cash flow positive or negative?
- What is the book value of your online business?
- How many units do you have to sell to break-even?

On the following page you will see an example of a cash-based income statement for a small online business. Please note that the financial statements prepared by large companies, including the newly public online companies, are based on accrual accounting and could not be compared to the following cash basis statement. However, cash basis accounting will give you an excellent idea of when to expect your online business to make money, and is also required by the Internal Revenue Service (IRS) for tax purposes.

> Financial statements that you must include in your business plan are an income statement, balance sheet, and statement of cash flow.

> Cash basis accounting will give you an excellent idea of when to expect your online business to make money.

Simple Cash Flow Statement

	JAN	FEB	MAR	APR	MAY	JUN	JUL
Sales							
Advertising				495	495	495	
Affiliate programs				150	150	150	150
E-commerce sales							
Total sales	0	0	0	645	645	645	150
Costs and expenses							
Phone line charges	12	12	12	12	12	12	12
Dial-up service	22	22	22	22	22	22	22
Web hosting service		50	50	50	50	50	50
Merchant account				25	25	25	25
Bank fees				25	25	25	25
Computer	1,195						
Web design software	149						
Advertising							
Submission service	15	15	15	15	15	15	15
Banner ads			200	200	200	200	200
Press release			250			250	
Print ad campaign				179	179	179	179
Direct mailing							1,300
Office supplies	200		50		50		50
Domain registration	70						
Trademark	890						
Computer	1,195						
Web design software	149						
Total costs and expenses	3,897	99	599	528	578	778	1,878
Net profit	(3,897)	(99)	(599)	117	67	(133)	(1,728)

Simple Cash Flow Statement

Aug	Sep	Oct	Nov	Dec	Total	Year 1	Year 2	Year 3
	990	990	990	990	5,445	10,890	21,780	
150	150	150	150	150	1,350	4,050	10,125	
	975	1,170	975	1,365	4,485	6,728	33,638	
150	2,115	2,310	2,115	2,505	11,280	21,668	65,543	
12	12	12	12	12	143	143	287	
22	22	22	22	22	263	263	527	
50	50	50	50	50	549	599	599	
25	49	54	49	59	337	468	1,141	
25	25	25	25	25	225	360	360	
					1,195	0	949	
					149	0	0	
15	15	15	15	15	180	180	180	
200	200	200	200	200	2,000	4,200	6,300	
	250			250	1,000	1,800	2,700	
179	179				1,074	3,000	4,500	
	2,750		4,000		8,050	10,500	13,000	
	50		50		450	675	1,350	
					70	0	0	
					890	0	0	
					1,195	0	0	
					149	0	0	
528	3,602	378	4,423	633	17,920	22,189	31,893	
(378)	(1,487)	1,932	(2,308)	1,872	(6,640)	(522)	33,650	

If you don't feel comfortable preparing financial statements, or you just want to learn more, both the Small Business Administration (*www.sba.gov*) and Edge Online (*www.edgeonline.com*) Web sites are worth visiting for more information. Additionally, you will definitely want to review your financial management plan with an accountant before launching your online business.

> You will definitely want to review your financial management plan with an accountant before launching your online business.

Managing Your Online Business

One thing many entrepreneurs lose sight of when starting an online business and writing up a business plan is the amount of work that is actually required once the business is "live" on the Internet. Since the initial Web site creating process is relatively straightforward and can be done in a minimal amount of time, these individuals develop a "build it and they will come" mentality that is far from the reality of running an online business.

In addition to creating a Web site and publishing it on the Internet via a Web host, numerous other tasks need to be performed in order to run a successful online business. Some of the job functions that you will either need to do yourself, or find someone else to do, include:

- Getting listed in search engines
- Creating banner advertisements
- Answering e-mails
- Maintaining links to other sites
- Updating content
- Filling orders
- Producing operational reports

Although not all of these functions apply to every online business, most do, and most will require more effort over time than the initial creation process of the Web site. For instance, you'll soon learn that links on your Web site, such as those for affiliate programs, will constantly need to be changed or updated as affiliate hosts change their Web sites. In your business plan you will need to identify the number of employees you are planning to hire and their functions.

Putting It All Together with Your Business Plan Outline

The best way to create a business plan is to prepare an outline that covers the four distinct sections recommended by the Small Business Administration. Again, those are:

1. The description of your online business
2. The marketing plan
3. The financial management plan
4. The management plan

Under each of these sections, you can then begin to answer the questions that will be of most interest to your intended audience. For instance, if you are writing a plan to get a bank loan, bankers will want to know how you are planning to secure the loan (what you are going to use for collateral), and when the funds will be repaid. Venture capitalists, on the other hand, are more interested in how and when you expect your business to become profitable.

See page 32 for an outline of a business plan that you can find on the SBA Web site. In general, it displays all of the elements that you should address in your plan. If you visit this page on the SBA Web site, you can get a complete description of each of the underlying elements shown in the outline.

Keep in mind that since every business is different, every business plan will be different. For your plan you will want to address areas that specifically relate to your online business. For instance, make sure you include your domain name ("www.yourbiz.com"); a description of your Web hosting plan including monthly fees; the types of computers, equipment, and software you will use to maintain your Web site; and the online advertising services you are planning to use to promote your online business.

> Your business plan should include the four main elements recommended by the Small Business Administration: a business description, marketing plan, financial management plan, and management plan.

> Keep in mind that since every business is different, every business plan will be different.

Elements of a Business Plan

1. Cover sheet
2. Statement of purpose
3. Table of contents
   - I. The Business
     - A. Description of business
     - B. Marketing
     - C. Competition
     - D. Operating procedures
     - E. Personnel
     - F. Business insurance
     - G. Financial data
   - II. Financial Data
     - A. Loan applications
     - B. Capital equipment and supply list
     - C. Balance sheet
     - D. Break-even analysis
     - E. Pro forma income projections (profit & loss statements)
       1. Three-year summary
       2. Detail by month, first year
       3. Detail by quarters, second and third years
       4. Assumptions upon which projections were based
     - F. Pro forma cash flow
   - III. Supporting Documents
     - A. Tax returns of principal owner(s) for last three years
     - B. Personal financial statement (all banks have these forms)
     - C. For franchises, a copy of franchise contract and all supporting documents provided by the franchiser
     - D. Copy of proposed lease or purchase agreement for building space
     - E. Copy of licenses and other legal documents
     - F. Copy of resumes of all principals
     - G. Copies of letters of intent from suppliers, etc.

U.S. Small Business Administration,
www.sbaonline.sba.gov/starting/businessplan.html

As the following table shows, the Web contains a wide variety of resources to help you create a business plan.

BUSINESS PLANNING RESOURCES	WEB ADDRESS
BizPlanIt.com	*www.bizplanit.com*
Bplans.com	*www.bplans.com*
Deloitte & Touche LLP	*www.dtonline.com/writing/wrcover.htm*
Edge Online Business Builders	*www.edgeonline.com*
Microsoft Small Business	*www.bcentral.com/directory/bizplan.html*

Answering Many Questions with Your Business Plan

Business plans are designed to answer lots of questions about a proposed venture. You can use the following list of questions to address almost every aspect of your online business. Feel free to add or delete some questions, so that you are only answering questions that are relevant to your online business and target audience.

Describing Your Online Business

- What is your online business? A transaction site? Content site? Paid subscription site?
- What is the name of your online business? The domain name ("www.yourbiz.com")?
- When did you start your online business?
- What is your business model? How are you going to make money?
- How fast will your online business grow? In revenue? In profits?
- What are your financial and operational goals and objectives?

Selling Your Products and Services Online

- What products and services are you going to sell online? What are their benefits?
- What makes your products better than your competitors'?

> What is your business model? How are you going to make money?

- Why would your customers rather buy from you online, than from your competitors offline?
- What do you expect your best-selling product to be?
- Are you launching a new product line or expanding an existing one?

Analyzing Your Market and Industry

- How big is the online market for your products and services?
- How big is the *offline* market for your products and services?
- How quickly is the online market for your products and services growing? Offline?
- How will technology changes impact your online business?
- Are there any barriers to entering or exiting your online industry?
- What trends are driving your online industry?

Identifying Prospects and Customers in Your Target Market

- How many prospects, or potential customers, are in your online market? In the offline market?
- What is your market share? Is it growing?
- How much do your prospects buy online? What are they buying online?
- What demographic variables can you use to segment your market?
- Are you getting a lot or repeat business from current customers?

Identifying Your Competitors

- What are the names of your direct and indirect competitors?
- How many online competitors are in your target market?
- What is the ratio of online to *offline* competitors?

What trends are driving your online industry?

- How big are your competitors? In revenue? In profitability?
- Why is your online business better than the competition?
- What are your competitive strengths? Their weaknesses?

Conducting Market Research

- What other products did your customers consider before buying yours online?
- Do your prospects have contracts with other suppliers that keep them from buying from you?
- Have you surveyed your prospects to determine what they like about your online business?
- Why did some of your prospects choose another online business to make a purchase?

Developing a Marketing Strategy

- Is your pricing above, below, or the same as your competitors?
- What benefits do your products and services offer consumers?
- Are you only going to sell online?
- What advertising services are you going to use for your online business?
- Where are you going to store your merchandise for distribution?
- How much money do you have to promote and advertise your Web site?

Managing Your Online Business

- What are the names and experience of your management team?
- Does your management team have any experience running an online business?
- Do you have all of the right management skills to run a business? An online business?
- Where are you going to get help to run your online business?
- How is your online business organized? What are the job functions?

> Why is your online business better than the competition?

Hiring Personnel to Run Your Online Business

- How many people currently work for your online business?
- How many more people will you need to hire?
- Where do you recruit your employees?
- Do you have a training program?

Financing Your Online Business

- How much money will you need to start your online business?
- When will your business be profitable?
- How quickly will your sales and profits grow over the next three years?
- What is the book value of your online business?
- Are you taking in more cash than you are spending?
- How many products do you need to sell to break even?

Every online business needs to be able to answer a detailed set of questions, such as those presented above, especially if it is looking for outside financing from bankers or venture capitalists. Many banks, and some venture capitalists, will give you a specific list of questions that must be answered before they will even consider you for a loan or an investment. Therefore it is important that you anticipate the questions and provide answers accordingly.

> You should set realistic goals and specific objectives for your online business that are based on the amount of time and resources you can devote to the effort.

Setting Goals and Objectives for Your Online Business

You should set realistic goals and specific objectives for your online business that are based on the amount of time and resources you can devote to the effort. Make these goals and objectives part of the description portion of your business plan. Normally, goals are general statements about where you would like to see your online business in a few years. Objectives, on the other hand, are specific quantifiable events that you can use to measure progress toward your goals. For instance, you might set some of the following goals for your online business:

- Our goal is to be the premier content site on the Internet.
- Our goal is to be the most profitable business on the Web.
- Our goal is to satisfy every customer that buys from us online.
- Our goal is to provide the most informative content about our industry.
- Our goal is to get more page views than any other Web site.

These goals can then be linked to specific objectives that will ultimately lead to their fulfillment. For instance, if your goal is to be the most profitable business on the Web, your first step must be to actually turn a profit. Therefore, your first objective toward achieving this goal might be for your online business to turn a profit in two years, with a return on capital of, say, 17.5 percent. Your next objective might be to triple your profits from current levels, all in an effort to reach your goal of being "the most profitable." Other types of objectives could include:

- Our objective is get our business online in six months.
- Our objective is to have 10,000 unique visitors after our first year of operation.
- Our objective is to be rated as one of the top 10 content sites in our industry.
- Our objective is to reach $2 million in online sales by the third quarter.
- Our objective is to have less that two returns per 500 online purchases.

Often, businesses will set many objectives to achieve a certain goal. For instance, if your goal is to get more page views than the competition, you could establish quantifiable objectives for your different advertising campaigns. The following three objectives could be used to meet a goal "of getting more page views than the competition."

> Often, businesses will set many objectives to achieve a certain goal.

- Hire an agency to coordinate our online and offline advertising
- Increase the click-through rate on our banner ads from 0.5 percent to 1.5 percent
- Increase our offline advertising budget by 25 percent in the fourth quarter

Early on, it was stated that not only must you establish goals and objectives but that your goals and objectives must be realistic. If your goal is to become the next Yahoo! or Amazon.com, your objectives must include raising millions of dollars to launch your online business. If you have lofty goals and objectives like this, you need to ask yourself whether they are realistic.

Measuring Your Operational and Financial Results

Once you create a business plan and set your goals and objectives, you need the capability to measure your results. Measuring your results is important because you will be able to see how your online business is progressing over time. For instance, if you want your online sales to grow 50 percent each year, you will need to know what your sales were last year, what they are today, and what they will likely be at the end of the coming year.

Results can be measured both operationally and financially. Operational results can be measured in terms of the number of customers you have; the number of click-throughs you receive; the number of page views you get; or the number of products you sell. Financial results, on the other hand, are measurements of money, and include your sales revenue, profits, assets, and liabilities.

One of the best ways to measure a Web site's operational results is by using hosting service reports. Web hosting services provide a number of reports about the number and type of visitors a Web site receives. For instance, these reports can tell you how many visitors you had during a specific time period, such as a day or month, during what hours they were visiting your site, and how they found your

> Measuring your results is important because you will be able to see how your online business is progressing over time.

Web site. By familiarizing yourself with the reports that your Web hosting service provides, you can set operational objectives such as the following:

- Our objective is to get 10,000 unique visitors per month.
- Our objective is to maintain a visitor repeat ratio of 70 percent throughout the year.
- Our objective is to get 150,000 page views per quarter.
- Our objective is to grow our "hits" by 100 percent in the next six months.

Operational results can also be measured with other statistics, such as the number of e-mails you answer every month, how many phone calls you receive during the week, or how many orders you fulfill during the quarter. No matter what operational activities you decide are important to measure, you will need a way to keep track of these activities. You can either do it yourself manually, build systems around the activities you want to track, use your Web hosting service, or try to extract some of this information out of your accounting system.

Accounting systems, such as Intuit's QuickBooks (*www.quickbooks.com*), are designed to help you keep track of your financial performance. When used properly, they allow you to see how many sales you've made, your profit levels, how much money you have in the bank, and to whom you owe money. When you create a business plan, potential investors will want to know your anticipated sales growth and profitability over the next few years. Financial objectives might include the following:

- Increase sales 50 percent each year
- Become profitable by our third year in business
- Reduce debt 10 percent each year
- Increase working capital from a ratio of 1.3 to 2.4 next year

You can also use an accounting system to measure some of your operational goals and objectives. For instance, you should be able to tell how many orders you are processing every month by

> You can also use an accounting system to measure some of your operational goals and objectives.

counting the number of invoices generated by your accounting system. Other operational results available from the typical accounting system include:

- Average selling price of your merchandise
- Number of customers you have
- Average sales per order, and per customer
- Number of items in inventory

As you begin to track your operational and financial results, try to tie the two together in a meaningful manner. For instance, there should be a correlation between the number of page views your Web site is getting and the sales you receive. The more page views you get, the more sales you should get. If you find this isn't the case, try looking at how many unique visitors come to your Web site. Your sales might be driven by a unique set of customers, rather than the total number of prospects visiting your Web site.

> As you begin to track your operational and financial results, try to tie the two together in a meaningful manner.

Online Business Planning Resources

American Express Small Business Exchange (*www.home3.americanexpress.com/smallbusiness/*)

Although the American Express Web site is designed primarily to familiarize people with its products and services, it does have a complete section on creating an effective business plan. It also includes an interactive workshop that "will teach you to create a compelling business plan through a series of exercises."

Bplans.com (*www.bplans.com*)

Bplans.com has a wide variety of business planning information on its Web site, including sample business and marketing plans. It also has *The Plan Wizard*, which allows you to "find the sample plans that are most relevant to your particular business."

EdgeOnline (*www.edgeonline.com*)

EdgeOnline is owned by the Edward Lowe Foundation, which is a nonprofit organization founded by Edward Lowe. On this site you will find Business Builders, "a series of self-paced, how-to modules, that

Developing a Business Plan for OfficeLinks.com

Q: Did you write a formal business plan for OfficeLinks.com?

A: I'm not exactly sure what you mean by formal, but I did create a business plan that included a business description, some ideas on marketing, and how I was going to pay for it.

Q: By formal, I mean did it include all of the Small Business Administration's (SBA) recommended elements of a business plan?

A: Generally it did, but I didn't write down some details like "pro forma income projections for the next three years by quarter."

Q: How come you didn't cover all of the SBA elements?

A: The business plan that I created was just for me. I used it to get my thoughts straight about what I was going to do in terms of marketing and financing. Also, I had to write a business description since I needed it for my site and for some of the search engine auto-submission services.

Q: When would you use all of the SBA elements?

A: When I go to get a loan, or search for additional financing, I'm definitely going to expand my plan and address all of the SBA's recommended elements. At that point, I'll also have a much better idea about the forward-looking projections based on my current experience.

Q: Did you set goals and objectives for your online business?

A: Absolutely. I wanted to get my business online in less than 30 days, and I wanted to get at least 5,000 hits per month.

Q: Did you achieve your goals and objectives?

A: Yes. It was pretty easy getting the Web site published in 30 days because I knew what I wanted it to look like and how it was going to operate. It took me a few months to reach my other objective of getting 5,000 hits per month.

Q: What types of systems do you use to track your results?

A: For operational results, like counting hits on my Web site, I rely on the reports that I get from my Web hosting service, the affiliate management reports, and also from the banner exchanges.

Q: What about your financial results?

A: I am just setting up Intuit's QuickBooks as my accounting system. This will be a big help in keeping track of my finances, and it will also help me with taxes at the end of the year. Also, I will be able to use its reporting capabilities when I am finally ready to get additional financing for the business.

walk you through the procedures of growing a business in key areas such as finance, marketing and sales, and leadership and management."

Garage.com (*www.garage.com*)

Garage.com describes itself as a select list of the individuals ("angels"), venture capital firms, and corporate investors who can view and may invest in investment opportunities posted on their site. Here you get help on creating a business plan and attempt to get financing from Garage.com's subscribers.

Intuit QuickBooks (*www.intuit.com*)

Intuit is the publisher of the highly popular QuickBooks accounting software. On its Web site, not only can you learn more about the product but it also has a complete small business section that includes a business plan template.

U.S. Small Business Administration (*www.sba.gov*)

The Small Business Administration (SBA) Web site contains a lot of useful general purpose business planning information for small businesses. Topics include starting, financing, and expanding a business. Additionally, the site provides a business plan outline and a complete workbook that shows how to apply for SBA-backed loans.

Summary

The most important thing you should have learned in this chapter is to create a business plan before you put your business online. A good plan will help you to identify the resources required to set up your online business, to forecast your sales and associated expenses, and to address your specific goals and objectives.

If you've never created a business plan, you can find plenty of advice online at Web sites like the U.S. Small Business Administration and the Edgar Lowe Foundation. Remember that your business plan should be written with your intended audience in mind. A plan that is just for you can be relatively simple and just cover the bare essentials, while a plan for a bank or an outside investor will have to be considerably more detailed.

For more information on this topic, visit our Web site at www.businesstown.com

Chapter 3

Identifying Your Target Market and Growth Opportunity

Topics Covered in this Chapter

- **Defining your online market and growth opportunity**
- **Understanding market segmentation variables**
- **Differentiating between online and offline customers**
- **Segmenting your online market to find ideal buyers**

Most marketers know that 20 percent of buyers consume 80 percent of product volume. If you could identify that key 20 percent and find others like them, you could sell much more product with much less effort.

BUSINESS OWNER'S TOOLKIT, *WWW.TOOLKIT.CCH.COM*

Don't design your Web site for everyone; design it only for your target audience.

There is a famous story, often taught in business schools, about how Ford Motor Company developed an automobile that was designed to meet the needs of all consumers. Through extensive market research, Ford asked everyone what they wanted in a car, and then proceeded to design the car around all of these different requirements. The result was the Edsel, one of the biggest automobile disasters of the twentieth century. Your lesson from Ford's mistake is not to create a Web site that meets the needs of everyone, but rather a site that will meet the needs of your target audience. Ultimately, Ford did learn from its Edsel mistake and created one of the most successful cars in the country. By identifying a specific target group of customers and designing a car that met their needs, Ford created the Mustang.

In an ideal world your Web site would present a different appearance and provide different content based on the unique preferences and needs of your visitors. For instance, if you were selling toys online and knew that a visitor was a grandparent looking for a present for a young grandchild, your Web pages might take on a conservative appearance and emphasize safety features in the product descriptions. On the other hand, if you knew that your visitor was a young child looking for the latest video game, your Web pages might take on the appearance of a Saturday morning cartoon and emphasize all the "cool" features in the product descriptions.

Unfortunately, unless you have the technological capability to provide a dynamic Web site that changes appearance for every visitor, you will have to rely on more practical methods to market your Web site. One of the simplest approaches is to identify visitors that will benefit most from your online business, and then put all of your promotional efforts into attracting them to your Web site. In marketing, the process of identifying your ideal customers is often called segmentation.

One of the simplest approaches is to identify visitors that will benefit most from your online business, and then put all of your promotional efforts into attracting them to your Web site.

Traditional marketing strategy has used market segmentation to divide larger markets into smaller, and thus more manageable, groups of prospects and customers. Today, most of the larger markets in the United States can be broken down into specific groups of customers, each having different needs and buying characteristics. Market segments are often identified using demographic and psychographic variables, such as age, gender, race, education, occupation, income, and needs. By employing market segmentation you can target the *20 percent of buyers* mentioned above and develop profitable relationships based on satisfying their needs.

By identifying your target market you will be able to develop a sales forecast for your online business and predict its growth rate for the coming years. Although this chapter makes the assumption that you are most interested in segmenting online markets, you should also learn about the corresponding offline market. It is important to know the market size, both online and offline, for your products and services. Additionally, you should understand whether the growth in your online market is coming at the expense of the offline market, or whether both online and offline markets are growing rapidly.

Defining Your Online Market and Growth Opportunity

As we've discussed, one of the most important parts of a business plan is to identify the size of your target market and how fast it is growing. You should do this not only for your online market but for your offline market as well. This will give you a good idea of the total market for your products and services, and you can use this information to prepare a sales forecast.

Begin by trying to determine the number of potential customers for your proposed online business, and how much you expect them to buy during the next three years. For example, if you were going to sell life insurance online, you would need to research some of the following questions in order to determine the number of potential online customers.

- What age group typically buys life insurance?
- Do life insurance buyers differ by race? By occupation?

> By identifying your target market you will be able to develop a sales forecast for your online business and predict its growth rate for the coming years.

> One of the most important parts of your business plan is to identify the size of your target market and how fast it is growing.

- Does annual income influence the purchase of life insurance?
- What percentage of men and women buy life insurance?
- Do people with children buy more life insurance than those without?

You should note that these questions are not specific to online customers. However, unless you have specific information about online customers, begin with data from the offline world. Once you can identify the buyers of life insurance, try to estimate how many potential customers are online today. For instance, as of this writing, there are about 25.2 million Americans online between the ages of 35 and 54 (a good target group for life insurance). If you know that 38 percent of this age group normally buys life insurance, then you can estimated that the total online market for life insurance is 9.6 million customers (25.2 million x 0.38).

> In addition to estimating the total number of online customers, you will need an estimate for potential online sales.

In addition to estimating the total number of online customers, you will need an estimate for potential online sales. This can be as simple as multiplying the total number of customers by the average annual spending per customer. Using the life insurance example, if the average insurance premium is $100 each year, you could estimate the annual sales amount to be $960 million (9.6 million x $100).

Finally, you will need to estimate the annual growth rate for your target market. For instance, suppose that the number of Internet users is growing 50 percent each year. From the previous example, you could then estimate that this market would be $1.44 billion next year ($960 million x 1.5) and $2.15 billion the next year ($1.44 billion x 1.5). A summary of the insurance example is presented below:

	1999	2000	2001
U.S. Internet users (35 to 54 years)	25.2 million	37.8 million	56.7 million
Percent who buy insurance	38%	38%	38%
Internet insurance customers	9.6 million	14.4 million	21.5 million
Average insurance premium	$100	$100	$100
Total online insurance market	$960 million	$1.44 billion	$2.15 billion

The best way to define your target market is to use segmentation. For instance, in the insurance example above, the market for potential purchasers of online insurance was segmented by customer age (U.S. Internet users between the ages of 35 and 54). Age is a popular demographic for segmenting markets.

As you will learn in the following sections, you can also segment markets, using a variety of demographic and psychographic variables.

Understanding Market Segmentation Variables

Traditional marketing strategies use market segmentation to divide larger markets into smaller, more manageable groups of prospects and customers. Today, most of the larger markets in the United States can be broken down into specific groups of customers, each having different needs and buying characteristics. For instance, the food market can be broken down into grocery stores, convenience stores, and restaurants; the computer market can be divided into mainframes, desktops, and laptops; and the clothing market can be segmented into men's, women's, and children's apparel.

Even within these subgroups of larger markets, there is still ample room for more segmentation. For example, restaurants can be broken down into formal dining establishments, pizza parlors, and fast-food joints; desktop computers can be divided into home and office applications; and the market for children's apparel can be segmented into toddler and preteen. A summary of these different market segments is presented in the following table:

> Most of the larger markets in the United States can be broken down into specific groups of customers, each having different needs and buying characteristics.

EXAMPLE MARKET	MARKET SEGMENTS	ADDITIONAL SEGMENTS
Food	Grocery stores, convenience stores, restaurants	Formal dining, fast food, pizza parlors
Computers	Mainframes, desktops, laptops	Home, office
Clothing	Men, women, children	Toddler, preteen

Segmentation is important because it gives you the ability to focus your limited resources, like advertising dollars, on a specific group of prospects and customers. By concentrating your efforts on a specific market segment, you will do a better job of meeting your customers' needs and you will also have a competitive advantage over another business that is less focused than yours. For instance, small convenience stores are able to compete with large grocery stores by providing customers the ability to buy certain products quickly. They have succeeded by capitalizing on customers who have only a limited amount of time.

When you segment a market, you divide a larger market into smaller markets using demographic and psychographic variables. For instance, if you wanted to segment the market for automobile buyers, you could use a person's age as a demographic variable. You might find that younger car buyers, say those between the ages of 25 and 30, look for different attributes in a car than older buyers. These younger buyers are probably more interested in two-door sports cars, than four-door family sedans.

By establishing that a relationship exists between a demographic variable and a product or its attributes, you can do a much more effective job of marketing. Using the car example, it could be as simple as directing younger car buyers that enter a showroom to a specific model or creating a full-blown advertising campaign that includes television commercials targeted at younger car buyers. As shown in the following table, there are many consumer demographic variables for segmenting a market.

> Segmentation is important because it gives you the ability to focus your limited resources, like advertising dollars, on a specific group of prospects and customers.

CONSUMER DEMOGRAPHIC VARIABLES	EXAMPLES
Age	Under 12 years old, 25–30, 55+, senior citizen
Gender	Male or female
Race	Hispanic, White, African-American
Education	High school, four-year college, graduate degree
Occupation	Professional, doctor, engineer, lawyer
Income	Less than $35,000/year, $75,000–$150,000, $150,000+

In addition to consumer demographics, some consumer psychographic variables can help identify your target audience. Psychographics identify groups of consumers in terms of their needs or motives, and are not usually as widely available as consumer demographic variables. For instance, using our car example, instead of just identifying buyers by age group, you might identify buyers that want to "feel younger." Obviously, an older consumer might feel younger in a "hot" two-door sports car than in a four-door family sedan. The following table shows some of the consumer psychographic variables for segmenting a target market.

> Psychographics identify groups of consumers in terms of their needs or motives.

CONSUMER PSYCHOGRAPHIC VARIABLES	EXAMPLES
Needs	People who want to look younger, feel thinner, or be prettier
Reference groups	Members of the same religion with common beliefs
Attitudes	Type-A personalities who feel superior to everyone else
Perceptions	Individuals who feel less fortunate than others

Businesses can also be segmented by many variables, such as their annual sales revenue or number of employees. As in the business-to-consumer market, business-to-business marketers use these variables to identify their most likely customers. For instance, if your business is selling medical billing software, you would want to segment the market for business software into smaller groups, like offices of doctors that do their own billing. If your business is to sell to other businesses, you will want to use one or more of the following variables to segment your market.

BUSINESS SEGMENTATION VARIABLES	EXAMPLES
Annual sales revenue	Less than $500K, $1M–$5M, $10M+
Number of employees	Under 5, 50–100, 500+
Geographic	City, State, Zip Code, Country
Type of business	Manufacturer or service
Standard Industrial Classification (SIC)	Coding system developed by U.S. government to identify majority of businesses by industry

Once you have identified your most promising prospects using market segmentation, you need the ability to target them with your advertising. In the offline world, this might including buying a mailing list where you can use these variables as selection criteria, placing an advertisement in a magazine that is read by your demographic group, or even running a commercial on a television program that is watched by your target audience.

Differentiating Between Online and Offline Customers

Modern marketing theory says that you must sell the products and services that customers want to buy, when and where they want to buy them. The "when and where" portion of this theory is one of the things that has made the Internet and e-commerce so successful. In the past, many businesses were limited to "when" they could be open and "where" they could be located. For instance, a small retail store might have had limited hours of operation, say 9:00 A.M. to 5:00 P.M., and only have been able to sell to a small percentage of the total market because of geographic limitations.

The advent of the Internet and e-commerce now gives any sized business the ability to be open 24 hours a day, 7 days a week, and the opportunity to reach almost any prospective customer in the world. That being said, keep in mind that there are still millions of consumers who only want to buy at offline retail stores during traditional business hours. Most of these consumers want the ability to "touch and feel" merchandise they are planning to purchase. Many people have little interest in buying something off the Internet in the middle of the night on the weekend.

A new and easy way to segment a market is to identify customers who buy offline, those who buy online, and those who buy through a combination of online and offline. Some markets could simply be segmented as follows:

- Buyers who make *all* of their purchases online
- Buyers who make *some* of their purchases online
- Buyers who make *none* of their purchases online

> A new and easy way to segment a market is to identify customers who buy offline, those who buy online, and those who buy through a combination of online and offline.

Most of the big consumer markets can now be segmented according to these simple criteria. For instance, you can now buy books, movies, electronics, and drugs either online through a Web site, offline through a retail outlet, or a combination of the two. In fact, if you had been one of the lucky ones to segment your market this way a few years ago, your online business might now be called Amazon.com or eBay. Both of these companies found a new segment of customers who wanted to buy online, and were among the first companies to capitalize on the opportunity.

Unfortunately, with every passing day your opportunity to use the "online" segmentation variable *alone* is diminishing. Today's trend is for most traditional offline business in the United States, and around the world, to set up shop online. As mentioned earlier, in the retail industry this is popularly called a "clicks and mortar" strategy, where consumers can buy online with a click of a mouse or offline at a store made out of "bricks and mortar." Therefore, if you currently run a traditional offline business, it's more than likely that your direct competitors, or even some completely new competitors, have already established their businesses online.

Although you have probably missed out on the "low hanging fruit" opportunities of simply opening your offline store online, there is still ample opportunity for you to create a successful online business. The key for you is to segment larger markets into smaller subgroups of prospects and customers. For instance, even though Amazon.com might sell more books than anyone else on the Web, there is still plenty of room for specialty retailers to sell books online to a more targeted online audience.

> If you want to sell products and services online, you will need to segment your market into customers who buy online.

Segmenting Your Online Market to Find Ideal Buyers

If you want to sell products and services online, you will need to segment your market into customers who buy online. Some of the questions you should research about your online market include:

- How many online buyers are there?
- How fast is this online market growing?

- What do they buy online?
- Where do they buy online today? Where will they be buying tomorrow?
- How will they benefit from your online business?

Your answers to these questions should take into account not only the online market but also address the offline market as well. For instance, if you want to sell personal computers online, your segmentation should identify the total market of personal computer buyers, and then break down that number into online and offline buyers of PCs.

As described previously, there are many demographic and psychographic variables available to segment your online market. Some variables used for consumer segmentation include age, gender, race, education, occupation, income, and needs. For business markets, you may want to consider the number of employees, sales revenue, and type of business. Some variables also are uniquely applicable to the online market, such as type of Web browser or Internet service provider.

Examples of where you can locate some of this market segmentation information appear in the following pages. Fortunately, much of this information can easily be accessed online from Web sites like eMarketer (*www.emarketer.com*), CyberAtlas (*www.cyberatlas.com*), and the Georgia Tech GVU surveys (*www.gvu.gatech.edu*).

Segmenting Your Online Market by Age

It is often useful to segment your market by age, particularly if you are selling products and services that benefit specific age groups. For instance, if you want to sell a special heart medication to the elderly, you would be interested in the number of potential online consumers that are over the age of 55. You might want to start with the following table that can be found on the eMarketer (*www.emarketer.com*) Web site.

> It is often useful to segment your market by age, particularly if you are selling products and services that benefit specific age groups.

**U.S. Internet User Population,
by Age Group, for 1999**

AGE GROUP	NUMBER OF PEOPLE	PERCENTAGE
1 to 12 years	11.7 million	14.5%
13 to 17 years	11.1 million	13.7%
18 to 34 years	23.0 million	28.5%
35 to 54 years	25.2 million	31.2%
55+ years	9.8 million	12.1%
Total	80.8 million	100.0%

Source: www.emarketer.com

From the preceding table you can see that as of 1999, there were nearly 81 million people online in the United States alone, or about 29 percent of the total population of the United States as identified by the U.S. Census Bureau (*www.census.gov*). Additionally, you can see that more than half of the online population falls between the ages of 18 and 54, or about the same percentage of the entire population within these age brackets.

eMarketer provides even more marketing information in its *eUser & Usage Report*, helping you answer questions such as:

- What are the income breakdowns for U.S. internet users?
- How many kids, teens, adults, and seniors surf the Web?
- What online activities are most popular with teens?
- How do people find sites on the Web?
- Which minorities have established a presence on the Web?
- How does African-American usage compare to other minorities?
- How many hours a week do seniors go online?

Much of the information available from eMarketer requires that you pay a fee to receive the complete research report. However, the site is definitely worth visiting to learn how some companies are segmenting the online market.

Falling Through the Net: Defining the Digital Divide

- Whites are more likely to have access to the Internet from home than Blacks or Hispanics have from any location.

- Black and Hispanic households are approximately one-third as likely to have home Internet access as households of Asian/Pacific Islander descent, and roughly two-fifths as likely as White households.

- The gaps between White and Hispanic households, and between White and Black households, are now more than six percentage points larger than they were in 1994.

Source: U.S. Department of Commerce,
www.ntia.doc.gov/ntiahome/fttn99/execsummary.html

Segmenting Your Online Market by Gender

Many online businesses have found success by catering to a specific gender. One example is iVillage (*www.ivillage.com*), which specializes in providing all types of information for women. You can find a great deal of research about women online at Web sites such as NetSmart (*www.netsmart.com*). For instance, one of the firm's reports showed the following:

What Makes Women Click?
Women are flocking to the Web in droves. Over 40 percent of online users are women—up from 25 percent in just two years. The average female user is 41 years old. Household income is $63,000. Sixty-four percent work full time; 56 percent have children. They are online six hours a week at home.

SOURCE: NETSMART,
WWW.NETSMARTAMERICA.COM/REPORT3.HTML

Another source for finding a gender breakdown of Internet usage can be found in the CyberAtlas (*www.cyberatlas.com*) *Stats Toolbox* under the heading, "Percentage of Males and Females Using the Internet." It provides a gender breakdown for many of the largest countries in the world, including the United States, Germany, Canada, and Australia.

> Some of the variables used for consumer segmentation include age, gender, race, education, occupation, income, and needs.

Segmenting Your Online Market by Race

The U.S. Department of Commerce (*www.doc.gov*) has done extensive research about online users and their respective demographic backgrounds. One online report is called "Falling Through the Net: Defining the Digital Divide," which presents many demographic statistics on online users, including race.

The U.S. Department of Commerce publishes statistics based on race and other demographics, including income level, education, gender, and age. If you are interested in learning more, go to *www.ntia.doc.gov/ntiahome/fttn99/charts.html* and click on any of the segmentation variables that are appropriate for your online business. Some of the other demographics presented on this Web site include:

- By race/origin and U.S. rural, urban, and central city areas
- At home, by race/origin and U.S. rural, urban, and central city areas
- With child at home by household type, income, and race

Segmenting Your Online Market by Education Level

Education level is an important demographic variable that is often used for market segmentation. As you can see in the following table, more than half of all Internet users in the United States have at least some college training.

Education Level of Internet Users

	FREQUENCY	PERCENT	VALID PERCENT	CUMULATIVE PERCENT
Grammar	50	1.2%	1.2%	1.2%
High School	290	6.8	6.8	8.0
Voc/Tech	133	3.1	3.1	11.1
Some College	1294	30.4	30.4	41.5
College	1,430	33.6	33.6	75.2
Master's	731	17.2	17.2	92.3
Doctoral	144	3.4	3.4	95.7
Professional	149	3.5	3.5	99.2
Other	33	0.8	0.8	100.0
Total	4,254	100.0%	100.0%	

Source: *www.gvu.gatech.edu/gvu/user_surveys/survey-1998-10/graphs/general/q46.htm*

The Graphics, Visualization, and Usability (GVU) Center surveys presented on the Georgia Tech Web site cover almost every demographic variable imaginable, including age, gender, race, location, household income, primary language, marital status, number of children in household, and disability.

> Education level is an important demographic variable that is often used for market segmentation.

Segmenting Your Online Market by Occupation

Have you seen the TV commercials that depict the head of a large corporation as being computer illiterate, or never having accessed the Internet? The World Wide Web surveys prepared by the GVU at Georgia Tech lend credence to these commercials, as shown in the following table of Internet users by profession. As you can see, only 6.8 percent of individuals that describe themselves as upper management (Mgmt) use the Internet as part of their professions. From this table, you might conclude that there are better ways to reach company presidents and other high-ranking executives than through the Internet.

Only 6.8 percent of individuals that describe themselves as upper management (Mgmt) use the Internet as part of their professions.

Internet Users by Profession

	FREQUENCY	PERCENT	VALID PERCENT	CUMULATIVE PERCENT
Upper Mgmt.	291	6.8%	6.8%	6.8%
Trained Prof.	1,212	28.5	28.5	35.3
Middle Mgmt.	467	11.0	11.0	46.3
Skilled Labor	134	3.1	3.1	49.5
Junior Mgmt.	165	3.9	3.9	53.3
Consultant	201	4.7	4.7	58.1
Administrative	189	4.4	4.4	62.5
Temporary	43	1.0	1.0	63.5
Support	317	7.5	7.5	71.0
Researcher	115	2.7	2.7	73.7
Student	402	9.4	9.4	83.1
Self-employed	423	9.9	9.9	93.1
Other	295	6.9	6.9	100.0
Total	4,254	100.0%	100.0%	

Source: *www.gvu.gatech.edu/user_surveys/survey-1998-10/graphs/general/q31.htm*

The Georgia Tech GVU WWW Surveys (*www.gvu.gatech.edu*) provide a whole series of market segments by industry and/or occupation, including primary industry, occupation, sector, professional correspondence, organization total budget, and revenues.

Segmenting Your Online Market by Income

Researchers often segment markets by income levels for an obvious reason—wealthier people have more money to spend on products and services. Therefore, instead of targeting an entire market that includes people of all income levels, you might consider advertising to just prospects in the higher income brackets.

As shown in the following table, prepared by the U.S. Department of Commerce (*www.doc.gov*), the percentage of online users increases across all races as personal income rises. For instance, only 3.8 percent of Hispanics with an income under $15,000 per year use the Internet, while 48.1 percent of Hispanics with an income over $75,000 per year use the Internet.

Percent of Internet Users by Income

	PERCENT UNDER $15,000	$15,000–34,999	$35,000–74,999	$75,000+
White non-Hispanic	8.9%	17.0%	39.0%	60.9%
Black non-Hispanic	1.9	7.9	22.2	53.7
Other non-Hispanic	16.4	24.7	39.9	64.8
Hispanic	3.8	7.6	26.8	48.1

Source: *www.ntia.doc.gov/ntiahome/fttn99/FTTN_I/Chart-I-24.html*

The preceding table is part of a larger study conducted by the U.S. Department of Commerce, called "Falling Through the Net: Defining the Digital Divide." One interesting conclusion of this study is that households with incomes of $75,000 and higher are more than *20 times* more likely to have access to the Internet than those at the lowest income levels, and more than *nine times* as likely to have a computer at home.

Small businesses are trying to get online as fast as they can.

Segmenting Your Online Business Market

Today, more than one million U.S. small businesses have their own Web site. Small businesses are trying to get online as fast as they can, as shown by some of the following statistics prepared by Wirthlin Worldwide for BellSouth.

The Wirthlin Worldwide study also concluded that small businesses were most interested in getting online to expand their geographic markets. Another good source for general business segmentation information is The Internet Economy Indicators Web site (*www.internetindicators.com*).

Segmenting the Market for OfficeLinks.com

Q: What is the market for OfficeLinks.com?

A: OfficeLinks.com provides information and services for the small business market.

Q: How do you define the small business market?

A: I like to go with the definition of any business that has less than $5 million in annual sales revenue but is usually a little bigger than someone working out of a bedroom.

Q: How fast is the small business market growing?

A: Online, the small business market is exploding. I read somewhere that a new small business Web site is going online almost every minute! Offline, I'm not sure the actual number of small businesses is growing that rapidly. What I think is happening is that small businesses are just expanding online.

Q: What variables did you use to segment the market for OfficeLinks.com?

A: I used annual sales revenue to define a small business.

Q: Did you consider using any other segmentation variables?

A: Although we could have used the number of employees and gotten a somewhat different result, I just decided to use sales. Also, at this point using the "type" of small business, like a manufacturer or service company, didn't really seem to matter. As the business grows, if I see that we are getting more customers from a particular industry, then I will definitely incorporate this information into the segmentation.

Q: Explain what you mean by "incorporate this information into the segmentation."

A: Markets change over time, and so do your customers and their underlying demographics. I try to monitor a few key variables about my customers and see if they change over time. When they do, I want to make sure that my future advertising and promotions take these changes into account.

Q: Where did you get your segment information?

A: Interestingly enough, you can find a huge amount of information online. Also, what's really neat is that a lot of this information is updated in real time.

Q: Did you analyze the offline market for OfficeLinks.com?

A: Yes. In fact some of the ideas for OfficeLinks.com came directly from traditional offline companies that are now starting to move online. However, I don't think OfficeLinks.com competes directly with the offline portions of these businesses.

Online Market Segmentation Resources

CyberAtlas (*www.cyberatlas.com*)

CyberAtlas is now part of the Internet.com portal, and includes a lot of good marketing segmentation articles and data. For instance, there is *The CyberAtlas Statistics Toolbox*, which is a "resource that allows CyberAtlas visitors to easily find statistics, numbers, and tables that have run on the site."

eMarketer (*www.emarketer.com*)

As you would expect, eMarketer is an online publication that covers topics that are of interest to marketers on the Internet, including many demographic reports on Web usage. Although many of its reports are not available in their entirety unless you pay for them, there is enough "teaser" information to make the site worth visiting.

Graphics, Visualization, & Usability (GVU) Center at Georgia Tech (*www.gvu.gatech.edu*)

According to their home page, "GVU's World Wide Web Surveys are produced periodically by the College of Computing. Though lacking the validity of a true scientifically selected random survey, the GVU survey of Web users has provided an interesting and widely respected snapshot of who's using the Internet."

ICONOCAST (*www.iconocast.com*)

ICONOCAST is written by Michael Tchong, the founder of MacWEEK and CyberAtlas. Its home page declares that it "is the definitive source for facts, figures, trends, and rumors in the Internet marketing industry." Make sure to check out "Internet at a Glance," which provides key Internet statistics on a single page.

Jupiter Communications (*www.jup.com*)

Jupiter Communications provides detailed research and analysis on the Internet and telecommunications industries. Although you have to pay for many of their reports, you can view some good samples on their Web site, like "Online Gift Buying" and "Inside the Mind of the Online Consumer."

Small Firms (under $5M annual sales) Realizing Net's Potential

- 75 percent have or will soon develop a Web site for their business
- More than 50 percent use the Internet to market their goods and services
- More than half conduct business outside of their local geographic area
- 71 percent use the Internet to communicate with clients and customers
- 77 percent use the Internet to conduct research for their business

Source: CyberAtlas/Wirthlin Worldwide, *www.cyberatlas.com*

Yahoo! Statistics and Demographics
(*www.yahoo.com/Computers_and_Internet/Internet/*
Statistics_and_Demographics/)
Under Yahoo!'s "Computers & Internet" on its home page, you can access all types of Internet statistics and demographics, including surveys and Web traffic data.

Summary

This chapter introduced you to one of the most important concepts in modern marketing—the process of segmenting larger markets into smaller, more manageable target markets. Online market segmentation gives you the ability to identify an audience that will be interested in buying the products and services you wish to promote through your Web site.

Today, markets can be segmented simply by separating online from offline buyers—online buyers prefer to buy products and services over the Internet, while offline buyers prefer to buy through traditional bricks and mortar outlets. However, as time progresses, your market segmentation will have to become more sophisticated as the "low hanging fruit" is picked by other online merchants.

For more information on this topic, visit our Web site at www.businesstown.com

Chapter 4

Getting Your Business Online in Less than 30 Days

Topics covered in this chapter

- **Putting your online business plan to work**
- **Getting connected to the Internet**
- **Publishing your online business with a Web host**
- **Marketing your online business to the world**

Build your site in just 5 minutes!

MAX PAGES, *WWW.MAXPAGES.COM*

Most children learn the story of the three little pigs at an early age. Two of the pigs are lazy and build their homes out of material that the Big Bad Wolf has no problem blowing down. The third pig is hard working and builds his house out of bricks, which gives him sufficient protection against the wind-blowing wolf. The moral of this children's story is that hard work pays off. As you begin to explore the various ways of setting up your online business, you will have plenty of opportunity to become one of the *lazy pigs*. However, once you realize that developing a quality Web site requires a lot of hard work, you will be much better prepared to survive any attacks from the Big Bad Wolf.

One of the greatest allures of the Internet for entrepreneurs is the speed at which an online business can be opened. In a matter of minutes, hours, or days, you can set up an online business for very little cost and begin marketing your products and services to the millions of other people who are already connected to the Internet. In fact, as you become more familiar with the process of establishing an online business, you will see numerous claims like the one from Max Pages, which states, "Build your site in just 5 minutes!"

Now it's time for a reality check. Yes, you can build a Web site in five minutes with Max Pages, or open an online retail store with Bigstep.com (*www.bigstep.com*) in a matter of hours, but this does not mean that you will have created anything of value for your prospective customers. Simply opening an online store, without providing your customers any benefits, means that you've simply opened an online store. Not until you figure out how your Web site will actually benefit customers can you consider it an online business.

As we've said, one of the best places to address how your online business is going to benefit customers, and actually make some money, is in your business plan. You can create a simple business plan that describes your online business, how it is going to make money, and how you plan to promote it, in a matter of days. This is time well spent, since it will make you think more about the fundamental aspects of business and not just about displaying pretty pages on the Web.

> As we've said, one of the best places to address how your online business is going to benefit customers, and actually make some money, is in your business plan.

After you have developed a well-thought-out business plan, then you can begin the process of building an online business. Many start by selecting a computer, choosing a dial-up service, and identifying any other software and peripherals they will need to get their business online. If you already have a computer and a connection to the Internet, your only concern should be whether you will need some off-the-shelf software to develop your Web site and perhaps a digital camera to take pictures of the merchandise you plan to sell online.

Once your computer equipment and connection to the Internet is in place, your next steps include selecting a Web site host, registering a domain name ("www.yourbiz.com"), and creating your Web site. These three steps are not mutually exclusive. They depend mainly on the service you are going to use to publish your Web site, and whether your site will be content oriented or e-commerce capable. It's important that you select a Web hosting service that is flexible enough to meet your needs, plus a domain name that is easy to spell and conveys the nature of your online business.

The last step, and one that is usually underestimated by most business owners, involves marketing your online business. Because the barriers to entry are so low on the Internet, you will find that you have many competitors, both large and small. In order for your online business to be successful, you will need to execute successful advertising and promotion strategies. These can include getting listed with the major search engines, starting a direct e-mail campaign, sending out a press release, running banner advertisements, and creating an affiliate program.

No matter whether you plan to get your business online in five minutes, 30 days, or six months, there are a series of steps you must take to accomplish this task. Think of this chapter as a synopsis of the rest of the book (a book that covers the most important aspects of getting your business online). It contains some of the same material and concepts that you will find elsewhere in the book in an abbreviated form.

> Once your computer equipment and connection to the Internet is in place, your next steps include selecting a Web site host, registering a domain name and creating your Web site.

Putting Your Online Business Plan to Work

In Chapter 2 we presented details for developing a business plan. To quickly review, every business plan should cover certain aspects of the proposed venture, including a description of the business, a marketing strategy, a financial budget, and a staffing plan. However, the format and content will primarily be determined by your target audience.

If you want to get your business online in less than 30 days, the amount of time that you will be able to devote to writing your online business plan will be limited. Nevertheless, a business plan is vital. Your business plan should not only describe the business, but it should address some of the advertising and promotion activities you are planning to use in order to get prospective customers to visit your online business. These might include banner advertisements, e-mail campaigns, press releases, and search engine listings.

When it comes to the finance portion of the business plan, many would-be entrepreneurs are intimidated by financial terms like balance sheet, income statement, and cash flow statement, all of which are usually required for a full-blown business plan. However, you can simplify things by estimating how much money you have in the bank, how much you are planning to spend for your online business, and how much you are planning to make. If you already have a computer, your significant expenses will be for Web hosting and advertising. At a minimum, these expenses will run you a few hundred dollars a month.

Finally, your business plan should account for who is going to build and maintain your Web site. As mentioned earlier, the amount of time you will have to maintain and advertise your Web site will be significantly greater than the time required to initially publish it. It takes time to update links, produce new content, add new products, and respond to e-mails. Your plan must address whether you are going to do this all by yourself, hire contractors, use outside services, or even take on a full-time employee or two.

Getting Connected to the Internet

Although it's getting increasingly harder to find people in the United States who aren't connected to the Internet, you might be surprised to learn that by the end of 1999, only about 30 percent of the popu-

A business plan is vital.

lation was online. If you aren't online yet, here are some of the things you will need:

- Personal computer (PC)
- Phone line
- Dial-up access to the Internet
- Web site development software
- Peripherals, such as a digital camera

For the purposes of establishing an online business, the most important tasks your personal computer (PC) will need to perform are getting connected to the Internet through a modem and having enough disk space and memory to run any Web site software development packages. The good news is, most PC packages under $1,000 provide enough features and functionality to perform these tasks. Your job, before deciding on a PC package, is to ensure that it comes equipped with an internal modem (capable of 56Kbps downloads), and that it at least meets the minimum RAM, processor speed, and hard disk space requirements recommended by the software manufacturer.

Many Internet users first go online with their existing phone line. This means that while they are online, normal phone calls either go unanswered, or must be forwarded to a voice mail system provided by the phone company. You will find that this solution is cumbersome and inconvenient for your online business. Therefore, you should plan on having at least one additional phone line installed for your online business. This way you won't miss any important phone calls while you are working with your Web site.

Today, America Online (AOL) is the company most associated with dial-up access to the Internet. AOL, or any other dial-up service, gives you the capability to access the Internet through a traditional phone line and a modem connected to your PC. Many PC packages now offer *free* Internet dial-up service and are certainly worth investigating if you do not already have access to the Internet. These dial-up services should also come equipped with Web browsing software, such as Microsoft Internet Explorer or Netscape Navigator.

> Most personal computer systems under $1,000 provide enough capability to get your business online.

> Many PC packages now offer free Internet dial-up service and are certainly worth investigating if you do not already have access to the Internet.

You do **not** need to buy Web site development software in order to get your business online. Once you have a computer system and a dial-up connection to the Internet, you can get your business online using the software tools provided by your Web hosting service, as described in the following section. However, Web site development software is strongly recommended for content sites, or sites where you want complete flexibility and control over your online business. On the other hand, if your site is going to be mainly for e-commerce, and you are willing to sacrifice some control and flexibility, try one of the e-commerce packages offered by your Web hosting service.

Most PC packages come equipped with the peripherals you will need for your online business, including a monitor, printer, keyboard, and mouse. However, if you want to display merchandise on your e-commerce site, or need to provide informative pictures for your content site, then you will need a digital camera or scanner. Digital cameras allow you to load pictures directly from the camera into your PC, while scanners load pictures using an existing photograph. Normally you can get higher quality pictures using a digital camera, but it will cost more than using a traditional camera in conjunction with a scanner.

Publishing Your Online Business with a Web Host

There are many options for getting your business online. Some of these are as simple as using the services provided by your dial-up service account, like AOL Personal Publisher, while others are as complicated as purchasing a dedicated computer system that is connected to the Internet with high speed telecommunications services. In the middle are Web hosting services that offer an affordable and easy-to-use method to get your business online.

In order to publish your Web site on the Internet with a Web host, you will need to select a Web hosting service (and corresponding hosting plan), choose a domain name ("www.yourbiz.com"), and actually create your Web site using software tools available off-the-shelf or from your Web hosting service. You should be aware that registering a domain name and choosing a Web hosting plan can usually be done online, and only takes a credit card and a matter of minutes. Therefore, it is important

> Web hosting services offer an affordable and easy-to-use method to get your business online.

that you take your time in choosing the *right* domain name for your online business, and get a Web hosting plan that meets your needs.

Selecting a Web Hosting Service

Think of a Web hosting service as providing a location in cyberspace for your online business. It is much like the landlord you would deal with in the offline world if you were setting up a retail store in a mall. For example, if you signed a lease with a landlord, a monthly fee would pay for a certain amount of square footage for your store, parking for your customers, electricity for your equipment, and certain other standard services to keep your business running smoothly.

In cyberspace, a Web host is the landlord for your online business. For a monthly fee your Web host provides a certain amount of disk space to house your Web site, bandwidth for your customers to visit, design capabilities to build your Web site, and many other services to help you run your online business. Your choice of a Web hosting service should be based on its monthly service charge, the amount of disk space you will receive, access to reports, phone support availability, and ancillary services like credit card processing.

Just as in the offline world, where there are many types of landlords, the online world has many different types of Web hosts. There are firms that specialize in hosting entire computer systems for very large and highly trafficked Web sites; there are firms that specialize in hosting thousands of small business Web sites; and there are even many free services that provide some sophisticated hosting capabilities.

> There are even many free services that provide some sophisticated hosting capabilities.

Small Business and Free Hosting Services

WEB HOSTING SERVICES	WEB ADDRESS	TYPE
Angelfire	*www.angelfire.com*	Free
Concentric Network	*www.concentric.com*	Monthly fee required
EarthLink	*www.earthlink.net*	Monthly fee required
GeoCities (Yahoo!)	*www.geocities.yahoo.com/home/*	Free
MindSpring	*www.mindspring.com*	Monthly fee required
Verio	*www.verio.com*	Monthly fee required
WebJump	*www.webjump.com*	Free
XOOM.com	*www.xoom.com*	Free

As you explore different Web hosting services, there are certain things you must consider. For instance, most free hosting services do not allow you to have your own domain name ("www.yourbiz.com"). Normally, your Web address will include their company name, and look something like "www.theirbiz.com/yourbiz." Other features and capabilities you should consider when selecting a Web hosting service, include:

- E commerce capabilities, including credit card processing
- Amount of the monthly fee
- Support for Web development software, such as Microsoft FrontPage
- Technical support via an 800-number

Before you decide to pay for a Web hosting service, try out one or two of the free services to see if they meet your needs. In most instances, you can set up a simple Web site in a matter of a few hours. From there you should be able to tell whether the free services are appropriate for your online business, or if you will need to pay for a monthly service that provides more capabilities.

Registering a Domain Name

A domain name is your dot-com, or your Web site address. It might look something like "www.yourbiz.com," "www.yourbiz.net," or "www.yourbiz.org." Your domain name uniquely identifies your Web site from all of the other Web sites in the world. Whenever someone types your domain name into their Web browser's address box, your Web site home page will appear on their computer monitor.

Today, there are two ways to get a domain name: You can register a new name with Network Solutions (*www.networksolutions.com*) that hasn't already been registered by anyone else; or you can buy one from a domain name broker. Registering a new domain name is a relatively easy and straightforward process that can be accomplished directly through Network Solutions, or indirectly through your Web host. Either way, you will have to pay $70 for a two-year license of the domain name.

Since the large Web hosting services, like Verio (*www.verio.com*) and MindSpring (*www.mindspring.com*), have

> Your domain name uniquely identifies your Web site from all of the other Web sites in the world.

direct links to the Network Solutions/InterNIC database of domain names, it is often easier to select your Web hosting plan before registering a domain name. These companies make registering a domain name part of their process for establishing a Web hosting account. However, you can always register a domain name, and then choose your Web hosting plan at a later date.

Today, domain names have become very valuable pieces of online real estate. It is not unheard of for a company to pay millions of dollars for the *right* domain name. Therefore it is important that you choose yours very carefully. Make sure that any name you choose is easy to spell and conveys the nature of your online business. Ultimately, your domain name may be more valuable in terms of a "brand" than your online business by itself.

Creating Your Web Site

If you were going to build a house, would you begin by chopping trees down in the forest? For most people, the answer is an emphatic "No." Likewise, if you want to build a Web site, you don't need to start by learning how to program with HTML or Java. There are plenty of software tools on the market that make Web site creation a relatively painless process.

You can visualize software tools as falling into two separate categories. The first category includes software tools and templates that are provided by your Internet service provider (ISP), Web hosting service, or online mall. These tools are integrated with the type of service you choose and are designed to get you up and running quickly. The second category consists of off-the-shelf software packages that are loaded onto your computer. These software packages provide more flexibility than the integrated tools but still give you the capability to get up and running quickly. Some of the more popular off-the-shelf Web site development software packages include:

- Microsoft FrontPage
- Adobe PageMill
- Macromedia Dreamweaver
- NetObjects Fusion

> It is not unheard of for a company to pay millions of dollars for the *right* domain name.

The nature of your online business will in large part determine which approach you take. If your site is going to be predominantly geared toward selling things (an e-commerce site), you should see if the templates provided by the Web hosting services will meet your needs. Often, many of the security and credit card processing features required for e-commerce are offered as standard features through their e-commerce plans. On the other hand, if your online business is going to be more content oriented, you should consider an off-the-shelf software package to create your Web site.

These are only general guidelines, since you can create a content oriented site with templates offered by your ISP, and you can create an e-commerce site using an off-the-shelf software package. The decision comes down to the amount of time you want to invest and the design flexibility you need to create your online business. Finally, you should be aware that e-commerce plans provided by Web hosting services tend to be more expensive than their simple Web site hosting plans.

Marketing Your Online Business to the World

If you already have an offline business, or have started a business before, it should not surprise you that you will need to devote considerable efforts to marketing your newly published online business. If you have never started or run a business, be aware that simply publishing a Web site on the Internet without backing it up with significant marketing efforts will be a waste of time.

Marketing online means getting your Web site listed with the major search engines and online directories, sending direct e-mails, notifying news publications via press releases, and running banner advertising campaigns. Additionally, many online marketers have found they can generate significant online traffic using traditional offline media, like direct mail, radio commercials, and television advertisements.

Notifying Internet Portals and Directories

Once you have published your Web site, it's time to begin the marketing process. Your first step will be to get listed with the large

To get your business online you can use the software tools provided by your Web hosting service or buy a separate software package.

portals, or search engines, such as Yahoo!, Excite, and Lycos. You also will want to get listed with many of the lesser known directories that can steer more traffic, or prospects, to your Web site. Before you begin this process, make sure that your Web site is very close to being final and you have created some well-written descriptions for your online business. Backtracking from this point can be very time consuming.

Similar to registering your domain name ("www.yourbiz.com"), getting listed with the portals and directories can be done easily using an auto-posting service. You simply type, or cut and paste, the keywords and description for your online business in the appropriate boxes of the notification forms, and the auto-posting service will take care of the rest. In addition to getting your Web site listed across the Internet, many of these services will also analyze your site for loading speed, browser compatibility, and its ability to distinguish itself from the "crowd."

> Getting listed with the portals and directories can be done easily using an auto-posting service.

Popular Auto-Posting Services

AUTO-POSTING SERVICES	WEB ADDRESS
SiteAnnounce.com	*www.siteannounce.com*
SubmitIt! (LinkExchange)	*www.submit-it.com*
Web Site Garage	*www.websitegarage.com*

Getting listed with portals, search engines, and directories is the beginning of your promotional campaign. By having your site properly indexed in these search engines, you stand a good chance of attracting visitors to your site. However, don't expect the world to knock at your door just because your site is listed in all of the major search engines. As you can imagine, the competition to be listed in the top spots is fierce, and search engines are struggling to keep up with the thousands of new sites that are coming online almost daily.

Finally, you should be aware that even after you submit your freshly minted site to the various portals, there will be a time lag before your site is indexed. This lag occurs because your site will either have to be reviewed by human eyes or visited by a software

> The first step in your marketing process is to get listed with the major search engines such as Yahoo! and AltaVista.

"spider" to see that it actually exists. With some search engines this process can take as long as eight weeks.

Promoting Your Site with Press Releases and Direct Mail

By now you have created a Web site, published it with a Web hosting service, and had it listed with the major portals and online directories. Your job is finished, right? Wrong! Within a few days of registering your site, you'll probably be asking yourself why the reports from your Web hosting service still aren't showing any appreciable increase in traffic or hits. In fact, except for a few "spider robots," you seem to be the only one visiting the site! Now it's time to start actively promoting your site to bring in prospects.

If you have ever conducted any promotion in the *real*, or *offline*, world, you are already familiar with some of the concepts and methods, including press releases and direct mailings. However, marketing on the Internet involves some nuances that must be understood before beginning a promotional campaign. Start with a press release to the major publications in your industry. If you can spare a few bucks, there are online services that will take care of the entire distribution process for you. For instance, the Internet News Bureau (*www.newsbureau.com*) "distributes press releases via e-mail to more than 2,600 journalists throughout the world."

Another alternative is to create an e-mailing list of prospective customers for your products and services. Send them your press release and any other material, like a newsletter, that might entice them to visit your site. You should be aware that sending volumes of unsolicited e-mail, often called "spam," in the online world can have detrimental effects on your online business. Therefore, make sure that your mailing list was developed from prospects that authorized you to send them e-mail.

Running Banner Advertising Campaigns

After you have listed your online business with the major portals and directories, sent out a press release announcing your new venture, and started to collect the names and e-mail addresses of

> Press releases are an excellent and cost-effective way to promote your Web site.

> You should be aware that sending volumes of unsolicited e-mail, often called "spam," in the online world can have detrimental effects on your online business.

visitors to your site, it's time to consider some online advertising. Probably the most popular method of online advertising is through the use of banner ads. These are the advertisements, most often in rectangular boxes, that seem to appear on almost every page you look at on the Web. In addition to banner ads, other ways you can advertise your online business include having your ad placed with a newsletter distribution service and inserting your domain name ("www.yourbiz.com") in offline advertisements.

If you are unfamiliar with the process of running a banner ad, you'll be surprised at how fast you can actually start pulling in visitors with this medium. While in the offline world it can take months to actually place an advertisement in a publication, in the online world the whole process can be accomplished in a matter of days. Another advantage of online advertising is that you can change your ad in the middle of a campaign. For instance, if your graphics or message are not generating an acceptable click-through rate, then you can change the entire banner in an effort to attract more visitors. The cost of running banner ads ranges from *free* to thousands of dollars per month.

> Probably the most popular method of online advertising is through the use of banner ads.

Popular Banner Advertising Services

BANNER AD SERVICES	WEB ADDRESS	TYPE
24/7 Media	*www.247media.com*	Paid advertising
Ad Smart	*www.adsmart.net*	Paid advertising
Beseen	*www.beseen.com*	Free banner exchange
Click Taxi	*www.clicktaxi.com*	Free banner exchange
DoubleClick	*www.doubleclick.net*	Paid advertising
Excite Affiliates Network	*www.affiliate.excite.com*	Free banner exchange
Flycast	*www.flycast.com*	Paid advertising
LinkExchange	*www.linkexchange.com*	Free banner exchange

In order to create an appropriate banner ad, you can either do it yourself or have one created by an outside agency. There are many services online that you can use to create a banner ad for free, such as Quick Banner (*www.quickbanner.com*). Alternatively, LinkExchange (*www.linkexchange.com*) provides a "pay" service from an outside agency that you can use when you register with their network. Finally,

> There are many *free* online services that you can use to design your banner ad.

many of the off-the-shelf software packages include tools to design banner ads, such as the Microsoft FrontPage Image Editor.

Joining Affiliate Programs

Affiliate programs offer a way for your online business to make money by advertising other online businesses on your Web site. In their simplest form, affiliate programs establish a business relationship between your business and another business, in which you will receive a percentage, or a fee, for the sales that you generate for the other business. In a sense, by joining an affiliate program you become an agent for another business and get a commission every time you sell something for that business. For instance, let's say that you joined an affiliate program that pays a 15 percent commission on every sale that you made. Sell an item worth $100, and you would receive a $15 commission from the affiliate program.

In order to join an affiliate program and begin earning commissions, you will be required to show a banner ad, or text link, for the other business on your Web site. For instance, if you join the Amazon.com affiliate program, you would place an Amazon.com banner ad on your Web site, with a special identification code, that links back to the Amazon.com site.

> In order to join an affiliate program and begin earning commissions, you will be required to show a banner ad, or text link, for the other business on your Web site.

AFFILIATE PROGRAM ADMINISTRATORS	WEB ADDRESS
LinkShare	*www.linkshare.com*
Refer-It	*www.refer-it.com*
RevenueAvenue (LinkExchange.com)	*www.linkexchange.com*
Webworker Top 10 List	*www.webworker.com/affiliates/top10w.html*

You can also set up your own affiliate program to enlist other online businesses to help you sell your products and services. In this instance, you would pay affiliates a percentage of sales, or a flat fee, for every sale they made for your online business. If you want to learn more about setting up an affiliate program for your online business, go to ClickTrade (*www.clicktrade.linkexchange.com*). This company can help you set up and administer an affiliate program for your Web site.

Getting OfficeLinks.com Online in Less than 30 Days

Q: How long did it take you to get OfficeLinks.com online?

A: It was about 20 days from the time I purchased Microsoft FrontPage until I actually had the site first published with the MindSpring Web hosting service.

Q: What took you the longest to get the site published?

A: I think developing the content for the site. Coming up with the written text for the various Web pages, like the Advertising page, was more time consuming than I had expected.

Q: How about the FrontPage software, was that hard to learn?

A: For me it was very simple. There are some easy-to-use templates that you can experiment with before deciding on the final layout. As soon as I had the software loaded and had registered a domain name with the Web hosting service, I practiced a couple of times on loading a "dummy" site. I think this experimentation really helped with the final design.

Q: Why did you choose the MindSpring Web hosting service?

A: It seemed like it offered most of the features and functions I wanted, and it also gave me the capability to get set up online. I never had to speak with anyone on the phone to get my first iteration up and running.

Q: Have you registered OfficeLinks.com with various search engines?

A: Yes. I've tried to get it listed with all of the major search engines like Yahoo!, Excite, AltaVista, and Lycos.

Q: How did you get the site listed with these search engines?

A: I used the SubmitIt! service from LinkExchange (*www.linkexchange.com*).

Q: Is it hard to use LinkExchange?

A: Not at all. You simply enter your domain name and the appropriate descriptions, and the service automatically posts your site to a variety of search engines and directories.

Q: Do you do any banner advertising?

A: Yes. I use the Banner Network from LinkExchange and ClickTaxi (*www.clicktaxi.com*). Both of these banner exchanges will show my banner ad for free. In return, I have to agree to show their banners on my Web site.

Q: Have you joined any affiliate programs?

A: Yes. I've joined a lot of affiliate programs through LinkShare (*www.linkshare.com*). They have a very comprehensive network of affiliate programs that are easy to join. Also, once you learn how to create the links for one company, the process is very similar for all of the others. This makes it easier than joining individual company affiliate programs, where all of the linking arrangements are different.

Online Business Resources

Bplans.com (*www.bplans.com*)

Bplans.com has a wide variety of business planning information on its Web site, including sample business and marketing plans. It also has *The Plan Wizard*, which allows you to find sample plans that are most relevant to your particular business.

CNET Web Services (*www.webhostlist.com*)

On its Web site, CNET publishes the *Ultimate Web Host List*, which provides a monthly ranking of the top 25 Web hosting companies based on value, customer service, quality, and flexibility. You will also find an A to Z listing of Web hosts, and many tips on building an e-commerce Web site.

Internet News Bureau (*www.newsbureau.com*)

The Internet News Bureau "distributes press releases via e-mail to more than 2,600 journalists throughout the world." Using your credit card and dial-up connection to the Internet, you can distribute your press release in a matter of hours to a nationwide audience.

LinkExchange (*www.linkexchange.com*)

LinkExchange is owned by Microsoft, and contains many invaluable resources for marketing a Web site. It includes the SubmitIt! service for auto-posting your site to search engines, the Banner Network for promoting your Web site with banner ads, Revenue Avenue for joining affiliate programs, and ClickTrade for setting up your own affiliate program.

LinkShare (*www.linkshare.com*)

LinkShare describes itself as "the worldwide leader in affiliate marketing programs for companies doing business on the Web," and boasts such members as Dell Computer, Disney, Avon, and Outpost.com. You can use LinkShare to join affiliate programs and to help you create and manage your own program.

U.S. Small Business Administration (*www.sba.gov*)

The Small Business Administration (SBA) Web site contains a lot of useful general purpose business planning information for small businesses. Topics include starting, financing, and expanding a business. Additionally, the site provides a business plan outline and a complete workbook that shows you how to apply for SBA-backed loans.

Summary

In this chapter you learned about some of the most important things you can do to get your business online quickly. The essential things that must be accomplished to set up your business were discussed, including writing a business plan, establishing a connection to the Internet, creating a Web site, and marketing to a worldwide audience.

Although getting online quickly might be an objective, it should not be your primary goal. Establishing a successful business model should be your primary goal. Therefore, don't get taken in by advertisements that claim you can set up shop online in a couple of hours. Getting your business online (successfully) takes a lot of hard work!

For more information on this topic, visit our Web site at www.businesstown.com

Evaluating the Technical Considerations of Going Online

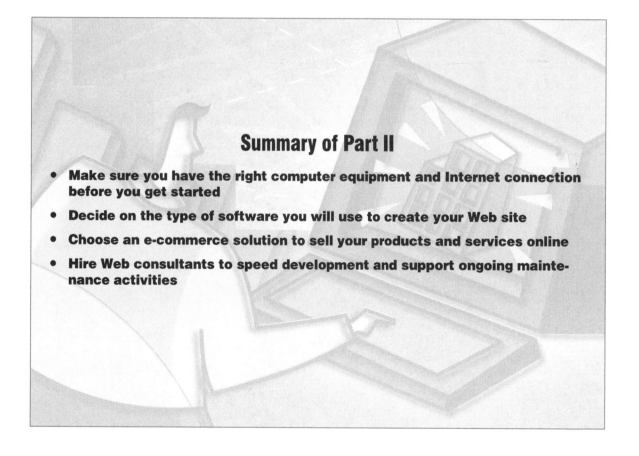

Summary of Part II

- **Make sure you have the right computer equipment and Internet connection before you get started**

- **Decide on the type of software you will use to create your Web site**

- **Choose an e-commerce solution to sell your products and services online**

- **Hire Web consultants to speed development and support ongoing maintenance activities**

Chapter 5

Selecting the Right Computer and Dial-Up Service to Get Connected

Topics covered in this chapter

- Selecting the right PC for your online business
- Creating a checklist for your hardware and software needs
- Connecting your computer to the Internet
- Selecting an Internet service provider (ISP) for your connection
- Getting a free PC, dial-up connection, or both

The free PC movement has boosted the slumping computer hardware market, but users still aren't buying into the ads.

JANE WEAVER, MSNBC

In order to get your business online you will need at least a personal computer and a dial-up connection to the Internet. Additionally, you might need some special Web site development software and a scanner, or digital camera. You don't need to spend a fortune on these items, and most packages advertised today in your local newspaper are adequate for building your business online. In fact, for less than $1,000 you can get a complete computer system, including a PC, scanner, printer, and dial-up connection to the Internet.

If you were to walk into a personal computer retailing store and ask a salesperson to help you pick out a PC, their first question might be "what do want to do with it?" For instance, they might ask if you are getting it for your children to play games, for your spouse to pay bills, or for you to surf the Web. Your answers will help the salesperson decide what type of PC hardware configuration will best meet your needs.

Today, most people will answer "yes" to all of these questions, and also want to perform a multitude of other tasks with their PCs, like listening to music and watching movies. However, for the purposes of this book, it will be assumed that you are going to get a separate PC just for your online business (a very good idea since you will need to use it daily and aren't going to have much time to watch movies). Also, as described earlier, this book assumes that you are going to use a Web hosting service for your online business, and therefore don't require a computer server and telecommunications network to connect to the Internet.

Once you have narrowed down the functions that you will need your PC to perform, your selection process will be much easier. It comes down to memory, disk space, peripherals, cost, and most importantly, technical support. Fortunately, since most Web sites are still just a combination of text and graphics, you will not need any heavy duty (and expensive) equipment to get your business online.

You will need at least a personal computer and a dial-up connection to the Internet to get your business online.

Since most Web sites are still just a combination of text and graphics, you will not need any heavy duty (and expensive) equipment to get your business online.

Since you will be using a Web hosting service to get your business online, your only other requirement is to select a "dial-up" service connection to the Internet. You will use your dial-up service to publish your Web site and monitor daily activity. The most popular dial-up service today is America Online, but there are many others, including MindSpring and Earthlink. You can also investigate whether your Web host provides a dial-up service to connect with their servers.

The costs of connecting to the Internet range from "free" to $21.95 per month to thousands of dollars. You should investigate as many of these alternatives as possible before making your final choice. Start-up businesses can now get a PC and a dial-up connection to the Internet for one low monthly fee through special promotions from hardware manufacturers and Internet service providers.

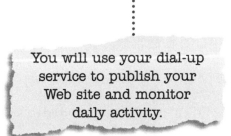

You will use your dial-up service to publish your Web site and monitor daily activity.

Selecting the Right PC for Your Online Business

In order to choose the right PC for your online business, you must answer the salesperson's question ("What are you going to do with it?") posed at the beginning of this chapter. You have to decide what type of software and peripherals you are going to use to build your Web site. After answering these questions, you can choose a computer.

Web Site Development Software

When selecting a computer, one of the first decisions you must make is what type of software you are going to use to develop your Web site. Are you going to use an off-the-shelf package, like Microsoft FrontPage, to create your site? Or, are you going to go with the canned software tools provided by your Web host, or another third party? While Web site development tools are discussed more fully in Chapter 6, you must be aware of their minimum system requirements before you select a PC.

There are literally hundreds of software choices available to build your Web site. You can use the tools included with your Web

One of the most important considerations in selecting a PC is the type of software you are planning to use.

browser, such as Netscape Composer or Microsoft Front Page Express; you can use word processing or presentation software, such as Microsoft Word or Corel Presentations; or you can use software specifically designed to build Web sites, such as Microsoft FrontPage, Adobe PageMill, or Macromedia Dreamweaver.

Your task is to determine what hardware will be required to run your software of choice. For instance, the following table presents the minimum system requirements for three of the most popular Web site design software packages.

WEB DESIGN SOFTWARE	MINIMUM COMPUTER SYSTEM REQUIREMENTS
Microsoft FrontPage 2000	Pentium 75MHz processor or higher
	Windows 95/98/NT 4.0 with Service Pack 3 or higher
	24MB RAM, 40MB RAM for Windows NT
	167MB disk space for typical installation
	CD-ROM Drive
	VGA or higher-resolution monitor
	14,400 or higher-baud modem recommended
	Multimedia computer required for some effects
	44MB disk space for typical installation
Adobe PageMill v3.0	80486 or higher processor
	Windows 95, NT 4.0 or higher
	16MB RAM
	20MB disk space
	VGA 8-bit or higher monitor, 800 x 600 recommended
	CD-ROM drive
Macromedia Dreamweaver v2.0	Pentium processor—90-MHz or higher processor
	Windows 95/98/NT 4.0 or higher
	32MB RAM
	20MB disk space
	256-color monitor capable of 800x600 resolution

Source: Beyond.com (*www.beyond.com*)

Knowing the minimum system requirements, you can begin to research PCs and determine if they match up. For example, you will notice that the three leading Web design software packages have minimum Random Access Memory (RAM) and disk space requirements. Microsoft FrontPage and Macromedia Dreamweaver require that your PC be equipped with a Pentium class processor and operate at minimum speeds of 75MHz and 90MHz, respectively. Additionally, all three of these packages require a version of Microsoft Windows, either Widows 95, 98, or NT 4.0 (a software package that normally comes preloaded on your PC).

There is no need to worry if you are not completely comfortable with all of these technical terms, like RAM and disk space, since these are the basic building blocks of all PCs. Your job is to simply look at the minimum system requirements of the software package and compare them to the hardware specifications of prospective PCs. However, if you need more information, check the following section "Creating a Checklist for Your Hardware and Software Needs" for brief descriptions of these terms. You can also get in-depth explanations of computer terms from the Webopedia (*www.webopedia.com*) Web site.

Web Browsing and Productivity Software

After choosing a Web site development software package, you should evaluate any other software applications that will be required for your online business. Since some applications use more than 400 megabytes of hard disk space when fully installed (for example, Microsoft Office 2000), it is important to pick these out before selecting your PC.

Other applications you should consider for your online business include Web browsers and anti-virus, productivity, and bookkeeping software packages.

You should plan on installing both Microsoft Internet Explorer and Netscape Navigator on your PC, as well as any other special browsers required for your dial-up Internet service. Currently, most browsers are free and can be downloaded from the Internet. For instance, on ZDNet (*www.zdnet.com/swlib/topics/browsers.html*) you can download Netscape Navigator, Microsoft Internet Explorer, and a few others.

> Other applications you should consider for your online business include Web browsers and anti-virus, productivity, and bookkeeping software packages.

APPLICATION SOFTWARE	MINIMUM COMPUTER SYSTEM REQUIREMENTS
Microsoft Internet Explorer	Windows 95, 98, NT
	16MB RAM standard or full installations
	98 MB disk space for full installation
Netscape Navigator	486/66 or higher processor (Pentium recommended)
	Windows 98, 95, or Windows NT 4.0
	16MB RAM
	25–35 MB hard-disk space
Norton AntiVirus 2000 by SYMANTEC	IBM PC or compatible, Intel 486/25 or higher
	Windows 95/98
	16MB RAM, 32MB recommended
	45MB disk space
Microsoft Office 2000	IBM PC or compatible with Pentium 75MHz or higher
	Windows 95/NT 4.0 Service Pack 3 or higher
	16MB RAM for Windows 95
	32MB RAM for Windows NT Workstation 4.0 or higher
	217MB: Word, Excel, Outlook, PowerPoint, Access
	174MB: Publisher, Small Business Tools
	CD-ROM drive
	VGA or higher-resolution monitor
QuickBooks 99 by INTUIT	IBM compatible 486 computer
	Windows 95/98/NT 4.0 or higher
	16MB RAM
	45MB disk space
	Internet access for online services
	256 color VGA or SVGA video
	Printers supported by Windows 95/NT 4.0 or higher

Source: Beyond.com (*www.beyond.com*)

The reason for planning to use multiple browsers is to test your Web site in as many environments as possible. For instance, if you develop your Web site using Microsoft FrontPage, some of the software's features only work with Microsoft Internet Explorer and should be avoided if you want your site to appeal to the largest audience possible.

PC Peripheral Equipment

In order to put your business online, you should consider buying a few peripherals, such as a printer, backup device, scanner, and digital camera (it's assumed that your base PC package includes a monitor, keyboard, mouse, and CD-ROM). Your selection of a scanner and digital camera is optional, and depends on the type of online business you are going to start.

You will definitely need a printer for your online business. You'll use it to print important documents for future reference, such as e-mails, orders, and Web pages. The two most common types of printers for small businesses are ink jet printers and laser jet printers. Unless, you will be using your printer for other functions, like direct mail campaigns, an ink jet should be fine. These printers are less expensive than comparable laser jet printers, and offer the added benefit of producing color copies (very useful for printing out Web pages).

At some point, the amount of time and effort that you will have invested in your Web site will be very significant, and you will want the capability to make backup copies. Depending on the size of your site, you may be able to store the entire site on a single floppy disk. However, if you are going to create a big site, with lots of pages and images, you should consider a Zip drive. A Zip disk holds 100MB of information, or nearly seventy regular floppy disks of information.

Do you need a scanner or digital camera for your online business? If you are going to sell products or produce content that will require photographs, you should consider these peripherals for your online business. You can take pictures with a digital camera and load them directly onto your Web site, or you can take pictures with a conventional camera and then scan them into your Web site. The advantages of a digital camera are convenience and quality. These devices connect directly to your PC and avoid the "taking a picture of a picture" quality problems that are inherent with scanners. However, digital cameras are still more expensive than using a scanner with a conventional camera. Additionally, scanners usually provide the added benefits of having fax and printer capabilities.

> In order to put your business online, you should consider buying a few peripherals, such as a printer, backup device, scanner, and digital camera.

The hardware options you select will have a bearing on the number and type of input/output slots you will need for your PC. For instance, if you buy a Zip drive to back up your Web site, you should be aware that it will require a slot, or connection, to your computer. Normally, Zip drives are connected to your parallel port, or the same slot as your printer. It is inconvenient if you always have to plug and unplug these various peripheral devices to accomplish certain tasks. Therefore, you should consider buying a Zip drive built into your computer from the beginning, or having enough input/output slots for all of your peripheral devices.

> The number of peripheral devices that you select for your online business will determine the number and type of input/output slots you will need for your PC.

Creating a Checklist for Your Hardware and Software Needs

Although you don't have to entirely understand computer terminology, some of the most important hardware and software specifications are described briefly in the following checklist. Additionally, the "suggested" column shows the minimum recommended hardware and software specifications for your online business PC.

PC Magazine recently completed a survey called "Where to Shop in PC Land," written by Bruce Brown. It reviewed the market for PCs costing less than $1,000. In the study they selected 16 sources of low-cost PCs, including office-supply superstores, computer superstores, a large discount store, two national electronics chains, a national buying club, and direct-sales PC merchants with catalogs and Web sites. Their choice for a personal computer was the Gateway Country: Gateway Essential 400c. You can read the entire article by selecting "The best places to buy a PC" on the ZDNet home page (*www.zdnet.com*).

> You can buy affordable high-quality PCs and peripherals on the Internet from many Web sites.

You can buy affordable high-quality PCs and peripherals on the Internet from many Web sites, including many of those reviewed by *PC Magazine*. However, if you don't have a computer or a connection to the Internet yet, you will need a catalog and an 800-number to place your order.

FEATURE/PERIPHERAL	DESCRIPTION	SUGGESTED
Central Processing Unit (CPU) and MHz	The brains and speed of the PC. The higher the MegaHertz, the faster your machine will operate.	266MHz Pentium class or higher
Random Access Memory (RAM)	Working area on the PC. The more Megabytes (MB) you have, the more programs you can run simultaneously.	32MB
Hard disk space	Storage area on the PC. The more Gigabytes (GB) you have, the more files and programs you can store on your PC.	2GB
Removable storage medium	Floppy disk or other backup device. Use to copy your most valuable files and store them separately from your PC.	A 1.44MB floppy drive and 100MB Zip drive should be built in.
CD-ROM	Read Only Memory (ROM). Reads software on a CD into your computer.	24X built in
Modem	Enables your computer to talk over phone lines to other computers.	Should be capable of speeds up to 56K, and pre-installed.
Monitor	The computer screen for your PC. Higher resolutions provide sharper images.	640 by 480 pixels; 15-inch
Operating system	The software that controls all of the programs and files on your PC.	Microsoft Windows should be preloaded
Preloaded software	Software that is already installed on your PC when you buy it.	MS Office 2000, Norton AntiVirus, QuickBooks
Web site development software	Software that you will use to build your Web site. Probably not preloaded.	Microsoft FrontPage 2000
Technical support	People you can call on the phone (preferably with an 800-number) that can help you fix problems.	24 hours per day

continued on following page

FEATURE/PERIPHERAL	DESCRIPTION	SUGGESTED
Printer	Ink jet printers are inexpensive and produce good quality color output. Higher resolution (dots per inch) and speed (pages per minute) are found in more expensive machines.	Ink jet resolution should be 300 by 600 dots per inch. 6–8 pages per minute
Scanner	Get offline pictures onto your Web site with a scanner. Higher resolution (bits) will give you better quality images.	24 or 30-bit color Built-in faxing and printing capability
Camera	Place pictures of your products on your Web site with a digital camera. Higher resolution will give you better pictures.	640 x 480 pixels

Source: ZDNet (*www.zdnet.com/smallbusiness/filters/buying_guide/desktops/September 1999*)

• • •

Online and Offline Outlets for Computers and Peripherals

COMPANY	PHONE NUMBER	WEB ADDRESS
Buy.Com	(888) 880-1030	*www.buy.com*
CDW Computer Centers	(800) 844-4239	*www.cdw.com*
Circuit City	(877) 932-2225	*www.circuitcity.com*
Compaq	(800) 888-0220	*www.compaq.com*
CompUSA	(800) 226-6772	*www.compusa.com*
Dell Computer	(800) 999-3355	*www.dell.com*
eMachines/Staples	(800) 378-2753	*www.staples.com*
Gateway	(800) 846-4208	*www.gateway.com*
NECX Direct	N/A	*www.necx.com*
PC Connection	(888) 213-0260	*www.pcconnection.com*
RadioShack	(800) 843-7422	*www.radioshack.com*
Sam's Club	(888) 746-7726	*www.samsclub.com*
ShopIBM	(888) 411-1932	*www.pc.ibm.com*
Tigerdirect.com	(800) 879-1597	*www.tigerdirect.com*
Value America	(888) 337-8258	*www.valueamerica.com*
Wal-Mart	(800) 966-6546	*www.wal-mart.com*

If you are hesitant to buy a computer through the mail from companies like Dell Computer or Gateway, don't be! These companies specialize in building PCs for small businesses, and offer technical service that is unmatched by traditional retailers. Their 24-hour 800-phone numbers for technical support can be a real lifesaver late at night or on the weekend.

Connecting Your Computer to the Internet

Today, the most popular way to connect to the Internet is through a dial-up connection to an Internet service provider (ISP), such as America Online. Usually, for a flat monthly fee, ISPs provide virtually unlimited access to the Internet by connecting your PC to their network through ordinary copper phone lines.

However, in addition to dial-up access, many ISPs are now offering homes and businesses speedier connections to the Internet with services such as Integrated Services Digital Network (ISDN), Digital Subscriber Line (DSL), T-1 Carrier, and cable modems.

> The most popular way to connect to the Internet is through a dial-up connection to an Internet service provider (ISP).

Dial-Up Access

Dial-up access connects your computer to an Internet service provider (ISP), such as America Online, through a modem and a telephone line. Since dial-up connections to the Internet use regular phone lines, the quality and data speeds are limited. Typical speeds for this type of connection range between 9.2Kbps (Kilobits per second) to a maximum of 56Kbps. Although, these modem connections are the most popular and inexpensive way for individual users to connect to the Internet, there are faster and more expensive connections available from your phone company or ISP, including ISDN, DSL, or T-1 Carrier.

Integrated Services Digital Network (ISDN)

In addition to dial-up service, your local phone company or Internet service provider can provide other connections to the Internet that are much faster, like ISDN. The "integrated" in ISDN means that this service has the capability to combine voice, video, and data over the regular phone lines running into your home or office. ISDN is normally set up to provide a data speed of 64Kbps but can be configured to run at twice that speed, or 128Kbps. ISDN will cost you more than traditional dial-up service and requires the installation of special equipment in your home or office.

Digital Subscriber Line (DSL)

Another service that your local phone company or ISP can provide is a digital subscriber line (DSL). Like dial-up and ISDN, DSL is provided over copper phone lines, but it is much faster. DSL can download data into your home or office at speeds up to 32Mbps (million bits per second), and take uploads in excess of 1Mbps. DSL is also more expensive than dial-up service and requires special equipment to be installed in your home or office.

T-1 Carrier

T-1 Carrier, also known as T1.5 or DS1 service, is another offering from your local phone company or ISP that can give you a faster connection to the Internet. A T-1 Carrier combines 24 individual channels, each at 64Kbps, to provide a data speed of 1.544Mbps (million bits per second). A T-1 Carrier is much more expensive than dial-up service and is usually sold to business consumers.

Cable Modem

The newest way to connect to the Internet is using a cable modem with your cable television service. Once this service becomes widely available, you will be able to establish a high speed 2Mbps connection to the Internet for about the same price as your dial-up service.

Selecting an Internet Service Provider (ISP) for Your Connection

In the preceding section you learned that there are a variety of ways to get online using an Internet service provider. For your online business, you can probably use dial-up access with little sacrifice in speed or quality. However, if you do a lot of surfing, or your online

> There are numerous ways that you can connect to the Internet, including dial-up, ISDN, DSL, T-1, and a cable modem.

> The newest way to connect to the Internet is using a cable modem with your cable television service.

business delivers a lot of audio, video, or other streaming media, you may want to consider a higher speed connection. Keep in mind, though, that most users still do not have high speed access, and therefore will be using your Web site with a "slow" connection.

In addition to regular activities such as sending and receiving e-mail, you will use your Internet connection for:

- Uploading your Web site onto your Web host
- Making updates to your Web site
- Checking daily Web site activity reports
- Receiving e-mail forwarded from your Web site

> Criteria widely used to select ISPs include price, reputation, recommendation from friends, content, range of services, availability of local access numbers, and speed of access.

According to a *PC Magazine* article featured on the ZDNet Web site (*www.zdnet.com*), criteria widely used to select ISPs include price, reputation, recommendation from friends, content, range of services, availability of local access numbers, and speed of access. Before you make a final decision on an ISP, review the following checklist.

ISP CRITERIA	DESCRIPTION
Pricing	Find out how you will be charged for your service. Is it a flat monthly charge for unlimited usage? Are there per-minute charges after you exceed a total number of hours in a month? Are there any free months?
Reputation	See how your ISP is ranked in customer satisfaction surveys. The most popular ISPs in the country are shown in the following table.
Recommendation from friends	Ask other users within your community which ISP they are using. Determine if they ever have any trouble connecting to the service.
Content	If you want more from your ISP than simply a connection to the Internet, evaluate any proprietary content they offer.
Range of services	Find out if your ISP offers any high speed access alternatives. Ask if they offer DSL.
Availability of local access numbers	This is a must. Your ISP must offer local access number(s), otherwise you will have to pay your phone company toll charges every time you use the service (this is on top of the monthly phone line charge).
Speed of access	As discussed, the fastest dial-up service your ISP can offer is 56Kbps. However, because of modem constraints, your service will probably be slower. Don't accept anything less than 24Kbps.

Top to Bottom (ranking of ISPs)

1. AT&T WorldNet
2. CWIX
3. MindSpring
4. America Online
5. CompuServe
6. Prodigy
7. IBM Internet Connection
8. Earthlink Sprint
9. MSN Internet Access
10. GTE.net

Your criteria for selecting a Web host will be different from that for selecting an ISP.

In the same *PC Magazine* article, the survey said most Web directories list more than 5,000 ISPs in the United States, and the top four among subscribers are America Online, AT&T WorldNet Service, MSN Internet Access, and CompuServe. Another article that appeared in the April 1999 issue of *Smart Money* magazine rated the top 10 ISPs according to network speed and reliability as shown in the accompanying sidebar.

The pace of change on the Internet is so dramatic that by the time you read this book, the rankings of ISPs and the services they offer will have changed. Therefore, do some research before you settle on your connection to the Internet. A good place to start is the ZDNet Product Guides found on *www.zdnet.com*.

Finally, if you don't already have a dial-up service, evaluate Web hosting services in conjunction with your search for an Internet service provider. Many ISPs, like MindSpring and Earthlink, provide Web hosting as part of their Internet services. However, your criteria for selecting a Web host will be different from that for selecting an ISP, because you are looking for two different types of services. It's much like deciding whether you want an interior house painter to paint the outside of your house, or whether you want your hairdresser to do your nails!

Getting a Free PC, Dial-Up Connection, or Both

One of the biggest changes taking place today is the combination of PCs and dial-up access to the Internet. PC manufacturers are offering free, or very low-cost, dial-up access with the purchase of one of their PCs. At the same time, Internet service providers are offering rebates on PCs if you sign up for their service for at least three years.

From a business standpoint, this gives you the opportunity to pay for Internet service and a PC with one low monthly fee over three years. For instance, you can get Internet service and a PC for about $30 each month. A good deal by almost any measure.

If you elect this route, you must ensure that the PC you select can run your Web site development software, and that the service provided will work with your Web host. In most instances, this should not be a problem, but check before you make a commitment.

Choosing the Equipment, Software, and Connections for OfficeLinks.com

Q: Did you buy a top-of-the-line computer to create OfficeLinks.com?

A: No. In fact I already had a relatively new sub-$1,000 PC that I'd purchased for another project, so I didn't need a new PC.

Q: How did you determine that you didn't need a new PC?

A: After doing a little research and deciding to use Microsoft FrontPage to create the site, I read the system requirements for the software package. From these I was able to determine that I could create OfficeLinks.com on my existing PC.

Q: What other peripherals do you use for your Web site?

A: Excluding the mouse, keyboard, and monitor, the only peripheral that I have is an ink jet printer. I use the printer to print out pages of my Web site and pages from other Web sites. I also use it for printing important e-mails and account information.

Q: What software do you use for OfficeLinks.com?

A: I developed OfficeLinks.com with Microsoft FrontPage 98. I also use Microsoft Office Professional for things like word processing, creating presentations, and maintaining a list of contacts. The other software that I use almost daily is Microsoft Internet Explorer and Netscape Navigator.

Q: Why do you use more than one Web browser?

A: I've learned that not all of the features available to create Web pages in Microsoft FrontPage 98 can be viewed properly with Netscape Navigator. I avoid those features to make sure that all of my visitors can get the most out of the Web site.

Q: Why did you choose Microsoft FrontPage 98 to create your Web site?

A: First, I read as many reviews as possible on Web sites like ZDNet (*www.zdnet.com*) and Beyond.com (*www.beyond.com*). All of these sources gave it good marks for ease of use and rapid development. Finally, I tried it out and determined that it met my needs.

Q: What type of connection do you have to the Internet?

A: I have dial-up service with America Online that is set up on a separate phone line provided by my local phone company.

Q: Are you thinking about getting a faster connection than dial-up service?

A: *Thinking* is a good word. Right now the dial-up connection works just fine for updating the Web site and checking daily activity reports. Sometimes I wish I had a connection that was always "on," since it usually takes a few minutes to log on. Normally, I log on to look at the site and activity reports many times during the day, and those few minutes can add up.

Online Computing and Dial-Up Resources

Beyond.com (*www.beyond.com*)

Beyond.com is an online computer store that carries a wide variety of software titles. On this site you can get complete product descriptions, system requirements, and customer reviews for most software titles.

ISPs.com (*www.isps.com*)

ISPs.com can help you "find the best deal from our database of over 4,000 ISPs." This site allows you to search by area code, price, ISP name, and ISPs with toll-free access numbers.

Outpost.com (*www.outpost.com*)

Outpost.com describes itself as "the cool place to shop for computer stuff." On their site you can buy computer hardware, software, peripherals, and accessories. You can also download software onto your computer.

Webopedia (*www.webopedia.com*)

Webopedia describes itself at the "the only online dictionary and search engine you need for computer and Internet technology." You can use this resource to look up almost any technical term you have about computers, software, telecommunications, or the Internet.

Yahoo!: Computers & Internet (*www.dir.yahoo.com/Computers_and_Internet/*)

Yahoo! has a wide variety of links to online computer and Internet resources that include buyer's guides for hardware and software, and Web directories.

ZDNet: How to Buy Index (*www.zdnet.com/computershopper/edit/howtobuy/index.html*)

On the ZDNet Web site you will find a wealth of information about PCs and peripherals, including articles on: desktops, notebooks,

CD-ROM/DVD-ROM drives, digital cameras, graphics cards, hard drives, modems, monitors, motherboards, printers, and scanners.

Summary

Your key takeaway from this chapter is that you don't need a lot of special hardware and software to create a Web site. As long as you have a PC that is connected to the Internet through a dial-up modem, then you can get your business online. Most of the sub-$1,000 PCs available from your local electronics retailer will suffice.

A PC selection should be based on the type of software you are going to use to create a Web site. In addition to a PC, there are a few other peripherals you should consider to get your business online. For instance, if your Web site is going to have a lot of pictures, then you might consider a digital camera or at least a good-quality scanner.

For more information on this topic, visit our Web site at www.businesstown.com

Using Software Tools to Create Your Web Site

Chapter 6

Topics covered in this chapter

- **Categorizing alternative software development tools**
- **Understanding HTML and other technical terms**
- **Selecting an integrated solution for your Web site**
- **Choosing an online mall for your online business**
- **Choosing an off-the-shelf package to develop your Web site**

Building a great Web site takes more than a "dot-com" in your name. It takes a great vision and the ability to pick products and services that can turn that vision into e-reality.

MICHAEL J. MILLER, *WWW.ZDNET.COM*

Remember, if you want to build a Web site, you don't need to start by learning how to program with HTML or Java. Most beginners either use the tools provided by their Web hosting service or choose an off-the-shelf software package to develop their Web site.

Software tools fall into two separate categories. The first category includes software tools provided by your Internet service provider (ISP), Web hosting service, or online mall. These tools are integrated with the type of service you choose and are designed to get you up and running quickly. The second category consists of off-the-shelf software packages that are loaded onto your computer. These software packages give you more flexibility than the integrated tools, but still give you the capability to get up and running quickly.

Whether you select an integrated solution from your software provider, or an off-the-shelf software package, there are a few technical terms that you must understand. Some of them are as simple as WYSIWYG (What-You-See-Is-What-You-Get). Others are more complicated, like the bits, bytes, megabytes, and gigabytes that are used to measure disk space or capacity.

Before making your final decision on the type of software tools you are going to use to create your Web site, evaluate your requirements thoroughly. If you don't want to pay for a separate domain name, Web hosting service, and software package, consider either a free service like Max Pages, or one provided by your Internet service provider, like AOL Personal Publisher. On the other hand, if you want complete design flexibility and powerful development tools, you will need to go with something like Microsoft FrontPage or Macromedia Dreamweaver.

This chapter is written to get you to think about different types of software you can use to get your business online. However, due to the nature of the industry, where new software revisions are

> Most beginners either use the tools provided by their Web hosting service or choose an off-the-shelf package.

published almost every six months, you should do some research to make sure that you have a current understanding of the alternatives. Investigate your choices with some of the great online information tools like ZDNet (*www.zdnet.com*) for software reviews, Beyond.com (*www.beyond.com*) for software pricing and descriptions, and Webopedia (*www.webopedia.com*) for technical descriptions.

Categorizing Alternative Software Development Tools

In a nutshell, there are two categories of software tools to choose from in order to get your business online. The first category includes software tools that are provided by your Internet service provider (ISP), Web hosting service, or online mall. These tools are integrated with the type of service you choose and are designed to get you up and running quickly. Normally, you access these tools and design your Web site while you are connected, or logged in, to your service provider.

The second category includes off-the-shelf software packages that are loaded onto your computer. These software packages traditionally give you more flexibility than the integrated tools provided by your Internet service but still give you the capability to get up and running quickly. Normally, you purchase these products from a third-party provider, such as a retail store, and then create your Web site offline before loading it on a Web hosting service.

> Off-the-shelf software packages traditionally give you more flexibility than the integrated tools provided by your Internet service but still give you the capability to get up and running quickly.

Web Site Development Software Alternatives

SOFTWARE DEVELOPMENT TOOL CATEGORY	EXAMPLES	BENEFIT
Integrated with ISP, Web host, or mall-type service	Max Pages AOL Personal Publisher Amazon.com zShops MindSpring Web Creator	Usually provided free of charge with associated service
Stand-alone, off-the-shelf software package	NetObjects Fusion Microsoft FrontPage Adobe PageMill Macromedia Dreamweaver	Complete design flexibility

Faced with these two categories of software development tools, your first question should be, "What is the best approach for my online business?" The answer rests in what you want to do and how much you want to spend. Although both categories of software tools give you the capability to get up and running quickly, you will definitely be able to get online faster using the integrated tools. However, this difference is only a matter of hours or days, and is largely determined by the time it takes you to order separate off-the-shelf software and load it onto your computer.

Off-the-shelf software will give you more flexibility in designing your site. Although most of the integrated services let you choose from a variety of Web site design templates, the only real control you have is in the text, fonts, images, and pictures that you can add to the Web site. Envision a "fill in the blanks" scenario where you have little control over the underlying page.

Also, remember that some integrated services like AOL Personal Publisher and Max Pages, will not allow you to have your own domain name, or dot-com. If you decide to use these services, your online business will be named something like "members.aol.com/yourbiz" or "maxpages.com/yourbiz," as opposed to "www.yourbiz.com." Therefore, if you want to have complete control over almost every design aspect of your Web site, including your domain name, choosing an off-the-shelf package is the way to go.

The other aspect you should consider is the cost difference between an integrated service and an off-the-shelf software package. Most of the integrated services are *free*. For instance, if you are a member of AOL, you can use their Personal Publisher service for free. To create a Web site with Max Pages, you only need to have access to the Internet (just enter "www.maxpages.com" in your Web browser and follow the on-screen directions). On the other hand, an off-the-shelf software package will cost between $50 and $300.

> Off-the-shelf software will give you more flexibility in designing your site.

Understanding HTML and Other Technical Terms

There is little need for you to fully comprehend most of the technical terms covered in this section before you start building an online business. However, if you can at least recognize some of these terms and get a feel for their meaning, you should be in a better position to choose your software development tool.

WYSIWYG

WYSIWYG is a software design term that means "what-you-see-is-what-you-get." If your software design tool gives you this capability (and most do), there is usually a graphical interface between you and the underlying programming language that allows you to design your Web site with a mouse. When your software is equipped with a WYSIWYG editor, there is no need for you to learn a programming language like HTML, because the software will convert your on-screen design to HTML.

Bit (or BInary digiT)

Every computer uses an instruction set that is composed of a series of "bits" or "on–off" signals that are usually represented by a "1" or a "0." A bit can be thought of as a single instruction that tells a computer processor whether it is "on" or "off." Think of this like the relationship between a light bulb and a light switch—when the switch is up, the light is on, and when it is down, the light is off. A computer language combines a series of bits into bytes and provides an instruction set that tells a computer processor what to do.

Byte (or 8 bits)

A byte is composed of eight bits or "on–off" signals. You can think of a byte as being the computer representation for a letter, like "A," a number like "7," or an instruction to multiply two numbers, like "3 x 6." For the purposes of creating a Web site, the

> WYSIWYG is a software design term that means "what-you-see-is-what-you-get."

number of bytes will measure the size of your site in terms of disk space. For instance, if your Web hosting plan allows you to publish a 2MB (megabytes or million bytes) Web site, essentially it can be made up of 2 million characters or instructions.

		EQUIVALENT MEASUREMENT	
MEASUREMENT	APPROXIMATE REPRESENTATION	ACTUAL MEASUREMENT
1 byte	1 byte	8 bits
1 kilobyte	1 thousand bytes	1,024 bytes
1 megabyte	1 million bytes	1,048,576 bytes
1 gigabyte	1 trillion bytes	1,073,741,824 bytes

Disk Space (a lot of bytes)

In the world of Web publishing, disk space normally refers to the amount of space that is provided by your Web hosting service. Whether you publish your Web site using a free service like Max Pages, or a paid service like Verio, the amount of disk space you get on their server will be limited to a certain amount of bytes (for example, megabytes or MB). Obviously, the more space you get, the larger your site can be. The amount of space you will need depends on the number of pages in your Web, and more importantly, on the number and size of your graphic images. If your site is going to have a lot of graphic images, you will need a hosting service that provides a lot of disk space.

Disk space normally ranges from a few megabytes (MB) to hundreds of MBs. For instance, if you use the AOL Personal Publisher for your Web site, you will get 2MB of disk space per screen name. If you go with a robust hosting plan from Verio, you can get up to 100MB of disk space on their servers. Although it is difficult to determine exactly how much space you will need, keep in mind that you can get about 100,000 words on a single floppy disk, or 1.44MB.

Bandwidth (the pipe to your Web site)

Bandwidth is the amount of bits that a connection to the Internet can carry in a certain amount of time. Think of bandwidth

> If your site is going to have a lot of graphic images, you will need a hosting service that provides a lot of disk space.

like a water pipe. The larger the water pipe, the more water it can carry in a specific period of time. Common measurements for bandwidth are bits per second (bps) and megabits per second (Mbps).

Sometimes bandwidth can also be measured in bytes per second. For instance, you might see a bandwidth measurement in megabytes (million bytes) per second, that would be abbreviated MBps. The only distinction is that the "B" is capitalized to represent "Byte," as opposed to "bit."

BANDWIDTH MEASUREMENT		EQUIVALENT MEASUREMENT
Bits per second	bps	1 bit
Kilobits per second	Kbps	1,000 bits
Megabits per second	Mbps	1,000,0000 bits
Gigabits per second	Gbps	1,000,000,000 bits
Bytes per second	Bps	8 bits
Kilobytes per second	KBps	1,024 Bytes
Megabytes per second	MBps	1,048,576 Bytes
Gigabytes per second	GBps	1,073,741,824 Bytes

Bandwidth is important for a Web hosting service because it determines the amount of traffic, or visitors, that can be handled simultaneously. For instance, if your Web host only has a few small pipes connected to the Internet (for example, a couple of DS3s), the amount of traffic that it can handle will be much less than a Web host that has a lot of larger pipes (for example, a few OC48 systems).

HTML (computer language)

According to Webopedia (*www.webopedia.com*), hypertext markup language (HTML) "is the authoring language used to create documents on the World Wide Web." This language uses a special set of "tags" to create Web pages that can be read by Web browsers like Microsoft Internet Explorer and Netscape Navigator.

> Bandwidth is important for a Web hosting service because it determines the amount of traffic, or visitors, that can be handled simultaneously.

Software companies such as Microsoft and Macromedia have done a great job in creating software packages that allow you to design Web sites without knowing much about HTML. However, in a few instances, you will need to at least be able to identify a few important HTML components and understand their importance to search engines.

Java (programming language)

Java is a programming language created by Sun Microsystems. Once you have created an HTML document, Java allows you to add sound and pictures to make your site more interactive. Small programs that can be interpreted by Web browsing software, like Microsoft Internet Explorer or Netscape Navigator, are called Java applets.

ActiveX Controls (technologies)

ActiveX, developed by Microsoft, allows you to add controls to your Web site, like scroll bars, drop down menus, and radio buttons. Once you add these controls to your Web pages, they can be downloaded and used by Web browsing software.

Selecting an Integrated Solution for Your Web Site

> An integrated solution involves using the tools provided by your Internet service provider (ISP), Web hosting service, or online mall to develop your Web site.

As described earlier, an integrated solution involves using the tools provided by your Internet service provider (ISP), Web hosting service, or online mall to develop your Web site. In this section you will find examples of how to use the software tools provided by Max Pages, AOL Personal Publisher, MindSpring Web Creator, and Amazon.com zShops.

All of these alternatives are best suited for quickly setting up your home page, getting your brochure on the Web, or trying to sell some of your products online. However, none give you the flexibility most professionals require to develop Web sites. If you are brand-new to the online world, you should definitely try a few of these solutions to see if they meet your immediate needs.

When you need more flexibility, or powerful programming solutions, then it's time to investigate the off-the-shelf software packages described later in this chapter.

Trying a Free Service Like Max Pages

Max Pages is a free service that provides a quick and easy way to get your business online in less than an hour (minutes, according to their home page). After you have finished designing your site it will have a name like "www.maxpages.com/yourbiz."

If you don't already have a Web site, you should definitely try Max Pages or one of the other free services shown in the following table:

> There are many *free* Web hosting services that provide their own integrated software tools.

FREE INTEGRATED WEB SERVICES	WEB ADDRESS
Angelfire	*www.angelfire.com*
Click2site	*www.click2site.com*
FreeUK	*www.freeuk.com*
GeoCities (Yahoo!)	*www.geocities.yahoo.com/home/*
Max Pages	*www.maxpages.com*
MoneyAvenue	*www.moneyave.com*
Myfreeoffice	*www.myfreeoffice.com*
WebJump	*www.webjump.com*
XOOM.com	*www.xoom.com*

To create a free Web site with Max Pages, do the following:

1. Type "www.maxpages.com" in your Web browser's address box and press Enter.
2. On the Max Pages home page, click on "Create Site."
3. After you get to the *Create Your Site* page, enter the name of your Web site and your e-mail address.

4. Once you enter this information, click on the "I Agree to Terms, Create Site" button. If you want to see the Max Pages terms and conditions, click on "View Terms and Conditions."
5. Next you will receive a password and confirmation that your Web site name is available. Print a copy of this information for future reference.
6. Now you can follow the series of on-screen directions to create your free Web site, including choosing a name for your site, selecting background colors, and inserting your content.

Using Your ISP Tools to Create a Web Site

Most Internet service providers (ISPs)s, such as AOL, MindSpring, and Earthlink, give their subscribers a way to create Web sites for no additional charge. For instance, if you subscribe to AOL, you can use its Personal Publisher service to create a home page or simple Web site.

As with the free services described earlier, the software tools provided by your ISP are normally easy to use and allow you to set up your site in less than an hour. The main limitations of these services are that your disk space will be limited (2MB for AOL), and your Web address will contain the name of your ISP ("members.aol.com/yourbiz/index.html").

To give you an idea of how easy it is to set up a site with your ISP, here are the steps required for AOL's Personal Publisher:

1. On the AOL Internet Connection page, click on the "Internet Extras" button.
2. Once you get to the *Internet Extras* page, click on the "Personal Publisher" button.
3. On the *Personal Publisher* page, you can now click on "Create a Page," then select a Personal, Business, or Greeting template.
4. Now follow the on-screen directions to complete your personal Web site.

> The software tools provided by your ISP are normally easy to use and allow you to set up your site in less than an hour.

Choosing an Online Mall for Your Online Business

There are a growing number of online malls that allow you to quickly set up shop on the Internet. Although your design capabilities will be limited with these services, they do offer the e-commerce benefits of shopping cart technology and credit card processing.

Popular Online Malls

ONLINE MALL	WEB ADDRESS
Amazon.com zShops	*www.amazon.com*
GO-SHOP™	*www.go-shop.com*
iMALL	*www.imall.com*
ShopNow.com	*www.shopnow.com*
The iCat Mall	*www.icatmall.com*
Yahoo! Shopping	*www.store.yahoo.com/ad.html*

To create your store with an online mall service, access their home page, select "Create Store," then follow the on-screen directions. Another alternative similar to online malls is the online auction sites, such as eBay (*www.ebay.com*). In fact, Amazon.com will let you place items in both their online auction and zShops for the same price.

Using the Software Provided by Your Web Host

If you want a full featured Web site, with lots of disk space and your own personal domain name ("www.yourbiz.com"), you will need to sign up for a Web hosting plan. This can either be with your ISP, such as Earthlink, or with a separate company, such as Verio. (See Chapter 10 for a complete description of Web hosting services.)

Most Web hosting services give you the capability of publishing a Web site with either an off-the-shelf software package, or with a set of their integrated design tools. For instance, if MindSpring is your Web host, you can either create a Web site with Microsoft FrontPage, or use the MindSpring Web Creator design tools.

If you want a full featured Web site, with lots of disk space and your own personal domain name ("www.yourbiz.com"), you will need to sign up for a Web hosting plan.

Popular Web Hosting Services

WEB HOST	WEB ADDRESS
9Net Avenue	*www.9netave.net*
C I Host	*www.cihost.com*
Concentric Network	*www.concentric.com*
Datarealm	*www.serve.com*
Earthlink	*www.earthlink.net*
MindSpring	*www.mindspring.com*
Verio	*www.verio.com*
Web 2010	*www.web2010.com*

Additionally, with a Web host you will have an option of setting up an online store and adding e-commerce capabilities that are not available with a free service like Max Pages, or with your ISP's publishing tools.

Choosing an Off-the-Shelf Package to Develop Your Web Site

If you really want to do more with your Web site than simply setting up a home page or publishing a brochure, then you seriously need to explore some of the off-the-shelf software packages on the market today. You will find that these packages are easy to use and give you many Web site development capabilities that are required by professionals.

All of the packages covered in this section have templates and wizards so that you can begin creating your site from the moment the software is loaded on your computer. They also come equipped with a WYSIWYG editor so that you don't need to learn HTML in order to create your Web site.

In an ideal world you would be able to buy all of the software packages, build your Web site with each one, and then decide which one works best for your application. Unfortunately, few people and organizations have that luxury. Therefore you will have to rely on some product descriptions and software reviews before making your decision.

It will help greatly to list all of the capabilities you will need for your Web site. For instance, ask yourself:

List all of the capabilities you will need for your Web site.

- How will credit card processing be handled?
- Does this package work with all Web hosts?
- Is there a way to handle large databases?
- How hard is it to add pictures to a Web page?
- What are the system requirements to use the software?

Once you have made your list, start to match up your requirements with specific off-the-shelf software packages.

Finally, you should consider price only after you have made a list of your requirements. If the least expensive software package does everything you want it to do, make your decision based on price. Go with the least expensive package. However, if a more expensive package provides features or functions that you need, don't buy a cheaper package. As of this writing, the following software titles range in price from $79 for Adobe PageMill 3.0 to $312.50 for NetObjects Fusion v3.0.

> Off-the-shelf software packages are easy to use and give you development capabilities that are required by professionals.

Microsoft FrontPage 2000

Edward Mendelson, writing in the June 1, 1999, issue of *PC Magazine,* says, "For beginning Webmasters and educational or small business users, Microsoft FrontPage 2000 ($150 street; $60 upgrade) is the simplest way to build complex Web sites, complete with discussion forums and database features."

In the following table you will find many key features and system requirements for Microsoft FrontPage 2000, as shown on Beyond.com (*www.beyond.com*). For more details, including a comprehensive list of all features, search for "Microsoft FrontPage 2000" on the Beyond.com Web site.

MICROSOFT FRONT PAGE 2000 FEATURES	SYSTEM REQUIREMENTS
Put graphics, text, and other elements anyplace you want them	Pentium 75MHz processor or higher
Choose from 60 new predesigned, ready-to-use themes	Windows 95/98/NT 4.0 with Service Pack 3 or higher
Edit existing HTML and scripts created with other tools	24MB RAM, 40MB RAM for Windows NT
Incorporate databases into your Web	167MB disk space for typical installation
Integrate other Microsoft products, like Excel and Word documents	CD-ROM Drive
	VGA or higher-resolution monitor
	List price $149

For Edward Mendelson's complete review of Microsoft FrontPage 2000:

1. Type "www.zdnet.com" into your Web browser's address box and press Enter.
2. On the ZDNet home page, click on "Product Reviews" located near the top of the page.
3. Once you get to the Product Reviews page, scroll down to the "Internet & Network" heading and click on "Web Authoring."

Adobe PageMill 3.0

Adobe says its PageMill 3.0 for Windows "provides the easiest way to get your business on the World Wide Web.... It's the only tool you need to design, build, post, and manage your Web pages, plus there's no need to learn HTML or master complex applications."

The following table shows a list of features and system requirements for Adobe PageMill 3.0, as found on Beyond.com (*www.beyond.com*). For more details, including a comprehensive list of all features, search for "Adobe PageMill 3.0" on the Beyond.com Web site.

ADOBE PAGEMILL 3.0 FEATURES	SYSTEM REQUIREMENTS
Includes drag-and-drop simplicity with WYSIWYG interface	80486 or higher processor
Offers more than 10,000 Web-ready images, sounds, video clips, animations, and customizable templates	Windows 95/NT 4.0 or higher
Editing capability for HTML	16MB RAM
Interface with e-commerce solutions from ICentral ShopSite Express	20MB disk space
	VGA 8-bit or higher monitor
	CD-ROM drive
	List price $79

If you would like to read a review about Adobe PageMill 3.0, visit the ZDNet (*www.zdnet.com*) Web site. A review by Sean Wagstaff, published in the November 2, 1998, issue of *MacWEEK*, describes Adobe PageMill as "a solid nuts-and-bolts editor aimed at small businesses with basic Web sites.... Overall, however, PageMill 3 is an elegantly constructed Web page design tool that offers most of the features most users will need most of the time."

Macromedia Dreamweaver v2.0

Macromedia describes Dreamweaver 2 as "the solution for professional Web site design and production. It is the only tool to offer Roundtrip HTML between visual and source editing for fast creation of great looking, cross browser Web sites."

The following table lists the features and system requirements for Macromedia Dreamweaver v2.0, as found on Beyond.com (*www.beyond.com*). For more details, including a comprehensive list of all features, search for "Macromedia Dreamweaver" on the Beyond.com Web site.

MACROMEDIA DREAMWEAVER V2.0 FEATURES	SYSTEM REQUIREMENTS
Offers "roundtrip" HTML between visual and source editing	Intel Pentium processor or equivalent 90MHz or higher processor
Supports other applications, like ASP, Apache, BroadVision, Cold Fusion, iCat, Tango	Windows 95/98/NT 4.0 or higher
Use drag-and-drop design features	32MB RAM
Separate content from design with XML	20MB disk space
Develop sites collaboratively	256-color monitor capable of 800x600 resolution
	List price $299

In an article titled "Build Your Dream Site," written by Rich Schwerin for *PC Computing* on June 14, 1999, a review for Macromedia Dreamweaver v2.0 begins: "Looks aren't everything–unless you're talking about the Web. At least for the first few seconds it takes to lure visitors onto your site and keep them there, looks are all that matter. So how do you design a knockout business online? You can go for broke and hire a consultant, or do it yourself with Macromedia Dreamweaver 2." To read this and other articles about Macromedia Dreamweaver, go to the ZDNet (*www.zdnet.com*) Web site and search for "Macromedia Dreamweaver."

NetObjects Fusion v4.0

According to an article by Jan Ozer in the May 12, 1999, issue of *PC Magazine*, NetObjects Fusion v4.0 "has evolved into a top-notch authoring and site management tool suitable for a broad range of developers, although novices may be deterred by the $300 price tag. Aside from a few weaknesses, NetObjects Fusion 4.0 delivers everything you'd expect and, as your site grows, a whole lot more."

The following table lists the features and system requirements for NetObjects Fusion v4.0, as found on Beyond.com (*www.beyond.com*). For more details, including a comprehensive list of all features, search for "NetObjects Fusion v4.0" on the Beyond.com Web site.

NETOBJECTS FUSION V4.0 FEATURES	SYSTEM REQUIREMENTS
Contains more than 600 pages of documentation (including tutorials) and tons of sample content, styles, and templates	90MHz or faster Pentium processor
Includes a SiteStructure editor to make layout easier	Windows 95/NT 3.51 or later
Links to ODBC-compatible databases like MS Access	32MB RAM
Centralized control of styles	50MB hard disk space (100MB required for full installation)
Database publishing capabilities	60MB hard disk space available
	Monitor capable of 800x600 at 256 colors
	CD-ROM drive
	List price $312.50

To read Jan Ozer's entire review, or see other articles on NetObjects Fusion, go to the ZDNet (*www.zdnet.com*) Web site and search for "NetObjects Fusion."

Selecting a Software Development Tool for OfficeLinks.com

Q: What software did you use to create OfficeLinks.com?

A: I used Microsoft FrontPage 98.

Q: How did you decide on Microsoft FrontPage 98 to create your site?

A: I researched the different software applications to create Web sites on ZDNet (*www.zdnet.com*) and on Beyond.com (*www.beyond.com*). After reading the reviews, and discovering that FrontPage seemed to do what I wanted, I went with that package. Also, the reality is that I am very familiar with many Microsoft products and felt comfortable in choosing them over the others. To me it was a "safe bet."

Q: Did you consider using any of the software tools that are integrated with your Internet service?

A: Yes. The first Web site that I ever created was with AOL Personal Publisher. However, I knew this wasn't an alternative since I wanted a "real" domain name (*www.officelinks.com*). Also, I needed more design flexibility than I was getting with AOL Personal Publisher.

Q: What were your biggest concerns in choosing FrontPage?

A: One thing that I spent a lot of time researching was whether FrontPage would work with my Web hosting service. In fact, after I had chosen Front page, I went looking for a hosting service that fully supported the product.

Q: How does a Web host fully support FrontPage?

A: As I understand it, in order for a Web host to fully support this product, they need to have computers that run the Microsoft Windows NT operating system. If your host doesn't have this operating system available, you cannot use all of the capabilities embedded in FrontPage.

Q: What else did you like about FrontPage?

A: It's very easy to create Web pages and publish them on my Web host. Also, the software figures out what pages I have changed since my last update, and then gives me the option of only updating those pages on my Web host.

Q: Are there any limitations for FrontPage?

A: Yes. I had read that not all of the FrontPage features and functions worked on all Internet browsers. Everything works on their Microsoft Internet Explorer but may not work on Netscape Navigator. Since I found this to be true, I made sure to test my site on a few different browsers, and then use only functions that worked on all of them.

Q: Are you going to upgrade to Microsoft FrontPage 2000?

A: Yes. I'm definitely going to try their newer product at some point in the future. But right now, the older version works fine.

Online Software Development Resources

Beyond.com (*www.beyond.com*)

Beyond.com is an online software store where you can buy the popular Web site development software tools, including Microsoft FrontPage, Adobe PageMill, Macromedia Dreamweaver, and NetObject Fusion. Additionally, on this site you can get complete product descriptions, pricing, and customer reviews of different software products.

"Build a Better Web Site" article (*www.zdnet.com/pcmag/stories/reviews/ 0,6755,2257024,00.html*)

This article, written by Michael J. Miller for *PC Magazine*, provides a good overview of the tools and technologies for building a Web site. Also, from this article you can access many links on the ZDNet Web site for other articles describing how to develop a Web site.

Developer.com (*www.developer.com*)

This site, owned by EarthWeb (*www.earthweb.com*), has an extensive resource directory that covers many software-related areas, including HTML/DHTML, ActiveX, e-commerce, Windows programming, operating systems, and JavaScript.

MSDN Online Web Workshop (*www.msdn.microsoft.com/workshop/*)

According to Microsoft's home page, "The MSDN Online Web Workshop provides the latest information about Internet technologies, including reference material and in-depth articles on all aspects of Web site design and development."

Netscape Web Building (*www.home.netscape.com/computing/webbuilding/*)

In their "Computing & Internet" directory, Netscape has numerous departments devoted to creating Web sites, including Web authoring, Web programming, Web graphics, Web servers, and Web business.

Web Monkey: A How-to Guide for Web Developers (*www.hotwired.com/webmonkey*)

Produced by Wired Digital, the Web Monkey site has an extensive set of information for Web site designers that is categorized as follows: e-business, design, HTML, JavaScript, databases, graphics and fonts, multimedia, browsers, Java, and stylesheets.

Summary

In this chapter you learned there are two types of software tools that can be used to create a Web site: an off-the-shelf software package like Microsoft FrontPage or template-based tools provided by your Web hosting service. Your selection will be based on cost and on the degree of flexibility you will require to build your online business.

Although the templates provided by a Web hosting service are usually more cost effective than buying an additional software package, they lack the flexibility required by some Web designers. Therefore, you must thoroughly evaluate how your Web site is going to work and what you want it to do before making the final selection.

For more information on this topic, visit our Web site at www.businesstown.com

Chapter 7

Choosing an E-Commerce Solution to Meet Your Needs

Topics covered in this chapter

- Selecting the e-commerce features you need
- Collecting money over the Internet
- Designing your back office operations to support your online business
- Choosing a prepackaged e-commerce solution

Carnegie Public Library
202 N. Animas St.
Trinidad, CO 81082-2643

The number of users who make purchases over the Web will jump from 31 million in 1998 to more than 183 million in 2003. Furthermore, there is ample opportunity to expand the 183 million as it will represent only 36% of all Web users.

INTERNATIONAL DATA CORPORATION (IDC), *WWW.IDC.COM*

Amazon.com became one of the early pioneers of e-commerce by selling books directly to millions of online consumers through its Web site. However, it has become increasingly difficult for other online e-tailers to successfully mimic the Amazon.com strategy, as witnessed by recent failures such as Value America. Even as this book goes to print, Amazon.com is still not planning to make any profits for the foreseeable future and other e-tailers like Beyond.com are re-evaluating their business strategy.

If you are reading this chapter with dollar signs in your eyes, seriously consider where those dollars are going to come from! Today, e-commerce is not so much about making money as it is about saving money. Yes, you can set up a business in record time on the Internet and begin collecting online payments with credit cards, but this still doesn't mean that you can start a successful business online—one in which you actually make a profit every month.

> E-commerce is not so much about making money as it is about saving money.

The great thing about e-commerce is that you can now start an online business for a fraction of the cost of its offline counterpart. For a couple of hundred dollars a month, you can open an online store and begin selling to anyone in the world who has a personal computer and a modem. Your expense is negligible when you compare it to doing the same thing in the offline world, for example by opening a chain of retail outlets.

Even if you already have a profitable offline "bricks and mortar" operation, you can still save money by transforming your business into a "clicks and mortar" operation. Nowhere is this more true than in the traditional mail order business. For example, before the Internet, mail order businesses had to publish thousands, or even millions, of catalogs each year and staff a call center with people to accept orders. The cost of processing these orders might range from $15 to $50 for every order. Now with e-commerce on the Internet, the cost of processing online orders is less than $1 each.

There should be no doubt in your mind that you can save money by opening a store online, or reducing your customer service expense, by using the latest e-commerce technologies. However, successful e-commerce usually results from many of the other topics discussed in this book, like Web site design and layout and conducting successful advertising campaigns.

In this chapter you will learn about many of the e-commerce technologies that online businesses are using to collect money online, such as credit card processing and electronic wallets. Additionally, we will discuss the many "back office" aspects of e-commerce, like order processing and customer service.

> Successful e-commerce on the Internet involves setting up both good "front-end" and "back-end" systems for your online business.

Selecting the E-Commerce Features You Need

Conducting successful e-commerce on the Internet involves setting up both good "front-end" and "back-end" systems for your online business. Front-end systems include the layout and navigational structure of your Web site (as discussed in Chapter 11), shopping carts, credit card payment methods, check guarantee services, and secure ordering technologies. Back-end systems include your warehousing and distribution, customer service, and return authorization policies.

This section gives you a brief overview of these features, and is followed by a more in-depth look at using merchant account providers to collect money online. If all of this seems too complicated, or overwhelming, for your business, consider one of the completely integrated e-commerce solutions discussed at the end of this chapter.

Getting a Shopping Cart for Your Online Store

A shopping cart system gives your customers a convenient way to buy multiple items from your online store during the same session. It is better than the traditional "grocery cart" system because it updates the shopping list and total price every time something is placed in the cart. Think how nice it would be if you knew how much your total grocery bill was going to be before you got to the checkout counter. Especially when you are on a tight budget!

If you are thinking about getting a shopping cart system for your Web site, some of the features you should look for include:

- Get a shopping cart system that provides all of the shipping cost alternatives you will need. For instance, if you are going to ship overseas, make sure that different costs are calculated for shipments to different countries. Likewise, you should be able to charge different rates for ground, air, and overnight delivery.
- Make sure your shopping cart can handle different tax rates for different states. Although pure online businesses are still not required to collect sales tax, offline businesses with an online presence are.
- Understand how you are going to get information from your shopping cart system. Find out whether you can load it into your database or spreadsheet program for additional processing and analysis.

There is no better way to learn about online shopping carts than to actually take a few for a "test drive." Almost every major shopping destination on the Web includes a shopping cart, and you can try them all without making a single purchase. Simply go to the large online retail sites, like Amazon.com, Outpost.com, or Drugstore.com, and fill up a basket of goods. After you are done, simply cancel your order or go to another Web site.

The prepackaged solutions discussed at the end of this chapter offer shopping cart technology that you can add to your Web site. Additionally, most Web hosting services offer shopping cart technology if you subscribe to one of their e-commerce packages.

Accepting Credit Cards Online

For the many online businesses that have a lot of customers or a wide selection of inventory, accepting credit cards online is a "must-have" e-commerce feature. However, before you can begin to accept credit cards online you will need to establish a business account with a bank, set up an additional merchant account (which can be with the same bank), and then establish a method to process credit cards.

> There is no better way to learn about online shopping carts than to actually take a few for a "test drive."

> In order to accept credit cards online, you will need to establish a merchant account.

Although the many merchant account providers (MAPs) say accepting credit cards online will dramatically increase your sales, be wary of the costs associated with these transactions. Normally, in addition to monthly account fees, MAPs will want a percentage of your sales and a separate fee for every transaction. Full details on credit card processing and MAPs are provided in the next section.

Making Your Customers Feel Secure

One of the great barriers that online businesses face is getting customers to actually buy something on their Web sites. Even if these sites are well designed, offer sufficient product descriptions, and make great product presentations, customers still may not buy anything because they fear their credit card information might be stolen. One thing you can do to alleviate this fear is to offer "secure" connections when you ask customers to provide their credit card number.

A secure connection gives you the ability to encrypt communication that occurs between your Web site and a customer's computer. Encryption technology uses mathematical formulas to turn this communication into a series of special codes that can only be read by computers that understand the encryption code. When a customer visits a secure area of your Web site, like the page that asks for their credit card number, you essentially share with them the secret code that they will use to send you their credit card information. This way they can be assured that no one else can see this information. One of the most common forms of online security uses the Secure Sockets Layer (SSL) protocol.

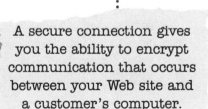

A secure connection gives you the ability to encrypt communication that occurs between your Web site and a customer's computer.

If you want to offer these secure connections for your online business customers, you will first need to apply for a digital ID from a company like VeriSign (*www.verisign.com*). According to VeriSign, "Digital IDs provide a means of proving your identity in electronic transactions, much like a driver's license or a passport does in face-to-face interactions. With a Digital ID, you can assure friends, business associates, and online services that the electronic information they receive from you are authentic."

As with shopping cart technology and credit card processing, the prepackaged solutions presented at the end of this chapter will give you the capability to provide secure connections for your customers. Additionally, most Web hosting services offer you secure technology if you subscribe to one of their e-commerce packages.

Collecting Money over the Internet

If you are planning to sell products and services over the Internet, you will need a way for customers to pay you. The most common way of accepting payment over the Internet is through a credit card; however, there are a couple of other alternatives, like taking a personal check or simply using an offline invoicing process.

The method you choose for collecting money over the Internet should be based on the type of items you are trying to sell, the quantity of items you are planning to sell, and the number of customers you anticipate. For instance, if you are planning to sell a lot of items to many different customers, you will want to establish a merchant account so that you can accept credit card payments online. On the other hand, if you are planning to sell "big ticket" items, like cars or prefabricated homes, you should consider taking a personal check online, or just keep the payment process offline.

Getting a Merchant Account to Accept Credit Cards

The most common way for e-tailers to accept online payments is through a credit card. By accepting credit cards online, you get the assurance that you will be paid (assuming the item isn't returned), and your customers get a sense of security that whatever they buy can be returned if they don't like it.

Unfortunately, especially for small businesses, accepting credit cards online or offline presents two challenges. First, you have to find a bank that will allow you to offer credit cards, and second, you need the technological capability to accept credit card payments. If you want to accept credit cards online, your first step is to establish a merchant account with your bank or a merchant account provider (MAP).

A merchant account is a special type of account that allows you to accept credit cards. A merchant account acts as the intermediary between your business bank account and your customer's

> The method you choose for collecting money over the Internet should be based on the type of items you are trying to sell, the quantity of items you are planning to sell, and the number of customers you anticipate.

credit card account. Think of it as a clearinghouse for credit card transactions. Money is transferred from your customer's credit card account, to the merchant account, and then finally to your business bank account.

Before for you select a MAP, there are some features you should consider for your merchant account. For instance, if you are going to have a high volume of transactions, you will want an account that offers "real-time transaction processing." A list of the features you should consider and their benefits are shown in the following table.

MERCHANT ACCOUNT FEATURES	DESCRIPTION OF BENEFITS
Offline manual transaction processing	Offline manual transaction processing gives you the capability to accept credit card payments over the Web. However, you cannot verify credit in real time. Credit card numbers are captured on your site, but then you must get authorization through a separate manual process, like calling the bank. This is a better alternative for a low volume of transactions since it is less expensive than real-time processing.
Real-time transaction processing	Real-time transaction processing allows you to verify credit online while your customer is still on your Web site. This is a good feature for high volumes of activity or for merchandise that is difficult to recover (like software downloads). This is more expensive than processing transactions manually offline.
Technological compatibility	Some MAPs only offer their complete line of features if you purchase their hosting plan and Web site building tools. If you are planning to use different software or hosting services, make sure to evaluate how your MAP will interface with your system. This is especially important for real-time processing, since your Web site must be able to communicate with the MAP in real (and fast) time.

In addition to evaluating different MAP features, you will also want to understand the different MAP fees, including discount rate, transaction fees, monthly fees, set-up costs, and charge-back contingencies.

Discount rate. This is a fixed percentage charged for every transaction you complete online. Discount rates can be as high as 3 percent per transaction. Expect to pay more for online sales than the traditional offline "swiping" systems.

Transaction fees. In addition to paying a discount rate, your MAP will probably charge you a fixed fee for every online transaction that is completed (between $0.25 and $0.75 per transaction). This fee is similar to the fee that you commonly have to pay to get money from a cash machine. Watch out for these fees if you are planning to sell a lot of low priced, or low margin, items.

Monthly fees. Most MAPs charge a flat monthly fee just for the merchant account itself. This means that even if you have very little activity in the form of transactions, you will still have to pay for the merchant account.

Set-up costs. There are usually many costs associated with the establishment of a merchant account. These set-up costs can cover any special software or telecommunications equipment that you will need to process transactions.

Charge-back contingencies. In order to protect themselves from having to process a lot of returns, MAPs will want to hold some of your money to give credit to your customers for any merchandise they decide to return. This is usually deducted as a percentage of your sales.

There are significant expenses associated with collecting payments online through credit card processing.

As you can see, there are significant expenses associated with collecting payments online through credit card processing. Therefore, it is important that you research many different MAPs before deciding which plan offers the best solution. The following is a sampling of MAPs that offer online credit card transaction processing services.

Merchant account provider (MAP)	Web address
First Merchant Solutions Agency	*www.safesolutions.com*
1st National BankCard Internet Services	*www.visamcwebsite.com*
Electronic Merchant Systems	*www.bankcardsystems.com*
EZ Merchant	*www.ezmerchantaccounts.com*
Total Merchant Services	*www.demerchantservices.com*
Chargc.Com	*www.chargo.com*
Plug 'n 'Pay Technologies	*www.plugnpay.com*
Signature Card Services	*www.signaturecard.com*
Heartland Payment Systems	*www.visa-mc.com*

Additionally, if you want to locate more MAPs, or just get a better understanding of how these services work, visit MerchantWorkz (*www.merchantworkz.com*). Page 128 features an example of the fees and types of services offered by EZ Merchant, a merchant account provider.

Taking a Personal Check over the Web

The popularity of taking a personal check in the offline world has not taken the online world by storm. The main reason is that taking a personal check from a complete stranger is risky business. Unlike credit cards, which can be authorized immediately, there is no easy way to verify credit on a personal check without actually depositing it in a bank and waiting for the funds to clear. Still, there are some online check guarantee services that operate in the same manner as credit card processing services.

As shown on page 129 in the service description from EZ Check Guarantee, you can give your customers the ability to pay online for your products and services with a personal check. Essentially, your customers will be asked to complete a blank check online, which the service provider will authorize (or reject) based on the information provided.

> There are some online check guarantee services that operate in the same manner as credit card processing services.

Sample Merchant Account Provider Service Description— from EZ Merchant (*www.ezmerchantaccounts.com*)

We have 2 separate and distinct programs available for the Internet merchant. The first is the ETC touch tone program that requires no equipment, software, or long term commitment. All transactions are processed through an automated 800 phone system. The second program available is Authorizenet real time on-line processing. This is the state of the art approach to Internet processing and includes a weblink which integrates into your website and a virtual terminal for your manual transactions.

ETC Touch Tone Program

- Discount Rate: 2.95%
- Transaction Fee: $0.40
- Monthly Minimum: $25.00
- Statement Fee: $9.50
- One Time Setup Fee: $295.00
- Monthly Recurring Fees: $34.50 = ($25.00 + $9.50)

Program Description: This program uses an automated touch tone phone system to process transactions and requires no software or equipment. Excellent for the start-up or Internet based business that needs a low cost entry level merchant account. For a full program description and pricing click on the Non-Real time link in the navigation bar, or the link in the header above.

Program Pros: Low cost, can be used from any phone.

Program Cons: For companies with large volume transactions, e.g., 50–100 a day, it would be tedious to manually enter.

Authorizenet Real Time

- Discount Rate: 2.30%–2.49%
- Transaction Fee: $0.35
- Monthly Minimum: $25.00
- Statement Fee: $9.50
- Secure Gateway Fee: $20.00
- One Time Setup Fee: $395.00
- Monthly Recurring Fees: $54.50 = ($25.00, $9.50, $20.00)

Program Description: Authorizenet is the state of the art real time processing system on the Internet today. With over 30,000 merchants on-line it offers both real time ability as well as access to a virtual terminal for manual transactions. Click on the header above or the real time link in the navigation bar for full program details and pricing.

Program Pros: On line real time processing, available fraud screen, eCheck option, virtual terminal for manual transaction. See program page for full details

Program Cons: If you are a very low volume merchant with no intention of offering real time transactions, this program may be more then you need.

Sample Online Check Guarantee Service Description—from EZ Check Guarantee (*www.ezcheckguarantee.com/checknet.htm*)

How ChecksByNet authorizes checks is quite unique. When a customer enters into a web store and wishes to purchase an item, they will navigate to the purchase screen which will include payment by check. The programming design here is completely self-supporting and will overlay any existing web store design or wallet product. In fact the consumer will be totally unaware that they are interfacing with any site other than the one on which they are shopping, other than the fact that they will see the security flag appear on the bottom of their PC screen.

Once the customer chooses the check payment option they will go directly to CrossCheck's Authorization Center (completely invisible to the consumer). At this point they will be asked a few questions, and they will simply fill out a blank check on the screen. The information will download to CrossCheck for authorization and seconds later the purchase will be approved. The customer will continue their order on the web page or at the cyber store. Minutes later, or on demand, the check will be recalled from CrossCheck by the cyber merchant and printed at the merchant's site, authorized and guaranteed.

As with accepting credit cards online, check guarantee services also charge their customers fees for processing checks over the Internet. Common fees usually include a percentage of sales, a fee per transaction, and an optional fee if you want to print the check. Additionally, some service providers charge a monthly account maintenance fee.

If you would like to learn more about online check guarantee services, visit some of the service providers shown in the following table. Also, you should be aware that most MAPs provide these services. Therefore, you might want to consider offering both online check acceptance and credit card authorizations from the same MAP.

> Most Merchant Account Providers (MAPs) offer check guarantee services for an additional fee.

CHECK AUTHORIZATION SERVICES	WEB ADDRESS
First Merchant Solutions Agency	*www.safesolutions.com*
Electronic Merchant Systems	*www.bankcardsystems.com*
Total Merchant Services	*www.demerchantservices.com*
MerchantChecks	*www.merchantchecks.com*
Vericard	*www.vericardsystems.com*
EZ Check Guarantee	*www.ezcheckguarantee.com*
E-Commerce Exchange	*www.ecx.com*
Point of Sale Services	*www.possinc.com*

Using Digital Cash and Electronic Wallets

In the past few years a couple of new alternatives have emerged to make electronic buying and selling over the Web easier and more secure. The first is a product called eCash, from eCash Technologies (*www.ecashtechnologies.com*), which lets consumers store electronic cash on their computers that can be used to buy merchandise over the Web from participating sellers. Essentially, the bank takes money out of a bank account and stores it as electronic cash on a customer's computer. Then, when a customer wants to make a purchase using their computer, they transfer the electronic cash to the seller as a payment. If you want to accept electronic cash as a payment method, you will need to get special software from eCash and join a bank that participates in the program.

Another way to collect money over the Web is through an electronic wallet service such as CyberCash (*www.cybercash.com*) or VeriFone (*www.verifone.com*). Electronic wallets store encrypted credit card numbers on a customer's computer that only need to be entered once. When a customer makes a purchase from a participating seller's Web site, the encrypted credit card information is transferred from the customer to the seller, and then from the seller to a bank. The seller and CyberCash never see the credit card information. Like digital cash, if you want to accept payments from electronic wallets, you will need special software from your vendor.

Processing Transactions Manually Offline

Many businesses do not need to offer credit card processing or check guarantee services online. As stated earlier, the way you decide to collect money from your online customers depends on the type and quality of items you are trying to sell, and the number of customers you anticipate. If you are selling only a few items to a small customer base, or selling "big ticket" items that wouldn't normally be charged to credit cards, you should be able to process your transactions manually offline.

One way to process transactions manually offline is to create an order form on your Web site that your customers can complete online (like the order form template provided with Microsoft

> Besides credit cards and personal checks, there are some other ways that you can collect money over the Internet.

> The way you decide to collect money from your online customers depends on the type and quality of items you are trying to sell, and the number of customers you anticipate.

FrontPage). This form should be set-up with an e-mail capability, so that once it is completed, your customers can automatically send it to you. At this point you can generate an invoice with your accounting software and send it to them using U.S. "snail" mail. Your customers will then pay you offline by mailing you a check.

Designing Your Back Office Operations to Support Your Online Business

Once you have settled on the "front-end" technologies for your online business, such as shopping carts, credit card processing, and secure connections, it's time to turn to the "back-end" systems that will ultimately determine your customer's buying experience. Consider your back-end systems as being everything that happens from the moment your customer places an order until it is finally delivered as promised.

Back-end systems, or back office operations, usually consist of order processing, shipping and handling, and return authorizations. Additionally, you can greatly enhance your customer's online buying experience if you give them the capability to communicate with you through as many means as possible, such as telephone support, e-mail support, and fax support.

> Back-end systems, or back office operations, usually consist of order processing, shipping and handling, and return authorizations.

Processing Orders As Promised

Once a customer decides to make a purchase from your online business, it is up to you to deliver the goods as promised. Your first step in the order processing system should be to send an acknowledgment of the order to the customer, including a special thanks for ordering from your online business. The acknowledgment should spell out what was ordered, the total price, shipping and handling charges, and applicable sales tax. Usually a simple e-mail containing these details will suffice.

Next you need to fulfill the customer's order. If you are running a small business, with only a few employees, this task should be relatively simple. For instance, you might print out a copy of the order form and give it to a shipping clerk, who in turn will mail the goods requested to the customer. However, if you are running a larger business, you may want to consider integrating your "back-end" accounting software, or order management system, with your "front-end" Web site. Ultimately, you will want these systems to communicate with each other so that orders flow directly from your Web site to your order management system.

A solution for a smaller business might be to incorporate orders received online with an accounting system like Intuit's QuickBooks (*www.quickbooks.com*). Larger businesses might explore some of the e-commerce capabilities of SAP (*www.mysap.com*). Fully integrated systems will update inventory records as orders are received and notify customers of "out-of-stock" situations.

> If you are expecting to take many orders online, consider integrating your Web site with your accounting system.

Shipping and Handling Capabilities

In today's competitive market, it is important to get merchandise delivered in the timeframe expected. Your online order form, or shopping cart software, should provide customers different shipping options, such as ground transportation or overnight air. Additionally, your customers should have some choice of carrier, for example, United States Postal Service, United Parcel Service, or Federal Express.

The shipping and handling section of your online order form should also set an expectation of when the products and services will be delivered. If the items ordered are currently out of stock, let your customers know when you expect the merchandise will be available, and ultimately when the items will be delivered.

> Clearly state your return policy on your Web site.

Making Returns Easy

Don't make it difficult for customers to return merchandise. Clearly state your return policy on your Web site, so that your customers can return items properly. For instance, tell your customers whether you will accept opened items, or items that were damaged in shipping. If you require a return authorization (usually a special number provided by your customer service department before accepting a return), mention it in your policy.

Amazon.com's return policy, for instance, is very straightforward and spells out each detail. In fact, Amazon.com's return

Sample Return Policy—from Amazon.com (www.amazon.com)

Our return policy is simple. Within 30 days of receipt of your order, you may return
- any book in its original condition, or any book we recommended (and you didn't enjoy) in any condition

- any unopened music CD, cassette tape, vinyl record, DVD, VHS tape, or software

- toys, electronics, and any other merchandise in new condition, with its original packaging and accessories for a full refund. Please note that we can process returns and refunds only for items purchased from Amazon.com.

How to Return Electronics

To return electronics merchandise for any reason, simply call us at 1-800-201-7575 or e-mail us at electronics-returns@amazon.com. An Amazon.com customer service representative will issue a return approval and assist you with return shipping. Please keep the original packaging and accessories to return with the item.

How to Return All Other Items

To return any book, CD, DVD, VHS tape, software, toy, or other non-electronic item, no call is required. Simply indicate the reason for your return, include the packing slip with your return, and wrap the package securely. Attach the return label from the front of your packing slip and ship to the address indicated on the label. For your protection, we recommend that you use UPS or Insured Parcel Post for shipment.

If you do not have your packing slip, please indicate the order number on a separate piece of paper and send the package to the following address [omitted].

policies vary according to the type of merchandise: electronics versus all other items.

Maintaining High Levels of Customer Satisfaction

There is no better way to improve customer satisfaction than to make it easy for customers to communicate with your online business. Many customers will prefer to call you before placing an order. Therefore you should provide adequate telephone support for your online business. For example, many online retailers now place an 800-number right at the top of their home page for everyone to see. Obviously, they have found that providing phone support has resulted in higher customer satisfaction, and undoubtedly more orders.

Although phone support is important, there probably will be customers who prefer to communicate or place orders via e-mail. For

> Many customers will want to call you before they place an order.

instance, they might want to send you an e-mail requesting more information about a product or service, or they might have a question about their latest bill. If you do provide e-mail capability on your Web site, make sure that you send an *automated* acknowledgment as soon as you receive the e-mail. Also, ensure that all e-mails are answered in 24 hours or less.

Another type of customer support that you may want to provide is to accept faxed orders. In business-to-business markets, for instance, some firms do not allow their employees to buy business supplies without proper authorizations and signatures. Finally, you should definitely encourage your customers to let you know what they think of your online business by providing a customer feedback form. On the form, ask how they found your site, what they liked about it, and what they disliked. Feedback forms also provide an opportunity to capture some key demographic market research, like customers' addresses, ages, genders, and income levels.

> Include a customer feedback form on your Web site.

Choosing a Prepackaged E-Commerce Solution

If you feel a bit overwhelmed at the thought of setting up a merchant account, worrying about encrypted secure IDs, and using electronic wallet services, you may want to consider a prepackaged e-commerce solution. Many online services—including some that are *free*—allow you to create an entire online business in a matter of minutes or hours. You only need to have dial-up access to the Internet and a Web browser to get started.

Most of these online services are well suited for online catalogs, where you can display products and services for sale. Most also allow the acceptance of credit card payments through a simplified merchant account process, and offer shopping cart services. Some services even allow you to add your own text content pages and provide supplemental marketing assistance.

The downside to using a prepackaged e-commerce solution is the loss in flexibility you suffer. For instance, you will have less control over where your items are displayed on the Web page than you would with a software design package like Microsoft FrontPage.

> If you feel a bit overwhelmed at the thought of setting up a merchant account, worrying about encrypted secure IDs, and using electronic wallet services, you may want to consider a prepackaged e-commerce solution.

However, if you want to start selling quickly, some of the following services are definitely worth investigating.

Bigstep.com (*www.bigstep.com*)

Bigstep.com is a free service that allows you to "create a catalog to sell products securely or display portfolio items efficiently." It offers an easy introduction to the service, including a 10-screen tutorial that shows exactly how to set up an online business. Additionally, Bigstep.com "features multiple pricing structures and a secure backend system that make it easy to create sales and specials."

Examples of businesses that might be interested in using Bigstep.com include a real estate agent who wants to show homes for sale, or a photographer who wants to display a portfolio online. Bigstep.com also gives you the capability to establish a merchant account (for a fee) through its partnership with Cardservice International.

Unlike some of the free Web hosting services discussed in Chapter 10, Bigstep.com allows you to create an online catalog with your own domain name ("www.yourbiz.com"). You still have to pay Network Solutions to register the name (currently $70), but you avoid including "bigstep" in your domain name.

eCongo.com (*www.econgo.com*)

eCongo.com, like Bigstep.com, is another free service that allows you to create an online business. It gives you the capability to establish a catalog for your products and services and provides a merchant account option. eCongo.com also has a banner network so that you can exchange advertisements with other merchants.

freemerchant.com (*www.freemerchant.com*)

By its name you can tell that freemerchant.com gives you the capability to set up an online store for free. However, right from the get-go, freemerchant.com lets people know that creating an effective online store takes more time than the 10 minutes touted by some services.

Beseen (*buyit.beseen.com*)

This service allows you to "accept credit card orders online and sell products from your web site or message board immediately and

> You can set up an online store quickly by using a prepackaged e-commerce solution.

The Myth of the 10-Minute Store

Our website builder is faster and easier than anything out there. And yes, you could build a fully functioning store in 10 minutes...but why would you? Look, I could paint my house in 10 minutes, but it would look like a 10-minute paint job. You want your customers to enjoy your site, so make it look nice and give it a thoughtful layout. In this respect, your Internet store is no different than a traditional "brick and mortar" store. Spend some time making your Internet store a place where people will want to come, look, and buy.

Source: freemerchant.com

securely with the free BUY IT! button." Although you don't have to set up a merchant account, you will have to give up a percentage of your sales.

Yahoo! Store (*www.store.yahoo.com*)

Yahoo! Store, unlike Bigstep.com, eCongo.com, and freemerchant.com, is a fee-based service.

YAHOO! STORE	CURRENT MONTHLY FEE	NUMBER OF ITEMS
Small Store	$100/month	Up to 50 items for sale
Large Store	$300/month	Up to 1,000 items for sale
Larger Stores	$300/month, plus $100/month for each additional 1000 items	A 5,000-item store would cost $700/month

Yahoo! Store will give you the capability to offer a very sophisticated "shopping basket," with features including monograms and inscriptions, sale pricing, quantity discounts, real-time totals as quantities change, cross-selling to make suggestions for your customers, and automatic tax and shipping calculations.

zShops (*www.amazon.com*)

zShops is a fee-based service from Amazon.com that allows you to sell your products and services online. According to the Amazon.com home page, "zShops is a place where retailers and independent sellers worldwide have a presence. zShops offer hundreds of thousands of new, used, and hard-to-find products from specialty retailers, small businesses, and individuals—things like buffalo steaks, office furniture, used books, maternity clothes, golf clubs, second-hand CDs and videos, car parts, and time-share accommodations at resorts."

To sell items with zShops you need an Amazon.com Pro Merchant Subscription. "A Pro Merchant Subscription lets you showcase up to 3,000 listings at a time for one flat monthly fee." Additionally, the service allows you to split your listings between Amazon.com Auctions and zShops. You should be aware that Pro Merchant Pricing covers insertion fees only, and that you will still be required to pay closing and merchandising fees (a percentage of sales).

Evaluating E-Commerce Solutions for OfficeLinks.com

Q: Is OfficeLinks.com an e-commerce business?

A: I think e-commerce means different things to different people. On the OfficeLinks.com Web site you can buy advertising from us. However, we still process payments offline by sending an invoice to our advertisers.

Q: How come you haven't added a credit card processing feature for your advertisers?

A: At this point our customer base, and advertising revenues, aren't large enough to justify the expense of setting up online credit card processing through a merchant account.

Q: Will you consider adding credit card processing in the future?

A: Yes. In fact, I am exploring this capability for early next year. I am coming out with a new service where I am expecting to get 100 to 200 orders per month. With this increased order volume and high average selling price, I will certainly be able to justify the expense associated with accepting credit cards online.

Q: Are you considering any other types of electronic transaction processing?

A: Not at this point. I definitely believe that the more payment options you offer your customers, the more likely you are to make sales. If I had a really big site, with millions of customers, then I would offer as many payment alternatives as I could.

Q: Does your site offer any other e-commerce capabilities?

A: Again, it depends how you define e-commerce. One portion of my business model is to refer users to other merchants, like Amazon.com, as a member of their affiliate program. Amazon.com pays me a fee based on these referrals. I'm not sure if you would define this as e-commerce, since I don't handle the payment processing or inventory involved with the sale.

Q: Does OfficeLinks.com have an order form?

A: Absolutely. We ask that our advertisers complete an order form for every buy they make. Once the order form is completed, it is simply e-mailed to us for processing. I think that anyone who wants to sell something, either online or offline, should make an order form part of their model.

Q: How else can your customers contact you?

A: Customers can call us, send us an e-mail, or complete a customer satisfaction survey.

Q: Do you think pure e-commerce businesses can be successful?

A: It's still not clear. Right now the biggest benefit of e-commerce is the cost savings that can be achieved by a business. Just think, the cost of processing each transaction is falling from $15 using a telemarketing call center to pennies online!

Online E-Commerce Resources

eBoz! (*www.eboz.com*)

eBoz!, "Your Guide To Creating Successful Websites," contains a wide variety of materials that you will find useful for creating your online business, including a series of articles on e-commerce, such as "Take Credit Card Orders On The Cheap," "The Deadly Sins Of E-Commerce Web Merchants," and "How To Use Email & Autoresponders To Communicate With Your Visitors."

The E-Commerce Guide (*www.ecommerce-guide.com*)

The E-Commerce Guide, published by Internet.com, provides a wide variety of articles and information on e-commerce. Additionally, you can participate in their discussion forums or subscribe to their e-newsletter to get answers about specific questions on e-commerce.

The E-Commerce Times (*www.ecommercetimes.com*)

As you would expect, the *E-Commerce Times* is a large content site that covers a wide variety of subjects on e-commerce. It contains current articles about e-commerce companies, trends, and legislation. For example, a recent article was titled "What does it take for an offline company to successfully launch an e-commerce site?"

MerchantWorkz (*www.merchantworkz.com*)

According to their home page, "MerchantWorkz is the most extensive Web site dedicated to helping small businesses attain a credit card merchant account." On their site you will find a wide variety of information about merchant accounts.

useit.com: Jakob Nielsen's Web site (*www.useit.com*)

As stated in his biography, "Jakob Nielsen, Ph.D., is a User Advocate and principal of the Nielsen Norman Group which he co-founded with Donald A. Norman (former VP of research at Apple Computer)." On Nielsen's Web site you will find many useful articles concerning Web site design and e-commerce, including "Good Web Site Design Can Lead to Healthy Sales" and "WebWord: Web Usability: Past, Present, and Future."

Workz.com (*www.workz.com*)

As described on their site, Workz.com "provides small business with a one-stop resource for marketing and managing a Web site, maximizing online e-commerce opportunities. Our network of sites provides the how-to checklists, utilities, resources, references, and tools needed to build, manage, promote, and maintain a profitable online business."

Summary

This chapter focused on the most important aspects of creating an e-commerce Web site, including credit card transaction processing and security considerations to protect your customers. Due to the technical nature of collecting payments online, you should seriously consider getting an e-commerce plan from a reputable Web hosting service provider.

Although the term *e-commerce* is most often associated with accepting credit card payments online, there are many other aspects to selling products and services online. Not only do you need to consider different Web site features, like shopping carts and secure servers, but you must also evaluate storing inventory, customer service, and alternative shipping methods.

For more information on this topic, visit our Web site at www.businesstown.com

Chapter 8

Finding Competent People to Build and Maintain Your Web Site

Topics covered in this chapter

- **Identifying the types of job functions your online business will require**

- **Designing and building your Web site**

- **Using a Webmaster to maintain your Web site**

- **Promoting and advertising your Web site**

- **Hiring the people to get the job done**

If you're trying to achieve excellent levels of performance in your organization, it's going to be a lot easier if you hire terrific people in the first place.

BUSINESSTOWN.COM,
WWW.BUSINESSTOWN.COM/HIRING/INDEX.ASP

The scope of your online business is going to determine whether you will need to hire additional employees to create and run your Web site. For instance, if you are going to develop a content site that features real-time news stories or topical articles, you may need to hire an editor to keep your site up to date. If you are planning to sell advertising, you might need a sales executive to negotiate contracts. By hiring someone to perform some of the editing and marketing job functions that are required for a good Web site, you can free yourself up to do other tasks, like raising money for your online business or managing the day-to-day aspects that are essential for any business.

Before hiring employees, you should understand the different types of job functions required to build and maintain a successful online business. As we've discussed, you will need to design and create your Web site using software tools, either from your Web host or using an off-the-shelf package. Naturally, you might consider hiring a contractor to do this initial work. However, you should be aware that once your Web site is built, it will need a lot of work to keep it updated and working as planned.

After your Web site is initially designed and published, the types of maintenance functions that are required include writing and updating new content, fixing broken hyperlinks, responding to e-mails, monitoring message boards, and reviewing site traffic reports. If you don't have the time to perform all of these functions on a routine basis, consider hiring a Webmaster to perform these job duties.

Another time-consuming aspect of running an online business can generally be categorized as marketing. The marketing job function of an online business covers a lot of territory, with many individual responsibilities such as competitive research and analysis, Web reporting, e-merchandising, program management, banner ad

> By hiring someone to perform some of the editing and marketing job functions that are required for a good Web site, you can free yourself up to do other tasks.

Hire someone to design your Web site if you want to concentrate on other aspects of running your business.

development, domain name registration, search engine submissions, and strategic content placements.

If you are planning to hire someone to help with the creation, maintenance, or marketing of your online business, one of the best places to post your job advertisement is on the Internet. You can post job ads on your own site, if you already have one, or you can use one of the many online recruiting services that are now available, such as Monster.com, CareerBuilder, HotJobs.com, and Guru.com.

> Before you hire anyone to help you with your online business, identify the types of job functions that will be required.

Identifying the Types of Job Functions Your Online Business Will Require

Before you hire anyone to help you with your online business, identify the types of job functions that will be required. Essentially, the three major functions that are required to set up and run an online business are design, maintenance, and marketing. Additionally, many other functions are required to run any business, for example, accounting, sales, manufacturing, and inventory control. Even so, this chapter focuses on job functions that relate directly to the creation, maintenance, and marketing of a Web site.

Designing and Building Your Web Site

Throughout this book it has been emphasized that creating a Web site is a relatively easy process for anyone that can move a mouse around in Microsoft Windows. Most of the software tools available, either from a Web host or an off-the-shelf package, give you the capability to create a Web site with no software development experience. Therefore, unless you are going to be developing a sophisticated site with *wiz-bang* database management features or *eye-popping* multimedia capability, it's unlikely that you will need to hire someone specifically to create your Web site.

With that said, you should be aware that there are many Web consultants and software developers who can add value to your site in the form of design and functionality. The thought process on whether you should do it yourself or hire someone else, is best summed up by Sal Favarolo of web2web design (*www.web2web.com*). When asked whether a novice should use an off-the-shelf software package, Sal said, "That question is like asking 'can a paint program make me an artist?' These packages do what you ask them to do (sometimes). Sure, some of them have templates and all that, but a professional web site does require a person(s) to have various talents. This includes experience or knowledge in layout, text positioning, copy writing (the text in your web site), graphic design, and in many cases computer programming."

Although Sal's point about Web professionals adding value in terms of knowledge and experience is very valid, a more important consideration is the amount of time you can devote to the effort. Designing and building your Web site can take anywhere from a couple of hours to hundreds of hours, and it will detract from your other responsibilities of running a business. Therefore, before you get started, ensure that this is something you want to do yourself and that you will have enough time to do it.

If you do decide to hire someone to create your Web site, make sure that person is going to use one of the popular off-the-shelf software packages such as Microsoft FrontPage, or use the tools from a national Web hosting company, such as Verio. The last thing you want is for someone to design your Web site from scratch, using HTML. Not only is this very time consuming but it will be very difficult to maintain, especially if your consultant goes out of business or your developer quits. Your site should be designed with software tools that many people already know how to use.

Once you have decided to get someone else to design and create your Web site, you will need to create an advertisement for the job.

As you can see from the SILCO job advertisement, there are a couple of key required skills for Web content developers. First, notice that competencies are required in HTML, JavaScript, and [Microsoft] FrontPage. Even if you are going to hire someone to build your Web site using FrontPage, it is a good idea that they have experience with HTML, because they can use these skills for getting your Web site listed with search engines, and placing affiliate banner advertisements on your site.

Second and maybe even more important, SILCO wants to see examples of previous work. If you decide to hire a consultant or an employee to build your Web site, make sure to review some of their

> Your site should be designed with software tools that many people already know how to use.

Sample Job Advertisement for Web Content Developer— from SILCO

The Ideal candidate for this position will enjoy the aspect of web development that deals with the look & feel of site and user interfaces. They will be creative and possess a desire & aptitude to learn. Must be a team player with excellent communication skills & must be detail oriented.

Required Skills:

- 2+ years hands-on Industry experience in Web Development.
- High competence in developing with HTML, JavaScript, & FrontPage for both Internet Explorer & Netscape.
- Experience in Search Engine positioning.
- Experience with ColdFusion, CSS, FTP/Telnet & DHTML are plus skills.
- Samples of Web Site work must be submitted.

Source: Monster.com (*www.monster.com*)

previous Web site designs. It is not unreasonable for you, and your prospective helper, to sit down in front of a computer and go through one of the sites they designed, page by page. You should inquire how the navigational structure was designed, who developed the content, where the graphics and images came from, and who was responsible for maintaining the site.

The implicit assumption here is that you will only need one person to design and build your Web site. However, it's certainly possible to hire one person to design the site, and another to actually build it. This is much like the offline relationship between advertising copywriters and printers. Copywriters create the text, and printers get it on paper. For very large sites, there can be teams of people responsible for creating specific areas of the site, such as the searching capability, message boards, and the content. However, large efforts like these are beyond the scope of most small business Web sites.

> Once you have built your Web site, be aware that it will require a lot of maintenance going forward.

Using a Webmaster to Maintain Your Web Site

Once you have built your Web site, be aware that it will require a lot of maintenance going forward. Content will need to be refreshed periodically, broken hyperlinks will need to be updated, e-mails will have to be answered, message boards need to be monitored, and traffic reports have to be created. You will either have to perform these maintenance functions yourself, or hire someone else.

If you hire a contractor to build your Web site, be sure to inquire how much they will charge for ongoing maintenance and how long it will take them to make updates. Keep in mind that many contractors, or outside consultants, will design your site for a nominal fee but expect to make the bulk of their money updating your site.

Another possibility for handling the ongoing maintenance of your Web site is to hire a Webmaster.

In the SalesLogix advertisement for a Webmaster, the job responsibilities go beyond just maintaining the Web site. This Webmaster will also be responsible for development activities and participate in some of the marketing functions, such as the development and maintenance of a "web-based lead generation system." It is not uncommon for many businesses, both large and small, to hire a Webmaster that has

> If you hire a contractor to build your Web site, be sure to inquire how much they will charge for ongoing maintenance and how long it will take them to make updates.

Sample Job Advertisement for a Webmaster— from SalesLogix

Responsibilities:

- Responsibilities include the development, maintenance, and support of our corporate websites, including planning, programming, implementation, and project management
- Interact with variety of users/audiences to fulfill project needs
- Also works with other departments to coordinate projects, determine best methods of implementation, and advise of process
- Will complete additions, changes, and maintenance of websites, develop and maintain web-based lead generation system
- Integrate with internal database and system
- The Webmaster will also monitor websites, respond to problems, and requests, advise of new developments, emerging technology that would supplement departmental productivity, and assist in structure and implementation of authoring system

Source: CareerBuilder (*www.careerbuilder.com*)

complete responsibility for all of the Web site job functions, including design, development, maintenance, and marketing.

If you will not have enough time to build and maintain your Web site, seriously consider hiring a Webmaster. Like SalesLogix, you can make the Webmaster responsible for all job functions relating to the Web site. However, make sure that you ask for examples of prospects' work, and inquire to what extent they have participated in the marketing of a Web site. Normally Webmasters are not experts in marketing but do participate in the advertising and promotion activities of the Web site.

Promoting and Advertising Your Web Site

Today, one of the most expensive aspects of setting up an online business is the amount of promotion and advertising that is required. It is not unreasonable to spend more money to market your Web site than on its design, development, and maintenance, combined. Therefore, if you are not going to perform the marketing functions yourself, find someone who can handle *all* of the responsibilities associated with marketing an online business.

Some of the skills required to market your online business include getting your site listed with the search engines and directories, administering promotional campaigns, writing and updating content, and creating banner advertisements. Additionally, depending on your business model, the marketing person may have to sell advertising for your site, or set prices for your products and services.

If you are going to hire someone to market your online business, it's worthwhile to look at some advertisements from other companies that are looking for the same set of skills.

As you can see from the sample Metasearch job advertisement for a copywriter, this particular job only covers the content development and editing aspect of marketing an online business. If you are going to produce a Web site that is primarily content oriented, you will need someone with good writing skills; someone who has the capability of making your content appeal to your target audience.

In addition to content skills, your online marketing job function will require some of the responsibilities shown in the following job

> It is not unreasonable to spend more money to market your Web site than on its design, development, and maintenance, combined.

Sample Job Advertisement for Marketing Copy Writer— Posted by Metasearch

Duties/Responsibilities:

- Create and manage the voice and editorial perspective for client's Web site, marketing and sales materials.
- Write copy and headlines for Web site pages. Keep content fresh. Work with Web site Producer to ensure that scheduled promotions are handled.
- Write copy and headlines for marketing and sales collateral materials. Work with Marketing Communications Manager.
- Create original content on a variety of subjects for the various pages within the site. This will range from customer testimonials to product data sheets and descriptions.
- Serve as the central editor and edit materials provided by internal content partners.
- Translate communication objectives into a compelling web presence.
- Create an environment that supports the brand attributes and encourages and fosters strong community participation
- Create copy for internal and third party promotions. Meet production deadlines. Build and publish style guidelines to provide a roadmap for content publishing partners.

Source: Headhunter.net (*www.headhunter.net*)

advertisement from Progress Software Corporation for an e-marketing program manager.

The e-marketing program manager description details most of the job skills required to do an effective job of marketing an online business. As always, make sure to ask for online examples of prospects' work. You can ask how they made search engine submissions (manually or with an auto-posting service?). What banner advertising services were used? How was the domain name registered? And what types of Web reports were generated?

Make sure to ask for online examples of prospects' work.

Hiring the People to Get the Job Done

As mentioned earlier, if you are planning to hire someone to help with the creation, maintenance, or marketing of your online business,

Sample Job Advertisement for E-Marketing Program Manager—Posted by Progress Software Corporation

As a key member of the e-Marketing team, this position requires a highly creative and energetic Internet Marketing Communications professional to develop and drive Web and electronic marketing initiatives that build awareness for our corporate Web site.

Responsibilities:

- Competitive research and analysis
- Web reporting
- E-merchandising
- Program management of corporate Web advertising
- Banner ad development
- Domain name registration
- Search engine submissions
- Strategic content placements, etc.

Gather requirements from multiple groups, set strategies, leverage outside agencies, and develop necessary content with Web and Marcom creative groups. Must be exceptionally well organized and have excellent writing and communication skills. Knowledge of competitive e-Marketing strategies a must. 3+ years Web marketing experience: Web content promotion, Web reporting, e-Merchandising, on-line marketing, advertising and seminars. Should have experience with Web site creation and development. Database application development a plus.

Source: HotJobs.com (*www.hotjobs.com*)

one of the best places to post job advertisements is on the Internet. You can post job ads on your own site, if you already have one, or you can use one of the many online recruiting services now available.

Online recruiting sites, such as Monster.com and CareerBuilder, charge about $100 to advertise a job opening. Some of the sites allow you to post your own job opening and pay online with a credit card. This is extremely convenient, and can usually be accomplished in less time than using traditional offline recruiting methods like newspaper classified ads.

Post job advertisements on the Internet.

ONLINE RECRUITING SITE	WEB ADDRESS
Monster.com	*www.monster.com*
CareerBuilder	*www.careerbuilder.com*
Headhunter.net	*www.headhunter.net*
HotJobs.com	*www.hotjobs.com*
CareerMosaic	*www.careermosaic.com*
TopJob	*www.topjob.com*
Dice.com (Earthweb.com)	*www.dice.com*
Guru.com (for contractors)	*www.guru.com*

In addition to checking out the online recruiting sites, try traditional recruiting venues such as college placement offices, local newspaper classified ads, and the yellow pages if you are looking for a contractor or temporary agency.

Before placing your job advertisement, develop an appropriate job description that outlines all of the duties and responsibilities for the position. If you need examples of current job descriptions, existing online job sites are a great place to start,. Simply go to the online recruiting sites listed previously, and do searches using some of the following keywords:

- Web site design
- E-marketing
- Content development
- Banner advertising
- Online sales
- Webmaster
- FrontPage software

Finally, you should try to get 10 to 15 resumes for every job opening you have. Rank your candidates from strongest to weakest according to the skills presented on each resume. Then, after you have conducted the interviews, re-rank everyone based on your assessment of the skills presented in person by each job candidate. If you need more advice on how to hire employees, you can find sites on the Web, such as BusinessTown.com (*www.businesstown.com*), that show you how to conduct interviews and check references.

> Try to get 10 to 15 resumes for every job opening you have.

Looking at the Job Functions for OfficeLinks.com

Q: How would you describe the job functions for OfficeLinks.com?

A: Generally, the job functions can be broken down into Web site design, building, maintenance, and marketing. However, each of these main job functions could be further broken down into sub job functions.

Q: What do you mean by sub job functions?

A: Well, although I say that OfficeLinks.com needs a marketing function, there are many aspects to marketing that can be identified by sub functions. For instance, there is content development, banner advertising, search engine positioning, and e-newsletter management.

Q: Why is it important to identify the job sub functions?

A: Take a large site, like one of the "four horsemen." They might have a whole group of people in the online marketing department who are simply responsible for managing their banner advertisements across the Internet. A small business site, on the other hand, might have only one person to perform all of the marketing functions. It's important to match a name with every job function and associated sub job function you are planning to perform.

Q: What job functions are the most time consuming at OfficeLinks.com?

A: The maintenance and advertising functions definitely are the most time consuming. I constantly have e-mails that need to be answered, broken hyperlinks that have to be fixed, banner ad campaigns that need to be created, and Web site traffic reports that need to be monitored.

Q: I'm surprised that you didn't say that design and development was time consuming.

A: Obviously, at the beginning, all of the effort went into the design and making of the Web site. But that was really a one-time deal. Once it was up and running, the other job functions become more time consuming.

Q: Have you been surprised by the amount of work that is required?

A: Definitely. You need to make a large commitment in terms of time if you want to do a good job of maintaining and marketing your Web site. Although it's easy to get your business online in less than 30 days, you'll need to devote much more time to the other aspects of running the online business.

Q: Did you hire anyone for OfficeLinks.com?

A: No.

Q: If you were to hire someone, what job function would you fill first?

A: Personally, I would hire a Webmaster to handle the routine maintenance of the Web site. However, that is only because I have a strong background in other business functions like marketing and finance. Generally, you need to hire people that complement your skills. For instance, if you are a Webmaster, you should maybe hire someone to help with the marketing. You need to evaluate your skills first, and then hire people to fill the gaps.

Online Personnel and Hiring Resources

BusinessTown.com (*www.businesstown.com*)
BusinessTown.com provides a lot of useful small business information, including a whole section on managing people. Here you can learn how to hire, compensate, and fire employees for your online business.

Business at Home (*www.gohome.com/Sections/ Finances-Taxes/index.html*)
As the name of this site suggests, Business at Home provides a lot of information for home-based businesses. This site has a couple of articles that discuss the different tax implications between hiring a contractor and an employee, titled "Can you do it all yourself?" and "Sometimes employees can provide much-needed relief, sometimes a big headache."

CareerBuilder (*www.careerbuilder.com*)
CareerBuilder is a recruiting site that you can use to post job advertisements. It claims, through its "mega job search" technology, to have more jobs than anyone else. This technology gives it the capability to search not only its own database listing of jobs but also those posted on other recruiting sites.

Headhunter.net (*www.headhunter.net*)
You can post a job advertisement on Headhunter.net for as little as $20 per month. Additionally, as of this writing, its Web site has over 245,000 "quality" resumes that you can search by keyword, salary, work experience, ability to travel, and education level. It also has an employer resource center that provides advice on skills testing, reference checking, and employee assessment.

Monster.com (*www.monster.com*)
With a credit card you can post a job advertisement on Monster.com's Recruiting Office. You can also search its database by keyword to find sample job advertisements for virtually every job

function, including Web site development, e-commerce marketing, and Webmaster.

HotJobs.com (*www.hotjobs.com*)

HotJobs.com allows employers to make up to 20 job postings for $600 per month. If you are really desperate, you can also buy a banner advertisement that will point prospective employees to your job listings on HotJobs.com.

Summary

Most of this book assumes that you will not be hiring outside contractors or additional employees to create and manage your Web site. However, if you don't have the time or desire to do all of this work yourself, then you are going to need some outside help. Before you make any hiring decisions, you should be aware of some of the key job functions that are required to build an online business, including design, maintenance, and marketing.

Business owners who are new to the Internet are inclined to start by hiring an outsider to create their Web site. Creating the initial Web site is actually far less time consuming than performing many of the maintenance and marketing functions that will be required to keep the online business running into the future. You will be far less vulnerable to making any bad hiring decisions once you understand how to build and operate a Web site.

For more information on this topic, visit our Web site at www.businesstown.com

Putting Your Business Up on the Web for Everyone to See

Summary of Part III

- **Brand your Web site by choosing a great domain name**
- **Find a Web host that provides the capabilities you will need for your Web site (at the right price)**
- **Design your Web site to be user-friendly and easy to navigate**
- **Understand why "content is king" on the Internet**

Chapter 9

Choosing a Domain Name, or Dot-Com, for your Online Business

Topics covered in this chapter

- **Developing an online brand name**
- **Understanding those dot-coms, dot-orgs, dot-nets, and all the others**
- **Registering your domain name with a Web host**
- **Buying your domain name at auction**
- **Seeking legal advice on your domain name**

A Venezuelan online casino doled out more than US$1 million to buy Wallstreet.com.

CRAIG BICKNELL, WIRED DIGITAL, INC.

> Why would someone pay more than $1 million for a domain name like Wallstreet.com?

In today's environment, your domain name, or dot-com, may ultimately be worth more than your online business itself. It is not unheard of for companies to spend thousands or even millions of dollars to acquire the "right" domain name. Just look at the Venezuelan online casino that doled out more than $1 million U.S. to buy www.wallstreet.com!

Why would someone pay more than $1 million for a domain name like Wallstreet.com? Why did Compaq computer pay more than $3 million to buy AltaVista.com? (This deal was especially interesting, because Compaq's purchase of Digital Equipment meant that it already owned the AltaVista Web site!) The simple fact is that these domain names, or dot-coms, represent valuable online real estate. If you own a widely recognized domain name, you will get more visitors to your Web site, be able to sell more products and services, and be able to charge higher advertising rates.

While domain names are becoming increasingly valuable, there is a distinct difference between simply owning a dot-com and actually owning a brand name. After all, what's in a name like Wallstreet.com or Drugs.com? Today, these are just names, or shells, for proposed online businesses. They are not recognizable brand names, like AltaVista.com or Amazon.com.

> A brand name conveys products, degrees of quality, and levels of service.

A brand name is much more than just a domain name, such as "www.yourbiz.com," because brands convey products, degrees of quality, and levels of service. When you think of the brand name Amazon.com, you think of something more than simply the domain name Bookstore.com. You think of a wide selection of inventory, an easy-to-use Web site, and great customer service. You can envision the complete buying experience. It is these characteristics of brand names that make them so valuable, and why they are often registered as trademarks with the U.S. Patent Office.

Before you can develop an online brand name, you will need to register a domain name ("www.yourbiz.com"), and publish your Web site on the Internet. Even if you already have an offline business that has an established brand name, you will still need to move your products and services to the Web and create an online brand name. This is much easier said than done. Look at some of the offline retailers like Toys-R-Us and Wal-Mart. These companies have established hugely successful brands and businesses in the offline world, but neither has become an online sensation.

Most of this chapter is devoted to the mechanics of establishing a domain name, or dot-com. You will learn about the different formats for domain names, registering the name with your Web host, locating sources to buy a domain name preregistered by someone else, and reviewing the legal implications of brand names or trademarks. Your ultimate goal will be to establish a recognizable brand for your online business.

Developing an Online Brand Name

What is a brand name? The American Marketing Association, in its dictionary of marketing terms, defines a brand as "a name, term, design or symbol, or any other feature that identifies one seller's good or service as distinct from those of other sellers. The legal term for brand is trademark." The key to this definition is that a brand identifies one seller's good or service from another.

Think about this definition in practical terms. If you go to a supermarket and have two choices of cookies, like Oreos and the store brand, which one would you choose? You might choose the store brand if you had tried those cookies before, were satisfied with their taste, and could save some money. You might also try the store-brand cookies if you are familiar with some of the store's other branded products. However, if you've never shopped in that store before, you would probably choose the Oreos because you were familiar with the brand name.

Now think about the Internet. Since it is such a new medium for many consumers, what do you think will be the primary motivator for selecting one product over another, or one Web site over another? That's right, brand name. When consumers have nothing else to rely on, they will choose the brand that they are familiar with.

"The legal term for brand is trademark."

> If your name is well known, like Max Factor or Chanel, stick with the brand name you have established in the "real" world.

> A compelling name is the soul of communicative identity. It embodies personality, culture and value. It is strategic in sight and sound. It is your best ally, positioning you above the noise. The name is undoubtedly one of the most important factors in both how quickly a company, product or service becomes successful, as well as the eventual degree of success it enjoys.
>
> Name Trade Home Page,
> *www.nametrade.com*

Using Your Offline Name Online

There is a fair amount of debate about whether you should use your offline brand or business name for your online business. For the most part, if you have already established a brand in the offline world that can be ported to the online world, you should choose that for your domain name, or dot-com. However, there are a few exceptions to consider.

First, will your online business be doing something different than your existing offline business? For instance, if you were currently running a beauty salon but thinking about starting to sell beauty supplies on the Internet, you may want to consider using a different online name. However, if your name is well known, like Max Factor or Chanel, stick with the brand name you have established in the "real" world. Established brand names are one of the strongest selling points you can have on the Internet. They give your business instant recognition and provide an element of trust for a user that might be thousands of miles away.

Second, if your offline business has a name that can't be easily ported to the Web because it is hard to spell or too long, consider a new name for your online business. Think about how people find your offline business today. Do they walk or drive by it? Do they call you on the telephone? Or do they read about it in newspaper or yellow page advertisements? Many of your prospects, especially repeat customers, are going to type your name into the Web browser's address box. You want to make your domain name as easy to spell and remember as possible.

Finally—and this is probably the most difficult situation— what do you do when you can't register your dot-com because someone else registered it first? For instance, if your offline business is called "My Store," and someone else has registered "www.mystore.com," what are your alternatives? Assuming there are no legal implications, you must either register another name like "www.mystore.net," or look for another name like "www.mybigstore.com," or buy the domain name from the person who registered "www.mystore.com."

Creating a New Online Brand Name

If you are starting a new business, selecting the right name is more difficult. Everyone would like to think that their online business is going to be the next Amazon.com or Yahoo! and get instant recognition once their Web site is published. However, the odds of that happening are minimal. Therefore, you should establish a name that meets the following criteria:

- Conveys what you do, or your type of business
- Will be easy for prospects and customers to remember
- Is not too long and is easy to spell
- Hasn't been trademarked by someone else

Begin by making a list of appropriate domain names for your online business. Test them out on your friends and colleagues to see which ones they like best. Confirm that your options are easily pronounced and spelled by your test audience. Finally, rank the names in order of popularity.

Once you have completed your list of name options, research them in the Network Solutions/InterNIC database (*www.networksolutions.com*) to make sure that no one else is using your carefully thought-out names.

Understanding Those Dot-Coms, Dot-Orgs, Dot-Nets, and All the Others

While your ultimate goal is to establish a brand name for your online business, your immediate need is to understand the mechanics of naming a Web site, or creating a domain name. Your domain name, or "www.yourbiz.com," is your Internet address. By using your domain name, anyone in the world connected to the Internet can come and visit your online business and purchase your products and services. Although most people are familiar with the dot-com (.com) extension, or top-level domain, there are currently quite a few other Internet extensions.

> Establish a brand name that conveys the nature of your business.

> Although most people are familiar with the dot-com (.com) extension, or top-level domain, there are currently quite a few other Internet extensions.

CURRENT TOP-LEVEL DOMAINS	DESCRIPTION
dot-com (.com)	Created for commercial entities like your business. Currently, anyone can register a dot-com.
dot-net (.net)	Created for Internet service providers and other entities involved with Internet operations. Currently, anyone can register a dot-net.
dot-org (.org)	Created for organizations such as nonprofit groups. Currently, anyone can register a dot-org.
dot-edu (.edu)	Created for colleges and universities.
dot-gov (.gov)	Created for U.S. Federal government.
dot-mil (.mil)	Created for U.S. military

In addition to these more familiar top-level domains, there are many others to indicate different countries, including (.co.uk) for the United Kingdom and (.co.nz.) for New Zealand. Usually, when you try to register a domain name, the registration service will provide appropriate alternatives if your first choice has already been taken. For more information on domain names, including those that differ by country, visit some of the following Web sites:

WEB PAGE NAME	WEB ADDRESS	DESCRIPTION
About Domains	*www.aboutdomains.com/News/FAQ.htm*	Has a complete FAQ sheet on domain names
Network Solutions	*www.networksolutions.com*	Learn about foreign domain names.
Domain Names 101	*www.interinc.com/WWW101/ Domains101/index.html*	Provides good overview of domain names
Register.com	*www.register.com*	Domain name rules for top-level domain names

Every Web address, or domain name, contains at least two parts that are separated by a "dot." For instance, if you want to create the *yourbiz.com* domain name, the key components are "yourbiz" and ".com." In this Web address, the top-level domain is "com" and "yourbiz" is the second-level domain. As discussed earlier, other top-level domains include "dot-org" and "dot-net." Although options for choosing a top-level domain are limited, you can use the following rules to create a second-level domain:

- Contains only letters, numbers, or a hyphen
- Doesn't use a dash at the beginning or end of the name

- Has no more than 26 characters
- Is not case sensitive

Finally, you should be aware of subdomains. Subdomains can be shown to the left of the second-level domain, or they can be followed by a "/" after the top-level domain. For instance, if your business had a customer service center, you might want to create the following subdomain: "service.yourbiz.com," or you might want to use "yourbiz.com/service." Unless you are registering for a "free" domain service, as described in later in this chapter, subdomains will not be necessary until you begin designing your Web site.

Visiting Network Solutions/InterNIC Before You Settle on a Domain Name

From 1993 until 1999, through a cooperative agreement with the National Science Foundation, Network Solutions/InterNIC acted as the exclusive registrar for all domain names within the dot-com, dot-org, and dot-net extensions. That means that all of the dot-coms, dot-nets, and dot-orgs were registered in the Network Solutions InterNIC database. By going directly to Network Solutions (*www.networksolutions.com*), or a third party registration service like Register.com (*www.register.com*), you can see what names are registered in their databases.

Network Solutions had registered five million names in its database at the time of this writing, and believed there was a potential to register 100 million names. In 1999 Network Solutions lost its monopoly on domain name registrations, and now a few other licensed companies provide this service, including America Online, Register.com, Internet Council of Registrars, Oléane, and Melbourne IT.

> Whois search provides a complete description of "Who" registered a dot-com.

Network Solutions' "Whois" Search

One service available on the home page of Network Solutions (*www.networksolutions.com*) is the "Whois" directory. The Whois search provides a complete description of "Who" registered a dot-com, including mailing, phone, fax, and Web hosting information.

Additionally, you can see when the domain name was registered and if and when it was updated.

To access the Whois information from the Network Solution home page, do the following:

1. Type "www.networksolutions.com" in your Web browser's address box and press Enter.
2. On the Network Solutions home page, click on the "WHOIS Search" button located on the left-hand side of the page under Additional Services.
3. After you get to the "Web Interface to Whois" page, you can look up the registration details for _____.

Sample Whois Search Results for OfficeLinks.com

Registrant: Office Links, Inc. (OFFICELINKS2-DOM) P.O. Box 131, Rocky Hill, NJ 08553-0131
    Domain Name: OFFICELINKS.COM

Administrative Contact: Goodman, Betsy (BG6738) officelynx
    @AOL.COM (609) 279-9039

Technical Contact, Zone Contact: Mindspring Domreg (MDP-ORG)
    domreg@MINDSPRING.COM (888) 932-1997, Fax (404)815-8805

Billing Contact:
    Domain Administrator (MDB5-ORG) domain.billing
        @MINDSPRING.COM (404) 815-0770, Fax (404) 287-0883

Record last updated on 27-Jan-99.
    Record created on 27-Jan-99.
    Database last updated on 3-Sep-99 09:14:06 EDT.

Domain servers in listed order:
    SPEAKEASY.MSPRING.NET   207.69.231.2
    HEARSAY.MSPRING.NET   207.69.231.3
    RUMOR.MSPRING.NET   165.121.2.31

Is Your Domain Name Available?

The simplest way to check if your domain name is available and hasn't been registered by someone else is to simply type it in your Web browser's address box and see what happens. For instance, if you wanted to call your new online business Cyberpet, you would type "www.cyberpet.com" in your Web browser's address box and press Enter. If a Web site appears, you are out of luck! If you get an error message, either the name has not been registered by anyone else, or the server hosting the site is not working.

The more precise way to see if your proposed domain name is still available is to use a registration service. For instance, to see if Cyberpet has been registered:

1. Type "www.networksolutions.com" in your Web browser's address box and press Enter.
2. On the Network Solutions home page, type "cyberpet.com" in the box titled "Get a Web Address or search our database for availability."
3. Then click on GO!

Momentarily, a new screen will appear that indicates whether the domain name you selected is available. If it isn't, you will have to try another name. Keep in mind that some companies that cannot get the dot-com (.com) they want, are still able to use the same name with dot-net (.net) instead. At the time of this writing, "www.cyberpet.com" and "www.cyberpet.net" are not available, but "www.cyberpet.org" is still available.

Registering Your Domain Name with a Web Host

After settling on a domain name for your online business and ensuring that it has not been registered in the Network Solutions database by someone else, you are ready to register it as your own. However, before registering your domain name, select a Web hosting service for your Web site. By doing this you

> Before registering your domain name, select a Web hosting service for your Web site.

will not have to worry about moving your domain name to a Web host later on.

WEB HOSTING COMPANIES THAT REGISTER DOMAIN NAMES	WEB ADDRESS
9Net Avenue	www.9netave.net
C I Host	www.cihost.com
Concentric Network	www.concentric.com
Datarealm	www.serve.com
Earthlink	www.earthlink.net
MindSpring	www.mindspring.com
Verio	www.verio.com
Web 2010	www.web2010.com

You should also be aware that in order to register your domain name you will be required to provide certain details about your business, including a contact name, address, and phone number. Therefore, it is suggested that you at least have a different mailing address and phone number than your principal residence because this information is readily accessible to anyone on the Internet.

What about Getting a *Free* Domain Name?

Most of the information in this chapter so far has been based on the assumption that you will register a domain name, like "www.yourbiz.com," with Network Solutions or another sanctioned registration service. By making this assumption, it is implied that you will register and pay for your own domain name and get a Web hosting account to publish your Web site. Your cost to register a domain name will be about $70, and depending on the type of account you get, your Web hosting fees will be $25 or more each month.

However, as you learn more about publishing your Web site on the Internet, you will come across many offers to publish your Web site for *free*. If you already have a dial-up account with an Internet service provider such as America Online, you may have

> Your cost to register a domain name will be about $70.

seen advertisements to "publish your own Web site for *free*." Unfortunately, as briefly mentioned earlier, in order to take advantage of these offers, you will have to include the service's top-level domain as part of your online business name. In other words, your online business name will be a subsubdomain to the service provider.

For instance, if you wanted to publish a Web site with Max Pages (*www.maxpages.com*), a popular free Web hosting service, your online business name would look something like "www.maxpages.com/yourbiz." The tradeoff is deciding whether you want a free Web site that requires you to include an advertisement for another business, like Max Pages, within your own online business name, or be autonomous and pay for your own domain name and Web hosting service.

The main advantage of a service like Max Pages is that it is *free*. Once you are connected to the Internet with a dial-up account, you can get a URL (Web address) and create a Web site for no additional charges. Some of the disadvantages of these free services include:

- Your URL ("www.maxpages.com/yourbiz") will be lengthy.
- Your URL will be hard to spell.
- Your URL will be difficult to remember.
- Your flexibility in Web site design will be limited—normally you must use their design tools.
- Your reporting capabilities (tracking visitors to your site) will be limited or nonexistent.
- You may be required to display advertisements you cannot control.

Although there are numerous disadvantages to using a free service, you should try one out to see if it meets your needs. If you currently only have dial-up service to the Internet, and are exploring the possibilities of establishing an online business, there is no better way to get your "feet wet" for the right price: *free*. Most of the services listed in the following table give you the capability to set up Web sites for free, and since they are relatively easy to use, you can get your business online in less than a few hours.

> Although there are numerous disadvantages to using a free service, you should try one out to see if it meets your needs.

FREE DOMAIN HOSTING COMPANIES	WEB ADDRESSES
Angelfire	*www.angelfire.com*
Click2site	*www.click2site.com*
FreeUK	*www.freeuk.com*
GeoCities (Yahoo!)	*www.geocities.yahoo.com/home/*
MoneyAvenue	*www.moneyave.com*
Myfreeoffice	*www.myfreeoffice.com*
WebJump	*www.webjump.com*
XOOM.com	*www.xoom.com*

To locate additional free domain hosting companies, try FreeLinks.org (*www.freelinks.org*) or FreeWebspace.net (*www.freewebspace.net*).

Buying Your Domain Name at Auction

This chapter started out by mentioning that a Venezuelan online casino spent more than $1 million to buy the Wallstreet.com domain name. This transaction was actually facilitated through GreatDomains.com, a domain name broker. GreatDomains.com describes its business as "a market for companies and individuals to buy and sell domain names, developed Web sites, and Internet-based businesses under the accepted industry practices that govern business opportunity and trademark sales."

GreatDomains.com is very similar to an online auction site, except it buys and sells domain names. GreatDomains.com acts as the broker and receives a percentage of the sale. To give you an idea of how important this market is, GreatDomains.com posts the following information on its Web site:

> You may need to buy the "right" name for your online business from a broker.

SITE STATISTICS FOR GREATDOMAINS.COM

Total number of domains listed	82,097
Average listing price	$32,338
Average selling price per domain	$10,170
Estimated value of all listed names	$834,926,490 [that's close to a billion!]
Drugs.com recently sold for	$823,456 [less than they were expecting]

Source: GreatDomains.com home page (*www.greatdomains.com*) September 1999

In addition to GreatDomains.com, there are many other places where domain names are being bought and sold online, including traditional online auctions sites, such as eBay and Amazon.com.

SPECIALTY WEB SITES THAT SELL DOMAIN NAMES	WEB ADDRESS
ALLFREEDOMAINS.COM	*www.allfreedomains.com*
CyberProperty	*www.cyberproperty.com*
Domain Station	*www.domainstation.com*
Ebiz Domain Names	*www.ebizdomainnames.com*
Names on Sale	*www.namesonsale.com*

Since prices for domain names purchased though brokers can easily reach thousands of dollars, many businesses decide to forgo this expense and just go with a "lesser" domain name. Less popular names can be purchased through Network Solutions/InterNIC (*www.networksolutions.com*) for $70, but they are not always a company's first choice. Obviously, if you can get the domain name you want from InterNIC, there is no need to use a broker. However, many companies are now facing the reality that part of doing business on the Web includes the cost of buying the right domain name.

Seeking Legal Advice on Your Domain Name

Once you have settled on a domain name and checked to see if it's still available for registration with Network Solutions (*www.network-solutions.com/cgi-bin/whois/whois/*), the last thing you should do is make sure that it isn't a registered trademark. At this point you may also want to consult with a trademark attorney to see whether you should trademark your domain name.

David G. Rosenbaum, in his book *Patents, Trademarks, and Copyrights* (Career Press, 1994), says, "Trademarks are used to protect names and symbols that are used to identify products. These can be registered under state or federal law.... A trademark owner acquires basic trademark protection simply by using his trademark on or in connection with his goods."

Since trademarks are protected by federal and state governments, you can expect some form of legal battle if you choose a domain name that has been registered as a trademark by someone else.

> You can expect some form of legal battle if you choose a domain name that has been registered as a trademark by someone else.

If you would like to learn more about trademarks, search the federal government's database (*www.uspto.gov*) for existing trademarks. This Web site also allows you to apply for a trademark and read some commentary on the registration of Internet domain names.

Selecting the Domain Name "OfficeLinks.com"

Q: How did you come up with the name OfficeLinks.com for your online business?

A: I wanted a name people could remember and a name that conveyed what type of online business I was in. I also wanted a name that prospects could spell.

Q: How did you test your domain name to see if people could pronounce and spell it before you registered it?

A: I found that a very effective way to test names is to call people on the phone and see if they could remember and spell the name without me repeating it. For instance I called a Web host and asked, "Hi. I'm think about registering OfficeLinks.com. Can you see if it's available?" Not one person that I spoke with misspelled the word. A few did confirm that it was L-I-N-K-Sdot-com.

Q: Was OfficeLinks your first choice for a domain name?

A: No. In fact, my first choice was OfficeMall.com and my second choice was OfficeLink.com, but both of these names were already taken.

Q: Did you consider using the dot-net or dot-org top-level domains for your first and second choices?

A: No. I wanted a dot-com (.com) for the top-level domain. I think the dot-coms are still more widely accepted and remembered than the other top-level domains. If this was not a new business, and I had already developed some brand equity for my existing business, I might have considered these alternative top-level domains.

Q: How did you register your domain name?

A: First of all I made sure that the domain name was still available using my MindSpring Web hosting service. Then, at the same time that I selected my Web hosting plan, MindSpring registered my domain name.

Q: What was the biggest mistake you made in registering your domain name?

A: I registered another name besides OfficeLinks with my Web host and then decided not to use it. This consumed some valuable time since I had to register another name and then get it pointed to my Web site. During this period InterNIC was overwhelmed with domain registrations and the whole process took nearly a week.

Q: How could you have avoided this mistake?

A: I should have been 100 percent certain of the name I was going to use before starting the registration process with my Web host.

Q: How much did it cost to register your domain name?

A: At the time I registered my domain name, the fee was $70 for a two-year period. This excluded the $50 set-up fee I had to pay MindSpring to establish my Web hosting account. Unfortunately, since I changed my mind after registering my first name, I had to pay the $70 fee again for the second domain name.

Online Domain Name Resources

CNET Web Services (*webhostlist.com*)

On its Web site, CNET publishes the *Ultimate Web Host List*, which provides a monthly ranking of the top 25 Web hosting companies based on value, customer service, quality and flexibility. You will also find an A to Z listing of Web hosts and many tips on building an e-commerce Web site.

FreeWebspace.net (*www.freewebspace.net*)

This Web site gives you the capability to search for free domains and Web hosts. There is also a list of free personal Web space providers. You can search the list by the amount of disk space you require and the host's language (for instance, Chinese Web hosts).

GreatDomains.com (*www.greatdomains.com*)

GreatDomains.com claims to be the largest domain name broker. On their Web site you can buy and sell domain names and Web sites through an auction process. GreatDomains.com sold Drugs.com for $823,456 in 1999.

Naming Guide (*www.namestormers.com/nameg.htm*)

On this site, created by the Namestormers, you will find the Naming Guide, which offers "free tips and advice on do-it-yourself naming." In addition to providing a checklist for creating a brand name, there is an entire section on how to create domain names.

U.S. Patent and Trademark Office (*www.uspto.gov*)

On the U.S. Patent and Trademark Office (USPTO) Web site you can search the United States' trademark database and also apply for a trademark online. There is also some excellent information on registering Internet domain names.

Web Interface to "Whois" (*www.networksolutions.com/cgi-bin/whois/whois/*)

From the Network Solutions home page you can access the Whois database. Here you can get a lot of information about "Who" registered a domain name, including contact information, when the domain was registered, when it was last modified, and what company is hosting the domain name.

Summary

In this chapter you learned that getting a Web address, or domain name, involves a lot more than simply registering it with Network Solutions. You must understand how you are going to turn your domain name into a brand name that will be recognizable and memorable for a worldwide Internet audience. You must also evaluate whether you need a dot.com as a top-level domain or whether you can settle for a dot.net or dot.org.

Once you have thoroughly evaluated different names, you can begin the registration process. Oftentimes, it is easier to use your Web hosting service to register a domain name than to register it separately with Network Solutions and then move it to a Web hosting service. Lastly, you should have learned that you may be forced to buy the right name from a domain name broker at an additional cost.

For more information on this topic, visit our Web site at www.businesstown.com

Selecting a Web Site Host to Support Your Business Strategy

Topics covered in this chapter

- **Understanding Web hosting terminology**
- **Choosing the right Web hosting plan for your online business**
- **Getting an e-commerce solution from your Web host**
- **Interpreting Web hosting reports**

Chapter 10

Web hosting is the term that refers to the service involving the placement of your Web site onto the Internet through a computer server. Once this is done, anyone anywhere in the World is able to access those Web pages and view the information that is provided there for them.

MINDSPRING BIZ, *WWW.MINDSPRING.COM*

> A Web host provides a location in cyberspace to store your Web site.

In order to get your business online, you will need a place to store your Web site. Most small online businesses are stored on shared Web hosting services such as Verio and Mindspring, while larger online businesses use dedicated hosting facilities provided by companies such as Exodus Communications and Applied Theory. Alternatively, it is possible, though technically challenging, to set up your own dedicated server to publish and maintain your Web site on the Internet.

One of the fastest growing Internet-related businesses today is that of Web site hosting. This trend is being driven in large part by people like you who want to get their businesses online but don't want the headaches of buying special computers and telecommunications equipment to set up their Web sites. Think of a Web hosting service as providing a location in cyberspace for your online business.

For a monthly fee, a Web host will provide a certain amount of disk space to house your Web site, bandwidth for your customers to visit, design capabilities to build your Web site, and many other services to help you run your online business. The choice of a Web hosting service should be based on its monthly service charge, the amount of disk space you will receive, access to reports, phone support availability, and ancillary services like credit card processing.

> There are many different types of Web hosting services.

There are many different types of Web hosting services. Some, like Exodus Communications, specialize in hosting the entire computer systems of very large and highly trafficked Web sites. Other firms, like Verio, specialize in hosting thousands of small business Web sites. This chapter is devoted to Web hosting services that typically cater to smaller businesses.

In order to provide service for its customers, a Web hosting company normally has numerous computers, or Web servers, attached to the Internet. On each computer, or server, resides a number of individual Web sites. For instance, a server might house hundreds or even thousands of Web sites. Each Web site is owned and published by a different small business, like yours. In effect, you are renting disk space and access to the Internet from a Web host.

Although this chapter is devoted to Web hosting services provided by other companies, it is entirely possible for you to set up your own server and connect it directly to the Internet. However, the costs and technical challenges of establishing an online business through this method are often prohibitive for smaller businesses. This is analogous to you building your own phone network rather than simply paying a phone company for service.

Understanding Web Hosting Terminology

With new technologies come new vocabularies, and Web hosting is no exception. Chapter 6 introduced general computer terms, such as bits, bytes, and bandwidth, which you must understand before you can select the right Web hosting plan for your online business. Even so, there are other terms specifically related to Web hosting services.

> With new technologies come new vocabularies, and Web hosting is no exception.

Common Gateway Interface (CGI) Scripts

Common gateway interface, or CGI, specifies how information is transferred between a server on the World Wide Web and a computer program. If a Web host provides CGI capability, it will be able to "talk" to any computer program that conforms to the CGI specification.

It is important that you select a Web host with CGI capabilities, because online forms are normally processed using this specification. For instance, if you put a customer feedback form on your Web site, you will need CGI capability to access the data from your Web host once the form has been completed and submitted.

Practical Extraction and Report Language (Perl)

Perl is a very popular text programming language developed by Larry Wall that is often used for writing CGI scripts.

Secure Sockets Layer (SSL)

If you are going to process credit cards online, or obtain other confidential information from your customers, then you will want to ensure them that this information can be transmitted securely over the Internet. One way to do this is to make sure that your Web host supports the secure sockets layer (SSL). As mentioned earlier in this book, SSL was developed by Netscape and is a protocol for transmitting encrypted documents over the Internet.

SSL establishes a secure connection been your customer's computer and your Web host's server, so that all information transmitted over the connection is secure. The Netscape Navigator and Microsoft Internet Explorer browsers can use SSL when communicating with a Web host that also supports the protocol. Part of the SSL protocol dictates that Web pages begin with "https://" rather than "http://."

File Transfer Protocol (FTP)

File transfer protocol (FTP) is a protocol used to send files over the Internet. If you are going to develop your Web site using an off-the-shelf software package like Microsoft FrontPage, you will need FTP to publish your site on your Web host. In this instance, FTP is used to transmit the files you create with Microsoft FrontPage on your PC over the Internet to your Web host.

Post Office Protocol (POP)

Not to be confused with the other POP, which the telecommunications industry uses for Point-of-Presence, post office protocol (POP) defines how e-mail is retrieved from an e-mail server. POP e-mail accounts receive e-mail on your Web host's server, as opposed to your dial-up account. E-mail sent to the POP would stay there until you read it. For instance, you could set up e-mail accounts for billing, sales, marketing, personnel, etc. on your Web host. There are two versions of this protocol: the newer POP3, which does not require SMTP to send messages; and the older POP2, which does require SMTP to send message.

If you are going to process credit cards online, or obtain other confidential information from your customers, then you will want to ensure them that this information can be transmitted securely over the Internet.

Disk Space

The size of your Web site will determine the amount of disk space that you will require on your Web host's server. If your site will contain mostly text and only a few graphic images, then 5–15MB is ample space. On the other hand, if your site will have many graphics, you should consider larger plans. Remember that a lot of graphics will slow down the loading time for your users. If the size of your Web site falls in between one of the standard plans offered by your Web host, normally you can purchase a little more disk space without having to pay the complete cost for the next larger plan. More information about estimating the disk space you will need is presented later in this chapter.

> The size of your Web site will determine the amount of disk space that you will require on your Web host's server.

Domain Mail Forwarding

In addition to having e-mail stored at the POP, you can have mail delivered to your dial-up account. Consider your dial-up account to be the place where e-mail is delivered when you connect to the Internet. For example, the famous America Online "you've got mail" indicates that you have received e-mail in your dial-up account. Once you establish a domain name ("www.yourbiz.com"), e-mail can be forwarded to your dial-up account when it is addressed to "anyone@yourbiz.com."

Control Panel

This tool allows you to view the activity on your Web site, change e-mail information, set up auto-responders, and set passwords. A control panel is a "must-have" for any Web master who wants to understand and control the activity on their Web site.

FrontPage Support

A Web host that provides FrontPage support can publish Web sites created with Microsoft FrontPage. In order for a Web host to provide this capability, it must have some computers that are using the Microsoft NT operating system.

Additional Traffic

If your Web site gets more traffic (or hits) in a given month than you were allotted, you will be charged an incremental fee by your Web hosting company. Some Web hosts give you the capability to shut your site down once your traffic limit has been exceeded. This might not be a bad idea when you first begin to market your Web site. Although unlikely, a million visitors to even a small site can add up quickly with additional traffic charges.

Set-up Fee

Most Web hosts will charge a fee to set up your Web hosting account. This covers the costs of mapping the disk space where your Web site will be stored, creating passwords, and initiating monthly billing.

InterNIC Fees

When you register your domain name ("www.yourbiz.com") with your Web host, you will be charged the fee that the host has to pay to Network Solutions to list the site in their InterNIC database. Currently, the registration fee is $70 for two years.

Choosing the Right Web Hosting Plan for Your Online Business

Most Web hosts offer a variety of plans that vary in price according to the amount of disk space you need for your Web site, the number of visitors you anticipate each month, and any special features that you will require, such as credit card processing or multimedia capabilities.

Web hosting companies differentiate themselves from the competition through their hosting plans, price points, customer service, and backbone infrastructure. As you consider Web hosts, research the following questions:

- What is the fee structure?
- Is technical support available 24 hours a day, 7 days a week?

Check with your Web host about the additional charges that you will incur if you exceed your monthly traffic allotment.

Web hosting companies differentiate themselves from the competition through their hosting plans, price points, customer service, and backbone infrastructure.

- Can I establish a Web hosting account online?
- How often can I update my site?
- Do you support Microsoft FrontPage in its entirety?
- Can I set up an online store?
- What types of credit card processing do you support?
- Can I shut my site down after a predetermined amount of bandwidth?
- What is your reliability record?
- How large is your network?
- What types of connections do you have to the Internet?
- What types of connections do you offer my online business?

Most of these questions can be answered by simply reading a description of the service on the Web host's site. If you need more information, or are unclear about something, make sure you call and find out. Selecting a Web hosting service that doesn't meet your needs will lead to a lot of rework later on.

Again, before you decide on a Web hosting service, you should at least know what types of features you will need for your online business, like credit card processing, and what your domain name ("www.yourbiz.com") is going to be. Additionally, you should have a rough idea of the size of your Web site, in terms of disk space, and how many visitors you expect each month.

As you begin exploring different Web hosting plans, be aware that the main variables used to determine the monthly charge are disk space, Web site traffic, and optional features like Secure Server technology and multimedia capabilities. For instance, in the three MindSpring plans that follow, the $80 difference in monthly cost between the QuickWeb and the CompleteWeb plans can be attributed to the additional disk space and Web site traffic you get with the CompleteWeb plan.

On the following pages you will see examples of the Web hosting plans provided by MindSpring and Verio. For the most part they offer a very similar set of features for comparable prices. (Chapter 9 contains information about free Web hosting sites.) MindSpring and Verio are currently the two largest domain-based

> Make sure your Web hosting service provides technical support 24 hours a day.

> As you begin exploring different Web hosting plans, be aware that the main variables used to determine the monthly charge are disk space, Web site traffic, and optional features like Secure Server technology and multimedia capabilities.

Web hosting companies for small businesses. However, as of this writing, MindSpring was about to merge with Earthlink, with the resulting company being called Earthlink.

Sample Web Hosting Plans from MindSpring (*www.mindspring.com*) March, 1999

FEATURES	QUICKWEB*	ENHANCEDWEB	COMPLETEWEB
Monthly Cost	$19.95	$49.95	$99.95
Disk Space	5–15 MB*	20 MB	50 MB
Web site Traffic	up to 675 MB	2,000 MB	6,000 MB
POP E-mail**			
(Receive Only)	1-3 POP3 accounts*	10 POP3 accounts	15 POP3 accounts
Domain Mail Forwarding	Unlimited	Unlimited	Unlimited
Technical Support	24 hr/7 days	24 hr/7 days	24 hr/7 days
Control Panel	n/a	Yes	Yes
E-commerce Capable	n/a	Yes	Yes
Custom CGI scripts	n/a	Yes	Yes
FrontPage Support	n/a	Yes	Yes
Secure Server (SSL)	n/a	Yes	Yes
Additional Disk Space	$4.95/5MB*	$4.95/ 5MB	$4.95/5MB
Additional Traffic	n/a	Yes ($.04–$.10/MB)	Yes ($.04–$.08/MB)
Set-up Fee***	$25	$50	$50
InterNIC Fees (nonrefundable)	$70	$70	$70

*User must have a MindSpring Internet access account to sign up for QuickWeb. Amount of disk space and number of physical or email@mindspring.com mailboxes depends on the dial-up plan. There is a 15MB total disk space limit.
** POP3 e-mail accounts are "receive only," you can send mail if dialing into MindSpring for your Internet connection.
***Set-up fee does not include $70 InterNIC fee. InterNIC fees are for the first two years of domain name usage and are nonrefundable. If you are transferring your domain to MindSpring, the domain set-up fee is waived with the purchase of a Web hosting account.

The following table features sample Web hosting plans from Verio (*www.verio.com*). If you compare them to the MindSpring Web hosting plans, you will see that the main difference in monthly charges can be attributed to disk space, Web site traffic, and additional features.

Sample Web Hosting Plans from Verio (*www.verio.com*)

FEATURES	BRONZE PLAN	SILVER PLAN	GOLD PLAN
Monthly Cost	$24.95/mo	$49.95/mo	$99.95/mo
Disk Space	40MB	60MB	100 MB
Web site Traffic	3,000MB/mo	4,000MB/mo	6,000MB/mo
POP E-mail** (Receive Only)	10 configurable POP3 accounts	20 configurable POP3 accounts	31 POP3 e-mail accounts
Domain Mail Forwarding	Unlimited	Unlimited	Unlimited
Technical Support	24 hrs/7 days	24 hrs/7 days	24 hrs/7 days
Control Panel	Yes	Yes	Yes
E-commerce Capable	n/a	n/a	n/a
Custom CGI scripts	Yes	Yes	Yes
FrontPage Support	Yes	Yes	Yes
Secure Server (SSL)	No	Yes	Yes
Additional Disk Space	n/a	n/a	n/a
Additional Traffic	n/a	n/a	n/a
Set-up Fee	$50	$50	$50
InterNIC Fees (nonrefundable)	$70	$70	$70
CyberCash support	No	Yes	Yes
RealAudio & RealVideo support	No	Yes	Yes

One thing not currently posted on the Verio plan descriptions is if there are additional costs for excess disk space or Web site traffic. It is important to determine what these costs are before publishing your Web site, since they can add up quickly on a highly trafficked Web site.

> As you plan your online business, a critical question to ask is, "How big is my Web site going to be?"

Sizing Your Web Site

As you plan your online business, a critical question to ask is, "How big is my Web site going to be?" The size of your Web site is important because it will determine the amount of disk space you will need and how many hits you can sustain with your Web hosting plan. Unfortunately, other than making some informed guesses, there is no way to know how big your Web site is going to be until you publish it on the Web host's server.

Understanding Disk Space

SIZE	EQUIVALENT	EXAMPLE
1 Byte	1 Character	Keyboard character
1 Kilobyte (KB)	1,024 Bytes	1 Amazon.com GIF image*
1 Megabyte (MB)	1,048,576 Bytes	70% of a 1.44 MB floppy disk
1 Gigabyte (GB)	1,073,741,824 Bytes	A billion characters

*You can see this size GIF image on the *www.officelinks.com* home page.

The size of individual pages within your Web site is also important because it will determine the amount of bandwidth that is used every time someone "hits" one of these pages. At MindSpring, "bandwidth" is determined by the following formula: (number of hits per file) x (file size).

Getting an E-Commerce Solution from Your Web Host

> Most Web hosting services offer e-commerce capabilities.

As you know from Chapter 7, most Web hosting services offer e-commerce capabilities. For example, MindSpring and Verio offer specific plans for businesses that want to create an online store. These plans make it easier for you to set up your store than simply using a traditional Web hosting plan, and usually offer additional services like secure connections and credit card processing.

One of the main differences between these e-commerce packages and the hosting plans is that your Web site design is already developed. You simply need to add pictures of your merchandise with appropriate descriptions, and the e-commerce package takes care of the rest of the details, like adding a shopping cart and incorporating credit card processing.

Pricing for the MindSpring and Verio e-commerce solutions is handled differently than their normal Web hosting plans. Charges for hosting plans is mainly driven by disk space usage and Web site traffic, while charges for their e-commerce solutions are based on the number of products you want to list. For instance, Verio charges a certain amount if you want to sell from one to 300 products, and another charge for 301 to 2,000 products.

Sample of MindSpring (*www.mindspring.com*) Biz E-Commerce Solutions

E-COMMERCE FEATURES	INTRO COMMERCE	COMMERCE ENHANCED	COMPLETE COMMERCE
Monthly Fee	$79.90	$109.90	$209.90
Set-up*	$50	$50	$50
No. of Products	50	100	Unlimited
Secure Browser Based Set-up + Admin	Yes	Yes	Yes
Store Building Wizard	Yes	Yes	Yes
Custom Page Creation	No	No	Yes
Online Credit Card Authorization	No	Yes	Yes
Shopping Basket	Yes	Yes	Yes
Secure Order Forms	Yes	Yes	Yes
Hot Deals Section	Yes	Yes	Yes
Discounting or Merchandising	No	No	Yes
Customer Feedback Forms	Yes	Yes	Yes
Secure Server	Yes	Yes	Yes
Password Protection	Yes	Yes	Yes

*Set-up fee does not include $70 InterNIC fee. InterNIC fees are for the first two years of domain name usage and are non-refundable. If you are transferring your domain to MindSpring, the domain set-up fee is waived with the purchase of a Web hosting account.

Sample Charges for Verio E-Business Plans

NUMBER OF PRODUCTS FOR SALE	COST PER MONTH
1–300	$199
301–2,000	$299
2,001–5,000	$399

If you select Verio for your e-business solution, you can use their software tools to create a Web site using only your Web browser, such as Netscape Navigator or Microsoft Internet Explorer. Some of the additional features of Verio e-business plans are shown in the following table.

Sample Description of Verio E-Business Plans (*www.verio.com*)

You get:

- **Store Main Page:** Includes your company name, information, and logo
- **Customer Service Page:** Summarizes ordering, shipping, customer service policies, and contact information
- **Store Catalog Pages:** Separate pages to display each category of products you offer
- **Shopping Cart:** All order taking and credit card processing is handled on our server
- **Merchant Account Services:** Apply online to enable credit card processing
- **Backroom Services:** Quick access to orders, credit card transactions, and traffic reports for your store site
- **Site Promotion:** Your products are listed in the Stuff.com search engine.

Interpreting Web Hosting Reports

Once you have published your Web site and started the marketing process, you will want to know how many prospects are visiting your online business. In other words, you will want to know how many "hits" your Web site is getting. While "hits" are good, this is a somewhat deceiving term. Let's assume that your home page contains text and five images. When a prospect visits that single home page, your Web hosting reports will register six hits, not just one, for that visitor. This is because the text and images are stored in six separate files and are loaded individually every time someone visits your home page.

Besides the number of hits your Web site is getting, you will also want to know many other key traffic statistics, including when prospects are visiting your site, what pages they are visiting, how they got to your site, and who your prospects are. Answers to these and other questions can be found by looking at your Web hosting reports. Through its control panel, MindSpring provides the following reports and associated descriptions:

Disk Usage: Provides the size of your Web site.

Bandwidth: Shows you the amount of bandwidth or traffic on your Web site.

Time Measured: Gives you a line graph that charts the hits and bytes transferred per-day and per-hour during a chosen time period.

> Once you have published your Web site and started the marketing process, you will want to know how many prospects are visiting your online business.

> Web hosting reports can tell a lot about your visitors, including how many you get each day, the most popular times for visiting your site, and which Web pages they visit the most in your site.

Single Page: Shows individual files and sorts them either by the number of requests made or the amount of bandwidth those requests have generated.

Browser Info: This shows you the types of browsers your visitors were using. "Mozilla" often means Netscape Navigator, but when you see "compatible; MSIE," your visitors were using Microsoft Internet Explorer. You may also see the type of operating system (i.e., Windows or Macintosh) they were using. An entry of "—" in the browser column means the server could not obtain any agent information from the visitor's browser.

Referrer Info: This shows how your visitors got to your Web site. A URL like "http://av.yahoo.com/bin/query?p=%22Front+Page+97%22&hc=0&hs=0" reveals that your visitor found your site by searching for "Front+Page+97" on Yahoo! Some, perhaps many, of the referrers may be from pages within your Web site. An entry of "UNKNOWN" means the visitor had no referrer. The person could have typed in the URL manually or used the bookmark to revisit your site.

Regional Info: This tracks where your visitors are connecting from. It shows the machine address, or the machine name, that people were using when they looked at your Web site. For example, "com.aol.proxy" means that you received visits from America Online; "com.compuserve.hil" means the visitors were from Compuserve; and "com.mindspring.dialup" reveals MindSpring dial-up customers.

> In addition to the reports provided by your Web hosting service, there are other reporting tools you might want to consider.

In addition to the reports provided by your Web hosting service, there are other reporting tools you might want to consider. One of the most popular tools is a software program called WebTrends. WebTrends is a statistical package designed to work with your log files, which can help you determine important information including your most popular products and services; the best page for placing advertisements; user activity by businesses, organizations, and the government; and visitor demographics.

Selecting a Web hosting Service for OfficeLinks.com

Q: What company is the Web host for OfficeLinks.com?

A: MindSpring.

Q: Why did you choose MindSpring to host OfficeLinks.com?

A: I looked at three Web hosting services, including MindSpring, and compared their rate plans. Since the costs for all three plans were about the same, and they all supported Microsoft FrontPage, it was the service level that finally sold me.

Q: How was the MindSpring service level different than the other hosts?

A: With one Web host, I could not speak to a service representative until 11:00 A.M. since they operated on West coast time (I live on the East coast). Also, with one of the other Web hosts I could not register and set up my business online. With this service it had to be done over the phone.

Q: Why was an automated sign-up process important in your decision?

A: I don't know about you, but I do a lot of my work late at night or on the weekends. Most of the time it is just easier to fill out forms online during these odd hours than to try to get someone on the phone. Also, I could see exactly what I was ordering and how much it would cost from the forms I had to complete. When you do this stuff over the phone, there are always some lingering doubts—in my mind, anyway.

Q: What MindSpring Web hosting plan did you choose for OfficeLinks.com?

A: I went with their EnhancedWeb, which is their middle-of-the-road program.

Q: Did this plan offer enough disk space and Web site traffic for you?

A: It has been plenty for me. In fact, I probably could have used their less expensive plan and still had plenty of room for more Web pages and visitors.

Q: Did you consider any e-commerce packages for your Web site?

A: No. OfficeLinks.com is not an online store and would not really benefit from this type of solution. However, I have been toying with the idea of accepting credit cards online, but I think I will just add this feature to my existing Web site.

Q: Do you use the MindSpring Web reporting capabilities?

A: Yes. Almost every day I log into their control panel to look at the activity on my Web site. I can check how many hits I got every hour on the previous day, and in many cases figure out where those hits were coming from.

Q: Are you satisfied with the Web reporting capabilities?

A: Yes. I can get the answers I want by using the control panel. Still, it's too bad there isn't an e-mail capability that would send me the reports daily. This would save me the time I spend logging in every day.

Online Web Hosting Resources

CNET Web Services (*webhostlist.com*)

As mentioned earlier, CNET publishes the *Ultimate Web Host List* on its Web site, which provides a monthly ranking of the top 25 Web hosting companies based on value, customer service, quality, and flexibility. You will also find an A to Z listing of Web hosts and many tips on building an e-commerce Web site.

Host Investigator (*www.hostinvestigator.com*)

Host Investigator provides a search tool "you can use to find a reliable host with the services, features, and pricing that best meets your needs." On its Web site you can also find a series of useful articles on Web hosting, like "What is Web Hosting?" and "What Are Web Hosting Services?"

Host Search (*www.hostsearch.com*)

Host Search features a search engine that allows you to find Web hosts that meet certain criteria, such as "Hosting services that are less than $5 per month." It also has hosting reviews (good and bad) that were written by its visitors who are current or past customers of the companies they reviewed.

The List (*thelist.internet.com*)

Internet.com claims it provides the definitive ISP buyer's guide with its trademarked List service. Here, you can search over 8,000 ISPs by area code, country code, and in the United States.

Web Host Guild (*www.whg.org*)

The Web Host Guild (WHG) was founded in 1998 "to make Web host certification a part of doing business on the Internet. Our mission statement is to protect consumers from unscrupulous hosts, and to help identify the honest, legitimate host companies that exist." On the WHG site you can get a list of members who have agreed to abide by their standards.

Yahoo! Directories of Access Providers
(*dir.yahoo.com/Business_and_Economy/Companies/Internet_Services/Access_Providers/Directories/*)
Under the "Business & Economy" heading on its home page, Yahoo! provides a list of directories of Internet service providers. There are also listings for free Internet access in the United States and elsewhere.

Summary

By now you should understand that a Web hosting service is where your Web site will be stored on the Internet. You can visualize it as a shared hard disk that stores all of the Web pages for your online business and makes them available for anyone on the Internet to access. Web hosts normally store thousands of different Web sites on their servers and collect a monthly fee for this service.

There are many different Web hosts and hosting plans available for a variety of online business needs. The right one for your business will depend on the nature of your Web site and the number of "hits" or page views you will be expecting every month. In addition to selecting a Web hosting service based on price, you should also consider other important things, like availability of technical support and network capacity.

For more information on this topic, visit our Web site at www.businesstown.com

Designing Your Web Site to be User-Friendly

Topics covered in this chapter

- Visiting other popular Web sites for design ideas
- Designing a clean Web site
- Incorporating key features in your Web site
- Getting help from professional Web site designers

Chapter 11

When it comes to home-page navigation, cleanliness is next to godliness.

JIM STERNE, *INC.* MAGAZINE

Many small business Web sites can look better and be more user friendly than those created by large multinational businesses. It is not unusual to find a Web site created by a large company with a household name that is slow, hard to under-stand, or difficult to navigate. Therefore, you should make every effort to understand some of the fundamentals of good Web site design before you begin creating your own Web site.

If you are developing your Web site using Microsoft FrontPage or another professional Web site development package, you are already ahead of the curve. These packages have sorted out much of what works, and does not work, in Web site design. However, you will still find it extremely helpful to investigate other Web sites in order to get additional design ideas and create a site that is dis-tinctively your own.

> Create a Web site that is clean and easy to use for your visitors.

One of the most important things for an online business is to create a Web site that is clean and easy to use for your visitors. Don't clutter your site with extraneous graphics, hard-to-read text, or superfluous sound. Everything you put on your Web site should help visitors to buy your products and services, or keep them returning for additional information.

Begin your design process by creating a logical layout for your Web pages. Decide how you are going to display your con-tent, and ensure that you include helpful features, such as a search engine, contact list, e-mail capability, and Frequently Asked Question (FAQ) sheet. You will greatly enhance your visitors' expe-riences by creating a user-friendly navigation system that helps them move around quickly, find what they are looking for, and return to your home page.

After you have created and published your site, test it out with as many Web browsers and versions of Windows as possible.

This will ensure that almost everyone will see what they are supposed to see on your Web site. In addition to testing your Web site for browser compatibility, you should also ensure that it loads quickly on even the slowest machine. Users will not wait long before clicking on STOP and moving on to the next Web site.

Although you can get your business online by using many of the software tools described earlier in this book, you may still want to seek an outside consultant or design firm to create your Web site. If you choose this route, be wary that Web sites need to be maintained and updated after the initial design phase, so decide whether you will retain your design firm to accomplish these tasks or do it in house.

> Test your Web site out with as many different Web browsers and Windows versions as possible.

Visiting Other Popular Web Sites for Design Ideas

Once you have decided what software you are going to use to develop your Web site, spend at least a few hours (days, if you have time) studying different Web sites for design ideas. Start with the most popular sites, as ranked by the Go2Net Hot 100 (*www.100hot.com*) or Media Metrix (*www.mediametrix.com*), and keep an eye on some of the following design characteristics:

- How is the home page structured?
- What type of fonts, colors, and graphics are being used?
- Are there any sound or other multimedia capabilities?
- How fast does the Web site load in your browser?
- Is complete contact information available on the home page?
- Where are the menu selections?
- Does the Web site uses frames or title bars?
- How many hot-links are shown on the home page?
- Does the home page include a search capability?

> Once you have decided what software you are going to use to develop your Web site, spend at least a few hours (days, if you have time) studying different Web sites for design ideas.

The Most Popular Web Sites

TOP 10 WEB SITES	WEB ADDRESS
1. Yahoo! and Four11	*www.yahoo.com*
2. Microsoft Corp., including MSN.com and LinkExchange	*www.microsoft.com*
3. AOL.com and Netscape	*www.aol.com*
4. Lycos Search Engine, Point, and WhoWhere	*www.lycos.com*
5. Go.com World Network	*www.go.com*
6. AltaVista Search Engine, Compaq, and Tandem	*www.altavista.com*
7. Excite, Magellan, City.Net, and WebCrawler	*www.excite.com*
8. CNN Interactive	*www.cnn.com*
9. NetTaxi Community	*www.nettaxi.com*
10. TUCOWS and www.freethemes.com	*www.tucows.com*

Source: Go2Net Hot 100 listing (*www.100hot.com/directory/100hot/ September 8, 1999*)

As you explore Web sites for different design ideas, notice that the most popular sites are portals, or gateways, to other sources of information on the Web. If your Web site is not going to be a portal but will specialize in selling products and services, dig a little deeper to find similar but, of course, larger e-tailers like Amazon.com (ranked #12 in this survey), or auctioneers like eBay (ranked #16).

Even if your Web site is not going to be a portal, you should still begin your study of popular sites with Yahoo!, which is usually ranked #1 in these surveys. It is important to study Yahoo! because you will immediately come to the conclusion that, in terms of appearance, it is one of the simplest sites on the Web. On its home page you will see only a few graphics across the top of the page, followed mostly by simple blue hot-links on a plain white background. What's more, Yahoo! maintains this simple theme throughout most of its site.

Your lesson from Yahoo! should be that great Web sites don't need a lot of fancy graphics, streaming audio, and other bells and whistles to make them popular. As Jim Sterne wrote in *Inc.* magazine, "When it comes to home-page navigation, cleanliness is next to godliness." By keeping your Web site clean and free of extraneous bells and whistles, your visitors will be able to load the site quickly, find what they are looking for, and move on to their next task.

> As you explore Web sites for different design ideas, notice that the most popular sites are portals, or gateways, to other sources of information on the Web.

Study some of the most popular Web sites on the Internet for good design ideas and navigational structure.

Designing a Clean Web Site

You shouldn't be surprised to learn that Web sites are simply a series of pages that are linked to each other. In fact, you can visualize the entire World Wide Web as millions, or billions, of individual pages that can be accessed through a Web browser. How you lay out these pages and what you place on them, will in large part determine the success of your Web site.

Although Web site content is more fully covered in the next chapter, you need to have an idea about what your Web site is going to contain before you can begin the design process. For instance, if you are going to sell products and services, you will need to decide whether to include a single page for every product and service, or whether multiple products and services will be displayed on a single page.

The framework, or Web site design, that you place around your content includes creating a Web site layout, establishing a navigation structure to help visitors to move around, selecting a theme for a consistent presentation, and adding links and graphics to make your site more interesting.

Laying Out Your Web site

A good Web site design begins with a logical layout of your individual Web pages. Get a piece of paper and start drawing a series of boxes, interconnected by lines, to represent the layout of your Web site. At the top will be your home page, followed by layers, or categories, of individual Web pages. Your drawing should resemble something like the diagram on page 194.

Think of your home page as being a table of contents for everything else in your Web site. Visitors will enter your Web site through your home page and will want to be able to find everything else on your site from that home page. If they can't get there directly with one click, you will need to provide categories for the content and steer them in the right direction as they click deeper into your site.

For instance, if the preceding layout was being used for an online hardware store, there might be categories on the home page for hand tools, power tools, hardware, plumbing, and paint. A visitor

> A good Web site design begins with a logical layout of your individual Web pages.

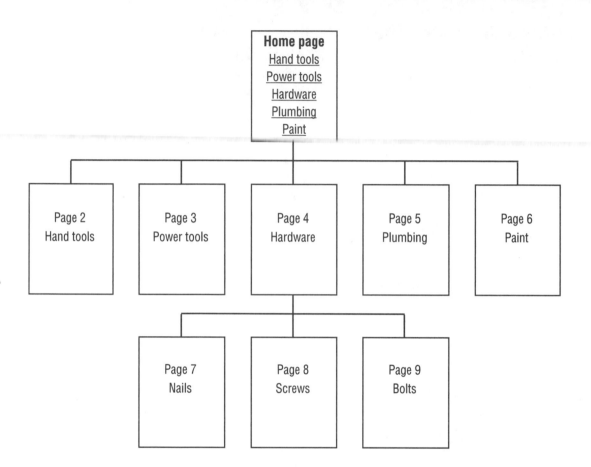

who clicked on "hardware" would now have a new set of choices, such as nails, screws, and bolts. If this visitor now clicks on "screws," there could be a complete description of all screws on page #8, or there could be additional lower layers covering different types of screws, like flat head, sheet metal, and so on.

In addition to creating separate pages for your content, there are also a few extra pages you should include within your site to make it more user friendly: an About page, a Frequently Asked Question (FAQ) page, and a contact information page. These and other Web site elements are discussed later in this chapter.

Your home page is the table of contents for everything else on your Web site.

All pages within your Web will be assigned a unique address, so that they can be accessed by other pages within your Web, and also by other Web sites that have links to yours.

Sample Addressing Scheme for a Hardware Web Site

PAGE NAME	WEB PAGE ADDRESS
Home page	*www.yourbiz.com*
Hand tools	*www.yourbiz.com/handtools.htm*
Hardware	*www.yourbiz.com/hardware.htm*
Screws	*www.yourbiz.com/hardware/screws.htm*

Fortunately, if you are using a Web site design tool such as Microsoft FrontPage, the process of laying out your Web site and naming the individual pages is completely automated. Not only does FrontPage take care of the individual page name hierarchy within your Web, but it also has a good graphical interface that shows the entire layout of your Web site.

Navigating Within Your Web Site

As you begin to develop the layout for your Web site, you will also want to consider how visitors are going to navigate, or move around, from one page to the next. Ideally, you would like to allow visitors to move from one page to any other page within your Web site. Unfortunately, as your Web site grows, this alternative will be too confusing and difficult to implement. For instance, if your site contained 500 individual pages, you would need to place 499 menu selections on every page of your Web site to provide this capability.

A well-designed navigational system allows visitors to easily move within your Web site, and find their way home from any page within the site. You want to make it as easy as possible for visitors to find what they are looking for, and then get back to your home page to begin their next search. If your visitors get lost, or don't understand what they are looking at, there is a good possibility that they will go to another Web site to get the information or make a purchase.

You can design a user-friendly navigation system by using either text links or graphical icons. Although you can make your site

> Most software packages will help you to name individual pages and create a navigational structure with in your Web.

> A well-designed navigational system allows visitors to easily move within your Web site.

more visually appealing by incorporating graphical icons, they are harder to implement and will offer little value in helping your visitors to move around. For instance, a pretty icon of a person entering a home (signifying how visitors can get back to your home page) offers little value versus a simple text link that says "Home." *Clear and simple* must be your guiding principles as you create your navigation system.

Visitors are usually given a few ways to move around a Web site. These include menus that are presented on the top, sides, or bottom of a page; hot-links in the body of a page; and a search box to find specific items within the Web site. You should use all three. Common menu choices include:

- Home
- Help
- Back to previous page
- Top of page
- Forward to next page
- Search entire Web site
- Contact us
- Send us an e-mail
- [Specific Web page names]

> The most important menu selection that you should include on, or near, the top of every page is "Home."

The most important menu selection that you should include on, or near, the top of every page is "Home." Additionally, if you have long Web pages, this menu selection should be included at the bottom of your Web pages. This is the easiest way for visitors to get back to your home page.

Hot-links within the body of your page allow users to get closer to their ultimate destination. They act much like the table of contents in a book, and break a large Web site down into smaller, more manageable parts. For instance, look at the hot-links that are included in the body of the Yahoo! home page. Yahoo! breaks its site down into categories that will appeal to specific users of the portal, such as "Computers & Internet," "Health," and "Society & Culture."

The other way to help your visitors find items easily is to include a "Search box" on your Web site. Your visitors will usually try this last if your menus or hot-links aren't helping. A search box can be incorporated into both your menu selections and on the body of your home page.

As you create your navigation system, the last item you should take into account is what happens after a visitor makes a menu selection, or clicks on a hot-link within your Web site. For instance, if a visitor clicks on a link within your site, say "Computers & Internet," the page that they are transported to should have a title that corresponds to the link—in this example, the page would have a "Computers & Internet" title.

Selecting a Theme for Your Web Site

One way to give your Web site a consistent look and feel is to select, or create, a theme for all of your pages. According to the Microsoft FrontPage 98 user manual, themes "are a collection of design elements—bullets, background patterns, table borders, fonts, and graphics—that you can apply to an entire FrontPage web or to a single page. A page with a theme applied to it has a consistent, professional appearance. Everything on it, from its bullets to its background pattern, fits together."

If you select an appropriate theme before you begin designing your Web, you will provide visitors a consistent, professional appearance. For example, decisions you should make concerning your theme, include:

- Background color for every Web page
- Appearance of page titles
- Location of menus
- Common page borders
- Placement of graphics
- Font style and size for text
- Bullet types for lists

Web site design software, like Microsoft FrontPage, makes the selection of themes easy—right from the beginning. For example, FrontPage provides a variety of theme options, including Automotive, Bubbles, Construction Zone, Fiesta, Highway, Industrial, Sunflower,

> A page with a theme applied to it has a consistent, professional appearance.

and World Finance. After you select one of these themes, every page on your Web site will be preformatted to match the chosen theme.

One thing you want to avoid is having your Web site look like another site—a problem that can occur when you select a predetermined theme. Therefore, you may want to modify the theme to incorporate a specific "look and feel" for your own Web site. However, even if you decide not to go with a predetermined theme from a software package, you should still have a theme for your Web site that incorporates common design variables.

Selecting Fonts for Your Web Site

Although you might be tempted to design your Web site using special fonts for your text, most visitors will not be able to see them because Web browsers are normally set to default settings, for instance, a 12-point size and Times New Roman font.

Because of this limitation, try to use the "Normal" font as you create text for your Web site. If you need to use larger fonts to separate topics or paragraphs, use a preset "Heading" format. This will increase the font size relative to the browser's default font. If you really need to control the appearance of some text (for instance, your logo or business name), you should create a graphics image. This is the only way to ensure that it will be displayed properly in your visitor's browser.

Choosing Colors for Your Web Site

One way to increase the visual appeal of your Web site is to limit the amount of colors you use on your Web pages. Again, you should return to Yahoo! and study the colors used throughout the site. With the exception of some colorful banner advertisements, and a few offsets to highlight navigation, Yahoo! currently uses four basic colors:

- Yahoo! is shown in red
- Links to different pages are colored blue
- Descriptive text is black
- All material is presented on a white background

One of the reasons that makes Yahoo! so easy to read is that it employs a large amount of white background on every page. This gives the site a clean and neat appearance, and contrasts well with

> Use the "Normal" font as you create text for your Web site.

everything actually shown on the page; the sea of white makes the site's content and advertisements stand out.

Yahoo! further enhances its image by using two of the most popular primary colors: red and blue. Research has shown that visitors are more likely to perceive integrity in a Web site that uses these colors than a site that doesn't. Naturally, if your Web site is named "www.purple.com," you will want to use purple as one of your predominant colors. However, make sure to limit your colors to no more than two or three.

Enhancing Your Site with Multimedia

One of the least utilized and most anticipated areas of Web site design is the incorporation of different types of media, such as sound and video. Today, you can find quite a few sites that have begun to broadcast sound, and others that provide some form of video download capability. The Disney site (*www.disney.com*) and some of the larger television network sites (like MSNBC, *www.msnbc.com*) are good examples of Web sites that have begun to offer full multimedia capability. However, because most users connected to the Internet still only have a slow dial-up connection, complete multimedia sites have yet to realize their full potential.

Don't add sound and video to your site unless it is going to benefit your visitors. You might think it's fun to play "Jingle Bells" at Christmas when someone visits your site, but after a minute or so it will become very annoying for them. On the other hand, if you are trying to sell holiday music on your site, your visitors might like to hear a portion of the music before they make a purchase. In this case, adding sound is a benefit, not an annoyance.

Web sites that have incorporated multimedia successfully are businesses primarily involved in sound or video. For instance, you can see clips of the latest movies on Web sites run by studios, you can listen to analyst conference calls about the stock market, and you can listen to music on CD retailing sites. In all of these instances, multimedia provides users with additional information that is relevant to the product being promoted.

If you want to add some multimedia capability to your Web site, you will need to purchase or download some additional software such as RealAudio, RealVideo, Flash, and MP3. To learn more about these

> Don't add sound and video to your site unless it is going to benefit your visitors.

technologies and how to get started, try "Adam's Multimedia Tutorial" available on Web Monkey (*www.hotwired.com/webmonkey/multimedia/*).

Including Pictures or Images on Your Web Pages

Most Web sites include graphic images, or pictures, on their pages to make them more visually appealing. Additionally, if you join affiliate programs or conduct other types of online advertising on your site, you may be required to include images on some of your Web pages. As long as you follow the basic design principles already discussed in this chapter, and don't clutter your site with too many images, your users should still have a good experience while visiting your Web site.

One thing to be wary of is the amount of time it takes your images to load in a Web browser. Large image files, or too many images, can significantly reduce the performance of your Web site. Sites that load slowly are usually avoided by Web users—they simply press the "Stop" button on their browser and look elsewhere for the desired information.

> Large image files, or too many images, can significantly reduce the performance of your Web site.

Popular Image File Formats

IMAGE FILE FORMAT	DESCRIPTION
GIF (graphic interchange format)	Developed by CompuServe, GIF images are very popular for displaying simple images, cartoons, text graphics, and logos. GIFs use a special compression technology that makes them smaller and load faster.
JPEG (joint photographic experts group)	JPEGs are best when you want to display photographs on your site, or other images that have many color and tone variations.
PNG (portable network graphics)	PNGs combine some of the best qualities of GIFs and JPEGs, but cannot be viewed by older browser versions. At some point they should replace the GIF format.

Checking the Performance of Your Web Site

After you have created and published your initial Web site, there a couple of good tools available on the Web that will run a diagnostic check for you, including SiteInspector (available through LinkExchange at *www.linkexchange.com*) and Web Site Garage Tune Up (*www.websitegarage.com*). Both of these services check for a variety of Web site performance characteristics, including:

- Your HTML validity
- What browsers can view your site correctly
- Whether you have any broken links
- Your spelling
- How quickly your site loads

Both of these diagnostic services are currently free and are definitely worth investigating to gauge the performance of your Web site. Unfortunately, they can't tell you whether your site is visually appealing or whether visitors will actually enjoy it!

Incorporating Key Features in Your Web Site

In addition to presenting a professional appearance on your Web site, you should include certain key features to make it user friendly. Some of these, like an easy-to-use navigation system and a search engine, have already been discussed. Other features that you should include in your site are e-mail capability, feedback form, FAQ sheet, registration form, complete contact information, message board, disclaimer information, and, where appropriate, order form.

With the exception of your navigation menus, most of the following key Web site features will probably require a separate page within your Web. Make sure you account for these pages as you develop your Web site layout.

Key Web site features	Description
Navigation menus	You need menus to help your visitors get around. Menus should be shown near the top of every page. For long pages, place menus at the bottom of the page, also. Every page must have a selection to get the user back to the home page.
Search engine	Give your visitors the capability to search your entire Web site with a search engine. Most software design tools give you this capability. You just need to add it to your site.
E-mail capability	Some visitors will want to send you an e-mail. You will get positive and negative feedback about your site, as well as inquiries about contacts and product information.
Feedback form	Encourage visitors to send feedback about your Web site. Ask them what they liked, and how it could be improved.
FAQ sheet	Compile a list of your most Frequently Asked Questions (FAQ) and post them on your Web site.
About page	Tell visitors about your Web site with an About page. Items you can include are a description of your business, types of products and services you sell, and even employee biographies.
Registration form	Every effort should be made to get more data from your visitors. For instance, where do they work? What does their business do? How did they hear about your site? Add a registration form for your mailing list or any special promotions (like a free e-newsletter).
Complete contact information	Your home page should include complete contact information for your business: phone and fax numbers, e-mail address, and street or PO Box mailing address.
Message board	Add a message board for visitors to ask you or other visitors specific questions. This makes your site more interactive, and will keep visitors returning.
Disclaimer document	Post a disclaimer document on your site that limits your liability for content and functionality. It's a good idea to review this with your lawyer.
Order form (if appropriate)	If you are going to sell products and services online, you'll need an order form that visitors can complete and e-mail to you.

Getting Help from Professional Web Site Designers

There is a fair amount of justifiable debate about whether you really need a professional to design your Web site. This can be best summarized in the accompanying Q&A, which appeared in the LinkExchange Digest #600 newsletter.

Most of the debate centers on whether using a prepackaged software program can give you professional results. Mr. Favarolo makes a good point with his analogy that giving paint to an amateur artist will produce an amateurish picture. Likewise, if you have no concept for the look and feel of Web sites, you will probably produce an unprofessional-looking Web site. However, you should be aware that many professional designers will actually use these packages to create your Web site. They use them as their starting point, and then add their own finishing touches to produce a professional result.

There are at least three things you should consider before you look for someone to design your Web site:

- What software tools will be used to create the Web site?
- Who will maintain the Web site after it's complete?
- How much can you afford to spend on Web site design?

As you begin to research different companies and consultants that might be able to design your Web site, find out what types of software tools they are planning to use to create the site. Again, many Web developers will use a package such as Microsoft FrontPage, and then add their own themes and graphics to complete a professional appearance. This is a good alternative, especially if you are going to contract for the initial design only but maintain the Web site using in-house resources. It is also a safer approach than getting a custom Web site designed from scratch; a Web site that only the original developer will be able to modify.

Web sites require ongoing maintenance after the initial design is created and published. It bears repeating: content must be updated, broken links need to be fixed, new affiliate programs must be added, and activity reports must be verified. You will need to

Commentary on professional Web site design

Q: Can site design software packages, such as Microsoft FrontPage 98, Adobe Pagemill and Allaire's Homesite, allow the user to achieve a professional outcome?

A: That question is like asking, "can a paint program make me an artist?" These packages do what you ask them to do (sometimes). Sure, some of them have templates and all that, but a professional web site does require a person(s) to have various talents. This includes experience or knowledge in layout, text positioning, copy writing (the text in your web site), graphic design, and in many cases computer programming.

Sal Favarolo
web2web design
(*www.web2web.com*)

If you are going to use a professional Web site designer, find out what software they are going to use to create your Web site.

decide who is going to perform these tasks once your design is complete. If you hire a consultant or design firm, expect to pay an hourly rate for these ongoing services.

Getting a Web site designed by an outside firm can be very expensive. This is especially true today where there is a shortage of qualified professional Web site designers. You should decide whether the additional design capabilities they offer will provide a larger benefit than the fees they charge. In other words, will their design help you to attract more visitors and sell more products and services?

Professional Web Site Designers

WEB SITE DESIGN SERVICES	WEB ADDRESS
Control V	www.controlv.com
Diamond Bullet Design	www.diamondbullet.com
Giant Step	www.giantstep.com
Ignition	www.ignitiondesign.com
NorthEast Internet Publishing	www.net-modules.com
Thoden Design	www.thodendesign.com
Webbs	www.webbsdesign.com
WWWebMasters	www.wwwebmasters.com

To locate other designers, including some in your geographic area, try some of the following keywords searches in the major portals, or search engines:

- Web site design
- Web site design service
- Web site design directory
- Multimedia Web designs

> Make sure that your domain name ("www.yourbiz.com") is registered in your name.

Finally, if you do decide to hire a professional Web site designer, make sure that your domain name (*"www.yourbiz.com"*) is registered in your name or the name of your business. Either register the name yourself, or insist that as part of your contract that the domain be registered in your name.

Designing the OfficeLinks.com Web Site

Q: How did you decide on the design for OfficeLinks.com?

A: Since the site is primarily a portal, I wanted to develop a Web site that had a similar look and feel as the other major portals, like Yahoo! and Excite. I studied their layouts and designs, and then incorporated my own ideas into the final design.

Q: Did you develop the site from scratch or use a software package?

A: Because I literally had no experience using HTML, I had to find a software package that made Web site design simple.

Q: What software design package did you choose?

A: I looked around and researched the different products that you can use to create Web sites, and finally decided on Microsoft FrontPage 98.

Q: Did you use a theme available in FrontPage for your Web site?

A: No. But I did go through and look at every theme provided with the software package. Unfortunately, I couldn't find one that totally satisfied my needs.

Q: Didn't this make your job harder?

A: Not at all. In fact, it is pretty easy to maintain a theme with FrontPage after you get your home page finished. Every time you want to add a new page, the software simply assumes that you want to maintain the same theme as the home page.

Q: Did you use any of the other features available in FrontPage?

A: Yes, in fact I used quite a few of them. One great thing is that the software comes with a bunch of pages that you can use as templates, like an order form. You just modify it for your own business and place it in your Web. That was a big time saver because I didn't have to totally figure out how to use drop down boxes and form fields.

Q: Where did you get all the graphics for your site?

A: Basically, the only graphics that I use are those created by the various affiliate programs that I've joined. To get those, you simply copy the GIF image from the host site and insert it into yours.

Q: Have you ever run any diagnostics on your Web site?

A: Yes. Every time that I register a new page with the search engines, using LinkExchange (*www.linkexchange.com*), I use their SiteInspector service. This looks at things like HTML validity, browser compatibility, spelling (U.S. English), and load time.

Q: How well does your site do on these diagnostic checks?

A: It does well because I have a pretty simple and clean Web site. There are not a lot of images, and things like HTML validity are already handled by FrontPage.

Online Web Design Resources

BigNoseBird.Com (*www.bignosebird.com*)

BigNoseBird (BNB) claims it has "everything you need to create a great Web site." It includes over two hundred tutorials, such as "Navigation Tricks: Getting around a site should be simple," and offers free scripts and free graphics.

Control V (*www.controlv.com*)

If you don't feel you have the time or skills to develop a professional-looking Web site, many companies like Control V are willing to help (for a fee, of course). On this site you can view many of the Web sites that Control V has developed for their clients, including some for businesses with a "small budget."

Designing a Business Web Site (*www.webmarketingtoday.com/webmarket/design.htm*)

Published by Wilson Internet, this site contains a series of informative articles on business Web site design, such as "Navigation Systems for Business Websites" and "7 Debilitating Diseases of Business Websites (and their cures)."

The Design & Publishing Center (*www.graphic-design.com*)

The Design & Publishing Center provides a lot of useful information for Web site designers, including "design, typography, graphics, illustration, writing, printing, publishing, advertising, signs, displays and information for graphic communicators of all kinds!"

Media Metrix (*www.mediametrix.com*)

According to their home page, Media Metrix is "the pioneer and leader in the field of Internet and digital media measurement services." From their home page you can access listings of the most popular Web sites on the Internet.

Web Monkey: A How-to Guide for Web Developers
(*www.hotwired.com/webmonkey*)

Produced by Wired Digital, the Web Monkey site has extensive information for Web site designers that is categorized as follows: e-business, design, HTML, JavaScript, databases, graphics and fonts, multimedia, browsers, Java, and stylesheets.

Summary

The most important thing you should have learned in this chapter is "clean is beautiful" when it comes to Web site design. Not only does eliminating a lot of clutter from your site make it easier for visitors to read, but it also significantly speeds up the speed at which your pages can be downloaded into a browser. One of the best places to get design ideas is to visit other popular sites on the Web, like Yahoo! and Amazon.com.

In addition to giving your Web pages eye-pleasing appeal with colors, pictures, and text, there are also some important design features you can incorporate to make it user-friendly. Start with the menu structure and make it easy for users to get around from page to page. Also include a way for users to get back quickly to your home page from anywhere within your Web site.

For more information on this topic, visit our Web site at www.businesstown.com

Developing Intriguing Content to Keep Users Returning

Topics covered in this chapter

- Categorizing Web sites by their content
- Making your Web site content informative
- Adding key content pages to your Web site
- Getting content from outside sources

Our network provides users with trusted healthcare content, services and tools to empower them to better manage their health.

DR. C. EVERETT KOOP, *WWW.DRKOOP.COM*

The merger between America Online (AOL) and Time Warner adds a lot of credence to the statement "Content is King" on the Internet. The folks at AOL know that in order to continue their network expansion, they must provide content that is useful and interesting for their customers. Through its acquisition, AOL gained access to all of Time Warner's content, including print (*Time* and *People* magazines), film (Warner Brothers and New Line Cinema), music (Warner Music), and television (CNN and HBO). For your Web site, you will also need to provide content that is useful and interesting for your visitors if you want them to keep returning.

> Content consists of the text, sound, and pictures that visitors read, hear, and see on your Web site.

Content consists of the text, sound, and pictures that visitors read, hear, and see on your Web site. Content gives Web publishers the ability to differentiate their Web sites from the competition, and provides visitors with valuable information that keeps them returning over and over. The expression "Content is King" still holds true today for the most popular Web sites on the Internet.

If you followed the design principles outlined in the previous chapter and start a marketing campaign as described in the next section, you will get some visitors to your Web site. Unfortunately, just getting visitors has little to do with the success of your Web site. In order for your site to be successful, it must provide certain benefits for your visitors that will keep them returning in the future. One of these benefits will be timely and informative content.

Think of your Web site as a restaurant. Once you are open for business, your restaurant will only be successful if your patrons enjoy their first meal, tell their friends about it, and occasionally return for another meal. Likewise, once you publish your Web site, it will only be successful if your visitors enjoy its content, tell other surfers about it, and keep returning for more of the same.

Although content includes, text, sound, and pictures, the written word is still the predominant form of successful communication on the Web. Surfers read and click, and click and read, as they move from page to page in your Web site. Therefore, it is important that you follow certain design principles as you develop content for your Web site. The other key factor is developing content that will be of interest to your target audience and lead to a personal relationship that you will find rewarding over time.

Before you start banging away on a word processor to create content for your Web site, look at the different types of content provided on the Web today. Just like in the offline world, Web content is presented in many forms. There are general interest Web sites that provide a broad array of content, and very specific sites that focus on specific subject areas.

> It is important that you follow certain design principles as you develop content for your Web site.

Categorizing Web Sites by Their Content

As described previously, some of the most popular sites on the Internet are portals, such as Yahoo! and Excite. These portals provide significant amounts of general interest content that appeals to a large audience, including:

- Breaking news stories
- Chat rooms
- Classifieds
- Entertainment and games
- Movie reviews
- Sports coverage
- Stock quotes
- Travel services
- Weather updates

Additionally, large Web portals have directories and search engines that will link you to thousands of other Web sites covering almost every subject imaginable.

There are also a wide variety of Web sites that cover specific topics in depth, like sports, medicine, and employment. Unlike the large Web portals that appeal to a broad audience, the specialized

> Your content should be designed to appeal to your target audience.

sites are targeted to narrower segments of Web users. This is analogous to the difference between newspapers and newsletters. Newspapers serve a large diverse audience, while newsletters focus on a particular niche.

Specialized Content Web Sites

CONTENT PROVIDER	WEB ADDRESS	TYPE OF CONTENT
Autobytel.com	*www.autobytel.com*	New and used cars
CareerBuilder	*www.careerbuilder.com*	Employers and job seekers
China.com	*www.china.com*	Chinese language audiences
Dr. Koop	*www.drkoop.com*	Health care network
EarthWeb	*www.earthweb.com*	Information technology industry
Internet.com	*www.internet.com*	Internet industry
OneSource	*www.onesource.com*	Business and financial information
Salon.com	*www.salon.com*	Demographic targeting
SportsLine.com	*www.sportsline.com*	Sports media
Talk City	*www.talkcity.com*	Online communities

As you can see, specialized Web sites provide a more narrow focus for their content than their portal counterparts. This is similar to the specialization in the magazine industry. For instance, there are general interest magazines, like *Time*; business-oriented magazines, like *Business Week*; and sports magazines, like *Sports Illustrated*. Each of these publications has found its own target audience.

As you begin to develop content for your Web site, you must have your target audience in mind. Although some of your visitors may watch the stock market, or be interested in the latest medical developments, you must decide if this type of content is appropriate for your Web site. Normally, you will provide expertise in one subject area and steer clear of most other subject areas. Think of it as a doctor—patient relationship, where you are the doctor providing professional advice to your patients (visitors to your Web site).

Generally, you should identify your target audience and then develop your content. Identify your target audience according to key

> Identify your target audience and then develop your content.

demographics and then determine what subjects will be of most interest. For instance, if your Web site is meant to appeal to children, you should investigate what subjects are most appealing to those children. Your demographics in this instance might be children between the ages of 8 and 12 who watch television on Saturday morning. From these demographics you can begin to develop content for your online audience, for instance, writing about their favorite characters, speculating on upcoming episodes, and identifying stores that sell related paraphernalia.

In addition to taking the target audience into account, your content will also be determined by the type of site that you are going to publish. If you expect your visitors to pay for your content, it must be timely and unavailable elsewhere for free. For instance, if you were going to publish a stock picking site, you would have to provide original commentary about the underlying companies that will benefit your subscribers.

On the other hand, if you were creating an e-tailing, or e-commerce, site, where you expected your visitors to buy products, you would want to include content about individual products. Content in this case might include a text description, a product review from a respected publication, a picture, and maybe even some appropriate sound or video.

> **Content Is King**
>
> On the Internet content is king! When creating your web pages keep in mind what attracts you to a web site. Sites that offer free or useful information will more than likely be the sites you visit again and again. The most popular web sites offer free and or useful information. Your web site should be rich in content and allow for updates.
>
> The TriMatrix Group,
> *www.trimatrix.com/tips.html*

Making Your Web Site Content Informative

As you become familiar with the different types of Web sites and their business models, you will often hear the expression "content is king."

If you begin to think of content as a feature, or benefit, of your Web site, you can use it to separate yourself from the competition. For instance, assume that you want to sell baby toys online. One way you can differentiate your site is to provide informative articles for parents on the different safety aspects of certain toys. You might also start an e-mailing list to notify parents of any product recalls from manufacturers, or consumer safety warnings issued by the government.

> As you become familiar with the different types of Web sites and their business models, you will often hear the expression "content is king."

The following quote, taken from The TriMatrix Group's Web site, indicates that you should "offer free and or useful information" as part of your content strategy. Even if you are planning to start a "pay per subscription" Web site, you can still offer free and useful information for your visitors in the form of "teasers." Instead of trying to sell all of your content, provide just enough to "tease," or get your visitors interested in your site, and then ask them to pay for the rest of your valuable information.

The other key aspect of content is that it must be dynamic. It must be constantly updated to keep your visitors returning "again and again." As developments take place in your industry or marketplace, you must update your content to keep your visitors well informed. If your first-time visitors find your content original and helpful, there is a good possibility that they will return again in the future for more information. If your content doesn't change between their first and second visits, they may get the "been there done that" syndrome and look elsewhere for better information.

> Your content must be dynamic, or constantly updated, to keep visitors returning.

Appealing to Your Target Audience

As we've discussed, you can differentiate your Web site from your competition by writing content specifically for your target audience. For example, take two online computer retailers that are trying to sell the same computer, at the same price, to different target audiences. The first online retailer is trying to reach the small business market, while the second is targeting the information services industry.

> As we've discussed, you can differentiate your Web site from your competition by writing content specifically for your target audience.

The small business online computer retailer could create content that would be beneficial to small businesses, such as reviews of popular accounting software or how to create promotional brochures with a color printer. This online retailer could take it a step further and provide general small business information, including business planning advice, effective marketing methods, starting an employee savings plan, and hiring practices for small business.

The information services online retailer, on the other hand, would take a completely different approach in creating content for its target audience. The content on this site might be more technical in nature and contain articles such as creating a local area network, or buying a server to manage a computer network. Additionally, this retailer could provide an online dictionary of computer related terms, and maybe links to other technical Web sites.

By differentiating their content to appeal to separate target audiences, both of these online businesses increase their chances of selling computers. They build a personal relationship with their prospective customers by providing relevant information that is useful and free.

> Use your content to build a relationship with your customers.

Writing Content That is Easy to Read

In addition to identifying content that is relevant for your target audience, it must also be written in a user-friendly format. Writing content for your Web site is different from writing content for a sales brochure or other types of offline media. The main difference is that your Web site provides an element of *interactivity* that is not available through most traditional offline media.

Since Internet users have a virtually limitless choice of content on the Web, you need to draw them into your Web site by making your content interactive. You must take advantage of the "scan and click" mindset that resides in most surfers. Give your visitors an opportunity to see pictures, click on links, and ask questions on your Web site. This way you will enhance the personal relationship that you are trying to develop with your prospects.

> Use a conversational style in your writing.

One way to make your content more appealing is to use a conversational style in your writing. Write in the first person, like you are talking to your visitors as a friend in a conversation. For instance, friends don't say, "This Web site is for people needing vacation information." Instead, they might say, "Welcome to my Web site. Here you will find plenty of information for planning your next vacation."

Making Your Content Easy to Read

TIPS FOR WEB SITE CONTENT	DESCRIPTION
Make it clear and concise.	Make whatever you are trying to say, or describe, be very clear and concise. Don't use a lot of extra words when you only need one or two. For instance, don't write "the great big dog bit me," when "the giant dog bit me" will do just as well.
Use a conversational style.	Write like you would speak to a friend. Use everyday words and phrases to tell your story.
Speak a language your audience understands.	Use words that are familiar to your target audience. This will help to build your relationship with them. Don't use a lot of technical terms if your audience won't understand them.
Write short sentences and short paragraphs.	Short sentences will give your message impact. Short paragraphs will keep your readers from feeling overwhelmed. Your paragraphs should be no longer than two or three sentences in length. There is no bigger turnoff than running into a screen filled entirely with words.
Check for spelling and grammatical errors.	There's no excuse for poor spelling. If your Web development software doesn't have a spell checker, cut and paste the text into your word processor and check the spelling.
Get someone to proofread your content.	Before you publish your site, get a few people to read your content for clarity, spelling, and grammatical errors.

Adding Key Content Pages to Your Web Site

Besides key content pages, such as a Contact Information page, an About page, and a Frequently Asked Questions (FAQ) page, many Web sites include other featured content to make them more interactive (a message board) and more believable (a testimonials page).

Although you don't need to include all of the following pages in your Web site, most will help to make your site more user friendly.

Adding a Contact Information Page

The reality of the Web is that once some people find your Web site, the first thing they want to do is pick up the phone and call you. They might want additional information, or it might make them feel more comfortable knowing there is a "real" business behind the Web site. Therefore, it is strongly recommended that you offer your visitors as many ways as possible to contact you. This can be through a phone number, fax number, street address, or e-mail address.

To create a contact information page, simply add a blank page to your Web site and then fill it in with all of your contact information. At the top of the page, encourage people to call or e-mail your business by simply including a sentence or two shown in "contact information."

If you want to add a degree of warmth to this page, you can include names and photographs of key contacts in your company. Also, don't forget to place links, such as "Contact us", on your home page for this contact information page. You should include at least one link near the top of your home page, and if your home page is very long, one at the bottom. Finally, it is becoming increasingly popular for many Web sites, especially e-tailers, to give an 800-phone number at the top of their home page.

> Offer your visitors as many ways as possible to contact you.

Telling Visitors about Your Web Site

Another common page that many sites incorporate in their Web is an About page. On your About page, you can describe for your visitors exactly what your online business does; you can include the description from your business plan; tell visitors more about your products and services; and include any other relevant information about your business that visitors might find useful.

Like the FAQ page described earlier, an About page is included in a variety of popular Web sites. Therefore, many Web surfers will know what to expect if they see an "About" link on your home page. Additionally, some search engines look specifically for this page through their indexing process to create a description for your Web site.

Your About page should not be the only place where you provide a description of your Web site. It should add more detail to the brief business description on your home page and the description placed between your HTML META tags (see Chapter 13 for more information).

> Create an About page to tell visitors exactly what your online business does.

Sample About Page—from OBGYN.net (*www.obgyn.net/about.htm*)

OBGYN.net has been designed for the specific needs of Professionals interested in Obstetrics and Gynecology, the medical industry, and women everywhere. Our goal is to continuously improve services to help in the delivery of Women's Healthcare.

- "Introducing OBGYN.net"
- "OBGYN.net Contact Information"
- "How You Can Get Involved in OBGYN.net"
- "Our Advisory Board"
- "Our International Council"
- "OBGYN.net Correspondents"
- "Our U.S. State Representatives"
- "Advisory Board—Women and Patients"
- "Women's Health Advisors"
- "Endometriosis Editorial Advisors"

If you would like to find other examples of About pages, simply type "About page" in the Search Engine of any of the major portals, such as AltaVista.com (*www.altavista.com*) or Excite (*www.excite.com*).

Answering Frequently Asked Questions (FAQs)

Once your Web site is open for business and you begin to get a steady stream of visitors, you will probably receive a few questions that are asked over and over again. Depending on your business model, these might concern warranties, registration profiles, returning merchandise, or directions to your offline business. These Frequently Asked Questions (FAQs), and their associated answers, should be placed on a separate page in your Web site.

Frequently Asked Questions (FAQs), and their associated answers, should be placed on a separate page in your Web site.

Placing a FAQ page within your Web site is important for two reasons. First, it will save you time from having to answer the same question repeatedly from every new visitor that comes to your site. Second, it will save your visitors time because they won't need to contact you to get an answer to these questions.

Most popular Web sites have at least one FAQ page that can be accessed from its home page through a FAQ link. Larger sites might have multiple FAQ pages relating to specific areas of the Web site. For instance, there may be a FAQ page for ordering, one for registration, and another for technical product information.

Ideally, your goal should be to have a Web site that is "so user friendly" and "easy to use" that your visitors won't have any questions. Therefore, if possible, you should try to modify your Web site design to eliminate any constantly occurring questions. For instance, if your visitors are having difficulty locating your order form, place a link at the top of your page that says "Click here to order."

> Most popular Web sites have at least one FAQ page that can be accessed from its home page through a FAQ link.

Sample FAQs—
from RealNetworks Software (*www.real.com*)

Have questions before you buy RealNetworks software?
Check below for the most commonly asked pre-purchase questions for RealNetworks Servers, Tools, and Players.

- "Where will I find the Streaming Media Buyer's Guide?"
- "Do I get different software if I pay for the Server as opposed to getting the free server?"
- "If I buy a RealServer, do I get a discount on any other products?"
- "If I buy a RealServer, how many clients will that handle simultaneously?"
- "How do I set up an Internet radio or TV station?"
- "Can I broadcast live content with this product? How do I accomplish this?"

Using Testimonials for Content

One traditional offline method you can use online is to share testimonials with your prospects. You can use testimonials to tell new prospects what others enjoy about your site, and what they like about your products and services.

Guidelines for getting and publishing testimonials on your Web site:

- Don't make up testimonials.
- Ask your existing customers for a testimonial through e-mail, warranty cards, or on a completed customer satisfaction survey.
- Make sure you ask if you can use the testimonial before putting it on your Web site. Find out if you can include their name and company name (when applicable).
- Keep testimonials short, one or two sentences. This means you may to have edit some testimonials.
- Publish as many testimonials as you can.
- Use testimonials that rave about specific products and services or content on your Web site.
- Don't publish any negative testimonials.

Starting a Bulletin or Message Board

You can greatly increase the interactivity of your Web site by incorporating a bulletin or message board. These boards allow users to post questions or comments that can either be answered by you, or by other users. Additionally, a successful message board will keep visitors returning to your site over and over again for the latest news and commentary on a particular topic.

One very successful application of message boards has been in the area of stock investments. For instance, investors come together daily to discuss the latest developments for a particular stock on the Yahoo! message boards. For some of the larger and more heavily traded stocks, messages are posted almost every minute by interested investors.

> You can use testimonials to tell new prospects what others enjoy about your site.

SAMPLE MESSAGE BOARDS	WEB ADDRESS
CyberFiber Newsgroups	*www.cyberfiber.com/index.html*
Deja.com	*www.deja.com*
Excite Message Boards	*boards.excite.com/boards*
Yahoo! Message Boards	*messages.yahoo.com/index.html*

Adding a message board to your Web site is easier than it might first appear. For instance, Microsoft FrontPage includes a message board application that you can add to your Web site (called the Discussion Web Wizard). There are also free message board services available on the Web that allow you to link to your own message board, such as *Inside the Web* (*www.InsideTheWeb.com*).

> Add a message board to your Web site to increase its *interactivity* for visitors.

Getting Content from Outside Sources

In order to add content to your Web site, you basically have three choices: do it yourself, link to other sites, or buy it from an outside agency. Sometimes a combination of all three provides the best results. Before making your final decision, you should be aware that creating content and keeping it up to date is time consuming. To some extent, it is just like publishing a newspaper or magazine that requires an editorial staff, photographers, and layout designers.

Creating Your Own Content

In the worst, or most time-consuming, case you might decide to create all of your own content. For instance, if you were developing a Web site to sell classical music, you might decide to write musical reviews about the composer, take pictures of the CD jackets, and even record some of your own music for embellishment. A huge job, certainly!

A better approach in this example might be to get the pictures of the CD jackets from the manufacturer and post them on your site,

> In order to add content to your Web site, you basically have three choices: do it yourself, link to other sites, or buy it from an outside agency.

see if you can also get free clips of music from the manufacturer or composer, and then create your own written reviews of the music itself. This would be a much less time-consuming approach for creating your content.

Linking to Other Sites for Content

Another way to add content to your site is to create links and brief descriptions to other sites that contain more information. For instance, using the previous classical music example, you might find a larger music retailing site (like Amazon.com) and create links from your site to specific pages within that site. On your site, you might write the review for a particular piece of classical music and then include a link to that selection on Amazon.com.

If you do decide to create links to other Web sites, be cautious about losing visitors and find out the other site's policy about linking. Every time you place a link on your site to another Web site, you face the risk of losing your visitor (forever) to the other site. Therefore, before you give your visitors an opportunity to go elsewhere, make sure you have given them everything of value on your site that you possibly can. Make sure they have to read your review and understand the benefits of your site before they can leave. This way they may return to your site in the future.

The other thing to be aware of when linking to another Web site, is whether it allows deep links. Most sites will allow you to link to their home page but often state that you cannot link to lower levels within their site, such as product reviews, specific articles, or commentary on a particular subject. This is especially true if you give the appearance that their content is actually yours by using Web frames or other technologies.

Buying Content from an Outside Agency

The final option for adding content to your Web site is to hire an outside agency or contractor. Today, you can hire agencies that

> If you do decide to create links to other Web sites, be cautious about losing visitors and find out the other site's policy about linking.

will create and manage your entire site, including the creation of all of your content. At the other end of the spectrum, you can hire someone to look at your site, much like an editor, and give you feedback about improving your content.

In between are companies and individuals who sell content about a particular subject area. For instance, you can purchase a stock quoting or news reporting service and place it on your site. In this instance, you pay for a feed from an outside agency, such as Reuters, and update your Web site as it comes across the newswire. However, because anybody can purchase this information, you have to decide why your visitors would benefit from getting it on your Web site, as opposed to getting it from one of your competitors.

Another way to buy content is to ask writers and columnists if they'd be interested in developing content for your site. If your site focuses on a narrow geographic area, or particular subject matter, look for experts in the field. Local newspapers or specialty magazines are an excellent starting place to locate these writers. Alternatively, if you have a very popular site, some writers might be willing to work for free, provided they believe the exposure will lead to bigger opportunities in the future.

> Approach experts in your field and ask them to develop content for your Web site.

COMPANIES THAT PRODUCE CONTENT	WEB ADDRESS
Content Exchange	www.content-exchange.com
Contentious	www.contentious.com
iSyndicate Express	www.isyndicate.com
JB McKee Creative!	www.jbmckee.com
The TriMatrix Group	www.trimatrix.com
TTL Communications	www.ttlweb.com
WordsWork	www.wordswork.com

> Before you sign a contract with an outside agency, make sure that you see examples of their work.

Before you sign a contract with an outside agency, make sure that you see examples of their work. Additionally, ask for references from existing and previous clients.

Creating Content for the OfficeLinks.com Web Site

Q: How would you describe your content?

A: The OfficeLinks.com content was developed to help small business owners find important and useful information on the Web. It includes articles, links, and advertisements to help these entrepreneurs market and manage their businesses.

Q: Is your content different than other small business sites?

A: Yes. Some of the big sites, like the Small Business Administration (*www.sba.gov*) and Edgar Lowe Foundation (*www.lowe.org*), are completely self contained. By that I mean they do not provide links to other sites. OfficeLinks.com, on the other hand, is more like a portal with links to many small business sites, including these two.

Q: Do you think the portal model for content is better?

A: Not necessarily, but I don't have the resources that the Federal government has to create a Web site for small businesses. Honestly, I would like to have a staff of 10 writers who could develop original content from scratch.

Q: Are there other differences between OfficeLinks.com and these sites?

A: Yes. The other main difference is that OfficeLinks.com is a dot-com, or commercial, site. I have joined many affiliate programs that sell products for small businesses. I get a percentage of the sales for anyone who buys something from these other sites after they visit mine.

Q: Do you offer any audio or video on your site?

A: No. There would be no real benefit for my visitors at this point if I provided sound or video. The only thing I could envision would be some book recordings, or seminars, that covered small business topics. However, those are not in my immediate plans.

Q: What is the most difficult thing about creating content for your site?

A: It's very time consuming. Although it's relatively easy to get a shell, or layout, on the Web, filling in the blank pages with useful information is time consuming.

Q: Do you have any advice for other Web site owners about creating content?

A: Yes. Your business plan should adequately address all of your content sources. Meaning: Are you going to hire someone or pay someone to create your content?

Q: Do you agree with the statement "content is king!"

A: Absolutely. There is no better way for a business to differentiate itself on the Web that through useful and timely content. The more valuable your visitors think your content is, the more often they will return for more information. Just ask Yahoo! how valuable content is!

Online Content Resources

Contentious (*www.contentious.com*)

Contentious describes itself as "the Web-zine for writers, editors and others who create content for online media."

Content Exchange (*www.content-exchange.com*)

If you are considering hiring someone to develop your content, try Content Exchange. It lets online writers, editors, and other content creators advertise their services.

Grantastic Designs (*www.grantasticdesigns.com/content.html*)

According to their "tips for website content" page, Grantastic Designs "provides website design, graphic design, and web copy writing tips to truly illustrate the concept 'Content is King.' Grantastic offers several tips for website design and illustrates how important content is by asking you three questions: 'Why should I visit your website (without spending any money)? Why should I return to your website? and What separates you from your competition?'"

The Webmaster's Toolbox (*www.marionia.com/toolbox/design.htm*)

This site includes "100's of Web design tips...so you can design sites like the pros!" You can find tips by topic, including: "Basic Site Design and Layout Tips," "Picking the Right Font," "Tips on Site Content," and "Don't Lose Your Credibility."

Wordbiz.Com (*www.wordbiz.com*)

According to their home page, "Wordbiz.Com provides marketing and communications solutions to high-tech startups and established Internet companies. We specialize in writing killer Web copy; in e-mail marketing; and in branding through a company's Web site." Make sure to check out their links to resources for online media.

Summary

In this chapter you learned that "content is king" on the Internet. Timely and informative content gives you an excellent way to differentiate your Web site from the millions of others on the Internet and will keep your visitors returning again and again. It's important that the content you develop for your site is appropriate and interesting for your target audience. Don't create a "me, too" site that provides a lot of general information that users can find elsewhere.

In addition to the words and pictures you use to deliver your message, there are many key content pages that you should include in your Web site. For instance, make sure you provide a contact information page that gives your business street address, phone number, and e-mail address; another important page is the "About" page that describes your online business.

For more information on this topic, visit our Web site at www.businesstown.com

PART IV

Marketing Your Online Business with New and Traditional Advertising Strategies

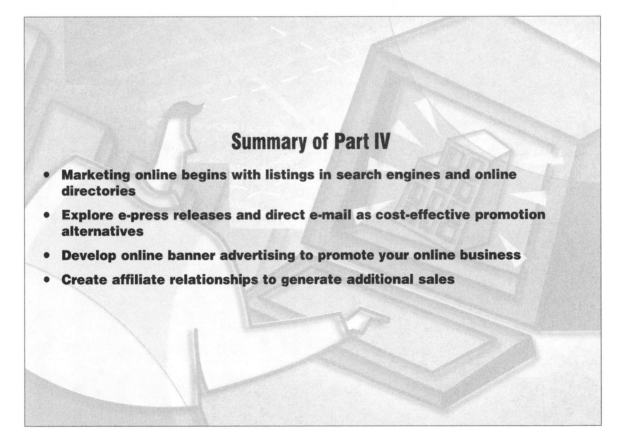

Summary of Part IV

- Marketing online begins with listings in search engines and online directories
- Explore e-press releases and direct e-mail as cost-effective promotion alternatives
- Develop online banner advertising to promote your online business
- Create affiliate relationships to generate additional sales

Getting Listed with Portals, Search Engines, and Directories

Topics covered in this chapter

- Looking at the different portals and their search engines
- Studying the portals and search engines
- Getting listed at the top of search engine results
- Announcing your online business on the Internet

Every little bit counts!
MINDSPRING MARKET DEVELOPMENT MANAGER,
WWW.MINDSPRING.COM

As the new owner of a Web-based business, your first concern will be to attract visitors to your Web site. Most online businesses begin their marketing process by getting listed in search engines and directories, such as Yahoo!, Excite, and AltaVista. Although these search engines will drive traffic to your Web site, getting your site listed with them is only the first step in the whole marketing process. Before you begin, make sure that your Web site is very close to being final and that you have written some good descriptions for your online business. Backtracking from this point can be very time consuming.

Similar to registering your domain name ("www.yourbiz.com"), getting listed with the portals and directories can be a completely automated process. You simply type, or cut and paste, the keywords and description for your online business in the appropriate boxes, and the registration service will take care of the rest. In addition to getting your Web site listed across the Internet, many of the registration services will also analyze your site for loading speed, browser compatibility, and its ability to distinguish itself from the "crowd."

Getting listed with portals, search engines, and directories is the beginning of your promotional campaign. By having your site properly indexed in these search engines, you stand a good chance of getting some visitors to your site. However, as you can imagine, the competition to be listed in the top spots is fierce, and the search engines are struggling to keep up with the thousands of new sites that are coming online almost daily.

Moreover, after you submit your freshly minted site to the various portals, there will be a time lag before your site is indexed. As previously mentioned, this lag occurs because your site must be reviewed by human eyes or visited by a software spider to see that it actually exists. With some search engines, this process can take as long as eight weeks.

> Getting listed with the portals and directories can be a completely automated process.

Looking at the Different Portals and Their Search Engines

Over the past few years, what essentially started out as search engines have now become Internet portals. Originally, Yahoo! was designed as a directory to help users search the Internet for information. Now, in addition to including a "Search box" prominently on its home page, Yahoo! provides numerous links and services for its user population, including chat rooms, stock quotes, retailing locations, and travel services, to name a few. It has become a portal, or gateway, for Internet users.

Webopedia (*www.webopedia.com*) defines a Web portal as "a Web site or service that offers a broad array of resources and services, such as e-mail, forums, search engines, and on-line shopping malls. The first Web portals were online services, such as AOL, that provided access to the Web, but by now most of the traditional search engines have transformed themselves into Web portals to attract and keep a larger audience."

Today, although there is a clear distinction between portals and search engines, you will often hear the terms used interchangeably. However, you should be aware that some portals, for example HotBot and GoTo.com, use the same search engine technology created by Inktomi. Therefore, when you search for the keyword "OfficeLinks" in these two portals, their search engines return the same or a similar listing of results.

Key Differences Between Search Engines

Just as most portals are different, so are most search engines. For instance, when you enter search keywords like "online business planning" in Yahoo!, you will notice that the search result is completely different from when you enter the same keywords in Excite. These differences occur because the search engines use different methods to assemble, index, and rank their databases.

Webopedia says a search engine is "a program that searches documents for specified keywords and returns a list of the documents

> Over the past few years, what essentially started out as search engines have now become Internet portals.

Getting a Site Listed on Yahoo!

The Yahoo! directory is organized by subject. Most sites in it are suggested to us by users. Sites are placed in categories by *Yahoo! Surfers* who visit and evaluate your suggestions and decide where they best belong. We do this to ensure that Yahoo! is organized in the best possible way, making the directory easy to use, intuitive, helpful, and fair to everyone.

Yahoo!
(*www.docs.yahoo.com/info/suggest/*)

where the keywords were found." Think of a search engine as a large spreadsheet, with Web addresses going down the left hand side and keywords at the top, as follows:

WEB ADDRESS	CHAIR	COMPUTER	DESK	PAPER	PENCIL
www.bizsite.com	Yes	Yes	Yes	Yes	Yes
www.toysite.com	No	No	No	Yes	Yes
www.booksite.com	No	No	No	No	No
www.computersite.com	No	Yes	No	Yes	No
www.foodsite.com	No	No	No	No	No

> Search engines create their databases using spiders, eyeballs, or a combination of the two.

If you were to type in the keyword "computer" for this particular search engine, the results would show that *www.bizsite.com* and *www.computersite.com* have Web pages that contain the word computer. Additionally, in this hypothetical example, the *www.computersite.com* listing would be shown first in the search result because the word computer is used twice: once on its Web page and once in its URL.

Search engines create their databases using spiders, eyeballs, or a combination of the two. A spider is a computer program that automatically crawls across the Web, from link to link, and sends information back to the search engine for indexing and ranking. One of the first search engines to use this technology is appropriately called Webcrawler. Other popular search engines that use this technology include AltaVista, Excite, and HotBot.

At the other extreme are search engines that use eyeballs (human, that is) to create their databases and indexes. Real live people review and categorize Web sites according to specific guidelines.

In reality, most search engine databases are created with some combination of spiders and eyeballs. For example, most search engines have spiders that traverse the Web looking for new and updated Web pages. Where appropriate, these pages may be reviewed by a set of eyeballs before they are entered into the database.

Studying the Portals and Search Engines

There is no better way to learn about the different search engines and their results than to actually start testing them with a few simple queries. Put yourself in your prospects' place and think about how they are going to find your Web site. What will they be looking for? What keywords or phrases are they going to use in their search? What benefits does your site offer them?

The following table lists the most popular portals and search engines on the Web, as of September 1, 1999. Select a few keywords that would be appropriate for your type of online business and test them on a cross-section of these search engines.

> Test your important keywords on the popular search engines and study the results.

PORTAL NAME	WEB ADDRESS	100HOT SITES RANKING
About.com	www.about.com	#78
AltaVista	www.altavista.com	#6
America Online (AOL)	www.aol.com	#3a
Ask Jeeves	www.askjeeves.com	#95
Excite	www.excite.com	#8a
HotBot	www.hotbot.com	N/A
InfoSpace.com	www.infospace.com	#40
GO (InfoSeek)	www.go.com	#5
GoTo.com	www.goto.com	#80
LookSmart	www.looksmart.com	#15
Lycos	www.lycos.com	#4
Magellan	www.magellan.excite.com	#8b
MSN (Microsoft Network)	www.msn.com	#2
Netscape	www.netcenter.com	#3b
CNET.com	www.cnet.com	#16
Snap.com	www.snap.com	#62
WebCrawler	www.webcrawler.com	#8c
Yahoo!	www.yahoo.com	#1

Source: 9/1/99 Rankings on *www.100hot.com*

Record the top 10 results from each search and see how they compare. Were some sites ranked higher on the spider search engines such as AltaVista and America Online? Did others do better on the eyeball engines such as Yahoo! or About.com? Were some of your query results exactly the same between search engines? Answering this list of questions will become important as you begin to select the appropriate title, keywords, and description for your Web site.

Getting Listed at the Top of Search Engine Results

Every Web site owner would like to have his or her site listed at the top of search engine results (or at least on the first page!). For instance, if you created an e-commerce site that specialized in selling antique clocks, you would want your site to appear on the first page of the search results whenever someone used the keywords "antique clocks." Unfortunately, since most search engines use different algorithms to index and rank the Web pages in their databases, you cannot get your Web site to appear at the beginning of *all* search engine queries.

Despite this, once you understand how search engines (especially spiders) use the information contained on Web sites to index and rank them in their database, you will have a better chance of improving the ranking for your Web site. Since spider engines have very little human intervention, they decide how to list and rank your site using about seven key pieces of information: Web page title, META keyword tag, META description tag, text on your site, keyword density, and number of other sites that link to yours. Before you can create all of these key attributes for your Web site, you should understand a little about Hypertext Markup Language (HTML).

Using HTML for Your Web Site Titles, Keywords, and Description

Software companies such as Microsoft and Macromedia have done a great job in creating software packages that allow Web

> Most search engines use different algorithms to index and rank the Web pages in their databases.

developers to design Web sites without knowing much about Hypertext Markup Language (HTML). However, in a few instances, you will need to at least be able to identify a few important HTML components and understand their importance to search engines.

According to Webopedia *(www.webopedia.com)*, HTML "is the authoring language used to create documents on the World Wide Web." This language uses a special set of "tags" to create Web pages that can be read by Web browsers such as Microsoft Internet Explorer and Netscape Navigator. Some of the HTML tags that you should be familiar with, include:

- <title>*your Web page title goes here*</title>
- <meta name="Description" content="*your Web site description goes here*">
- <meta name="keywords" content="*your Web site keywords are inserted here*">

To learn more about HTML and its various tags, try the HTML Dictionary *(www.htmldictionary.com)* for a complete description. Additionally, if you want to see some of these tags, open up a Web page, click your right mouse button, and select *View Source* from the menu. These HTML tags will appear at the top of your screen between the <HEAD> </HEAD>, or header tags, which define items that apply to the entire Web page.

Creating Web Page Titles

Every page of your Web site should contain a title. This title should be included on your Web page and between the HTML <TITLE> </TITLE> tags. Although these titles can be different, the title appearing on your Web page is usually shown at the top of the page in a different font and color than the rest of the document—much the same way a headline appears at the top of a newspaper. You should avoid creating this title with graphics software, since search engines can only recognize text.

In addition to having a title appear on your Web page, you should also ensure that a title appears between the HTML title tags.

> Every page of your Web site should contain a title.

These HTML titles are important for a few reasons: they will appear in the title bar of a Web browser, like Microsoft Internet Explorer or Netscape Navigator; they are often the underlined, or linked, words in search engine results; and they can be used by keyword density algorithms to determine your search engine rankings.

The HTML code for your title appears between the <HEAD> </HEAD> tags of the document, and would look something like <TITLE>*your title text*</TITLE>. For instance, the Realtor.com home page might have the following title:

<TITLE>REALTOR.COM: Real Estate–Homes for Sale</TITLE>

If you are using a Web site development tool such as Microsoft FrontPage, these HTML codes are created automatically. You can view the title tags in FrontPage by simply clicking on the HTML tab at the bottom of your screen. You can also see these tags for existing Web pages by going to the *View* menu in your Web browser, and selecting *Source*.

The following table shows the Web page titles for some popular destinations on the Web. To locate these titles, enter the domain name in your browser, and then click on *View Source* once the Web site loads. You will find these between the <TITLE> </TITLE> tags at the top of your screen.

DOMAIN NAME	WEB PAGE TITLE	PAGE
www.realtor.com	Realtor.com: Real Estate–Homes for Sale	Home
www.amazon.com	Amazon.com–Earth's Biggest Selection	Welcome
www.amazon.com	Amazon.com: Toys	Toys & Games
www.etrade.com	E*Trade	Home
www.beyond.com	Beyond.com–A Better Place to Buy Software	Home

You have the capability of changing these titles on every page of your Web site. For instance, Amazon.com uses "Amazon.com–Earth's Biggest Selection" for its Welcome page, and "Amazon.com: Toys" for its Toys & Games page.

Writing a Description for Your Web Site

Every Web page should have its own description in addition to its own title. This description should be included on your Web page and between the HTML META tags. Also, like titles, your Web page description can be different from the one that appears between the HTML META tags. Since your Web page description will be used by prospects to figure out what they are looking at, it should be short and to the point. A couple of clear sentences that describe your online business should suffice. Also, some search engines use the written description on your visible page for indexing and listing your site.

In addition to having a description appear on your Web page, you should also ensure that a description appears between the HTML META tags. However, the description that you use between these tags will not be seen by visitors to your site, but rather used by some search engines as a description for your site. Therefore, this description can be different and longer than the one that appears visibly on your Web site.

The HTML code for your description appears between the META tags of the document, and looks like <meta name="Description" content="*your Web site description goes here*">.

Although the OfficeLinks.com home page has a visible description that is very similar to its META description, there are a couple of differences. The main one is that the domain name is included in the META description but excluded from the description that appears on the visible page. This was done to increase the OfficeLinks keyword density and to make it easier to find in different search engines. Many of the other OfficeLinks.com Web pages have META descriptions that are completely different from those appearing on the visible page.

It's important to know that some search engines place more importance on words that appear toward the top of your page than those that appear further down. Therefore, you should put your most important information at the beginning of both your Web page and META descriptions. Additionally, the description should contain your top three or four keywords, since some search engines use word repetition (keyword density) in their Web site ranking algorithms.

Sample META Description Tag— for OfficeLinks.com Home Page

<meta name="Description" content="Welcome to OfficeLinks. This is your source for the best business products, services and advice available on the Web. No matter whether you are looking for office supplies; the latest in computer hardware and software; innovative telephone calling plans; a Web hosting service; or information to help you create and manage your business; OfficeLinks can help!— http://www.officelinks.com">

Some search engines place more importance on words that appear toward the top of your page.

Developing Your List of Keywords

Keywords are another important aspect of your Web pages, since many search engines will use keywords to rank your Web site in their listings. Keywords should be used in your title, description, and between the HTML META tags. Keywords convey what your business does and the benefits of your products and services. They also can determine how your site will be found by prospects.

Start by making a list of about fifty keywords, and then rank them in order of importance. Make sure to clearly identify your top five keywords, since you will want to include these in your title and description. For instance, if you were starting an online travel agency, your top five keywords might be travel, agency, airfares, hotels, and vacation. After you have made your list, check your keywords with as many search engines as possible and see what sites are listed at the top of the results. You may also want to see how these sites are using your keywords by checking their META description and keyword tags (use *Source* from the *View* menu in your browser).

Once you have completed your list, you will want to include your keywords between the keyword META tags of the document. The format for this tag is <meta name="keywords" content="*your Web site keywords are inserted here*">.

In the past, some Web site developers were successful at getting high rankings on search engines by repeating keywords as often as possible. This method worked because rankings were determined by keyword density, or by the number of times a word was repeated on the document. Higher search engine rankings were given to Web sites that had multiple occurrences of the same keyword. However, search engine administrators are now wise to this practice and may penalize sites if a certain keyword is repeated too many times.

Putting It All Together

Search engines, especially robot spider engines, use title, description, keywords, and keyword density to create their database rankings. Additionally, some search engines give higher rankings to sites that are popular. Popularity is determined by the number of other Web sites that link to yours. For instance, if 10 other Web sites

---

Sample META Keywords Tag— for OfficeLinks.com Home Page

<meta name="keywords" content="Small Business, Information, Office Resources, Business Plans, E-Commerce, Marketing, Advertising, Loans, Finance, Accounting, Legal, Internet, Electronic Commerce, Web Site Hosting, Affiliate Programs, Banner Advertising, Hits, Buy, Purchase, Office Supplies, Telecommunications, Direct Mail, DMDR, Online Business Planning, Rocky Hill, New Jersey">

Search engines, especially robot spider engines, use title, description, keywords, and keyword density to create their database rankings.

contain a hot-link to your site, it will get a higher ranking than a site that has only one hot-link from another site.

By combining these factors, search engine algorithms create rankings for all of the Web sites contained in their database. Unfortunately, search engine administrators don't publish their exact algorithms, and this makes it impossible to predict where your Web site will fall in the rankings. Add to this the fact that getting your Web site listed can take many weeks, and even a trial and error approach can be very time consuming.

Your best approach is to incorporate the following tips in your Web site, and see what happens. Also, because search engines are going to find and list your site (sooner or later), make sure to include a keyword that is either obscure or "nonsense" that will help you

> Include a keyword that is either obscure or "nonsense" that will help you find your Web site.

Tips for Improving Your Search Engine Rankings

Title

- Use your best keywords in your title
- Make your title descriptive
- Include your company name in your title
- On your Web page, create a visible title
- Use the HTML title tags

Description

- Place some descriptive text at the top of your pages
- Use your keywords in the description
- Include the HTML META description tags

Keywords

- Repeat your most important keywords
- Use keywords in your title and description
- Include a "nonsense" word that only you will recognize

Popularity

- Get other sites to hot-link to yours

find your Web site. For instance, you can use something like "rypotwghti" in your META description and keywords.

How Some Popular Search Engines Index Sites

By now you should know that all search engines create and index their databases differently. These differences will influence your site's ranking and how it will be displayed in search results. These differences also mean that you cannot get a high ranking in every search engine. Therefore, you should select one or two search engines and try to optimize your rankings.

The following table will give you an idea of some of the key differences between popular search engines. Use this table as a guide only, since search engines are constantly changing their algorithms for site ranking and appearance.

Select one or two search engines and try to optimize your rankings.

SEARCH ENGINE	<META> TAGS	KEY CONSIDERATIONS FOR INDEXING
Excite *www.excite.com*	No	• Uses artificial intelligence • Looks for common words and themes on page • Favors complete punctuated sentences
GO (InfoSeek) *www.go.com*	Yes	• Uses both the keyword and description <META> tags • Don't repeat words more than 7 times
HotBot *www.hotbot.com*	Yes	• Uses both the keyword and description <META> tags
Lycos *www.lycos.com*	No	• Uses text on your Web page • Incorporates artificial intelligence
Yahoo! *www.yahoo.com*	No	• Hierarchical index based on your selection • Uses text you submit through the master form

For more information on Web site ranking, review the Search Engine Tips in the "SubmitIt!" heading of LinkExchange (*www.linkexchange.com*). Other topics discussed in SubmitIt! include the following.

- General tips for getting listed in search engines
- Indexing characteristics specific to individual search engines
- How long does it take a search engine to list my site?
- Why should I submit inside pages of my site?
- How do I optimize my announcement with a directory?
- When will I need to inform search engines and directories of updates to my Web pages?

> Sooner or later your Web site is going to be discovered by the robots and spiders.

Announcing Your Online Business on the Internet

After you have published your site on the Internet, even if you do nothing, it is going to be found by the spiders and robots that constantly traverse the Web looking for new information. However, you can speed up this process by submitting your domain name to different search engines and by using announce sites.

You can submit your Web site, or domain name, to hundreds of search engines and directories either manually or automatically by using an auto-posting service. The main benefit of doing your submission manually is that it gives you greater control over your listing, while submitting automatically reduces the amount of time required to make hundreds of submissions.

Submitting Your Web Site Manually

Submitting your Web site manually to search engines and directories will give you greater control over your database listing and should improve your Web site's ranking. The downside to manually submitting your Web site is the length of time it takes to submit your Web site to all of the different search engines and directories. This becomes especially inconvenient if you want to submit multiple pages, or domains, to many different search engines.

Probably the best approach, at least at the outset, is to use a combination of both manual and automatic submissions. Choose a

> Use a combination of both manual and automatic submissions.

couple of search engines where you want to get your highest rankings, like Yahoo! and AltaVista, and submit your site manually. For all of the others, use an automatic submission service like LinkExchange as described in the next section.

Remember that with either the manual or automatic submission process, the time between actually submitting your Web site and its eventual appearance on a search engine can be many weeks. Therefore, to save time later on, make sure you have done the following before starting the registration process:

- Develop a good set of 5 to 50 keywords
- Write a description for your Web site
- Have your Web site near completion

Submitting your site manually to a couple of search engines is quite simple. On the search engine's home page (for instance, www.altavista.com), look for headings or links described as "Add a Page" or "Add URL" and click on the appropriate link or button. Now follow the on-screen directions to get your site added to the database. Currently, if you want to submit to Yahoo!, scroll down to the bottom of the home page and click on "How to Suggest a Site."

Using an Automatic Submission Service

As mentioned previously, probably the best way to register your site with different search engines is to use a combination of manual and automatic submissions. Use the manual method for the sites where you want to get the highest rankings, and use an automatic submission service for all the rest. This does not mean that you can't get high rankings with an automatic submission service; it just means that you should use your valuable time with just a few manual submissions. As of today you can register your site with well over one thousand different search engines and directories!

There are many automatic submission, or auto-posting, services on the Web. SubmitIt! (*www.submit-it.com*) is one of the

> There are many automatic submission, or auto-posting, services on the Web.

most famous auto-posting services and is now part of LinkExchange. It allows you to register your Web site with over four hundred search engines and directories. For other auto-posting services see the following list, or check Yahoo! under their "Computers & Internet" heading at *www.dir.yahoo.com/ Computers_and_Internet/Internet/*

> The big search engines will send a spider to visit your Web site once it has been submitted.

AUTO-POSTING SERVICES	WEB ADDRESS
Search Engine Guide	*www.searchengineguide.org/addurl.htm*
SiteAnnounce.com	*www.siteannounce.com*
SubmitIt! (LinkExchange)	*www.submit-it.com*
Web Site Garage	*www.websitegarage.com*

In order to submit a site to all the search engines and directories through SubmitIt!, you will follow a four-step process. The first step is to complete the SubmitIt! Master form that contains information about you, your business, and your Web site. While most of the information required on the form is straightforward, you will be asked to provide a short (70 characters) and long (255 characters) description of your Web site, and a list of 10 keywords. To save time and rework, have these descriptions and keywords ready before you start the Master form.

The second step involves having your site reviewed by SiteInspector, a Web site analyzer. This tool will visit your Web site in real time (it may take a minute or so), and check it for HTML validity, spelling, popularity, META tags, and broken hyperlinks. Although you don't need to do this every time, it is well worth getting the feedback the first time you register.

The third step is to send your domain name, or URL, to the list of search engines shown in the following table. SubmitIt! makes it very clear that the descriptions and keywords you enter on the Master form will not be used by the search engines on this list. Only your URL is submitted to the search engines, which will then send a spider to visit your site and develop a description.

Search Engines Available Through SubmitIt!

AltaVista (all languages)
Anzwers
Excite/NetFind
Magellan
HotBot
InfoSeek
Lycos
Microsoft Network Web Search
NationalDirectory
NetSearch
Northern Light
PlanetSearch
WebCrawler
What-U-Seek

Your fourth and final step is to register with Yahoo! and all the other directories that will appeal to your target audience. Unlike the first step, in which just your URL is required, this step is going to use much of the information on your Master form. Also, you should be aware that if you submit to a large number of directories, the process can be time consuming. Therefore, as SubmitIt! suggests, choose only those directories that will appeal to your target audience. For instance, if your site is going to sell Beanie Babies, there's no need to register with the travel service directories.

Announce Sites

Announce sites were created to let surfers know about new Web sites added to the Internet, and also give marketers another way to promote their sites. Announce sites are a hybrid of press releases that list new Web sites, fresh articles, and online developments in general.

Announce Sites to Promote Your Web Site Launch

ANNOUNCE SITE	WEB ADDRESS
Announce It America!	*www.announceitamerica.com*
Epage	*www.ep.com/faq/webannounce.html*
Net-Announce!	*www.erspros.com/net-announce/*
Netsurfer Digest: The Pressroom	*www.netsurf.com/nsd/pressroom.html*
What's New Too!	*www.newtoo.com*

You should be aware that many of the traditional announce sites, like Netscape What's New, have disappeared, been transformed into portals, or now offer a broad array of promotion alternatives for Web businesses. Therefore, it is becoming harder to distinguish between announce sites and the registration services described earlier.

> Announce sites were created to let surfers know about new Web sites added to the Internet, and also give marketers another way to promote their sites.

Getting OfficeLinks.com Listed with Search Engines

Q: Is OfficeLinks.com listed with any of the major portals or search engines?

A: Yes. You can find the Web site in most major portals, including Yahoo!, AOL, Excite, and Lycos, by simply using the keyword "officelinks" in the search box.

Q: How did you submit your Web site?

A: I used the LinkExchange (*www.linkexchange.com*) SubmitIt! service.

Q: Is LinkExchange difficult to use?

A: No. LinkExchange lets you submit your site to multiple search engines with a click of a button. The only part of the submission process that was time-consuming was completing all of the fields on the submission form.

Q: Why was this form time-consuming?

A: Part of the LinkExchange form requires a couple of descriptions of your Web site [a short one and a long one] and your list of keywords. Unfortunately, I did not have these prepared before I started.

Q: It sounds like you wish you had written these before you started.

A: No doubt. After that first submission, I always have the descriptions and keywords ready to go before I start.

Q: Why have you used SubmitIt! more than once?

A: There are a couple of reasons. First, I submitted more than one page through the service so that people would have a better chance of finding at least one page on my site; and second, I resubmitted some pages after I changed the titles and keywords.

Q: Have you gotten any high ranking keywords?

A: Yes. But they have tended to be phrases instead of just individual keywords themselves. For instance, if you try "Get your business online" in AltaVista, you should find my site in the first few pages.

Q: Do your search engine listings bring visitors to OfficeLinks.com?

A: Absolutely. Whenever I check my Web hosting activity reports, I can see that Inktomi [used by many portals] and Infoseek have referred a steady stream of prospects to my site. The key here is steady. I get a few hits daily from the search engines, but I have to rely on many other types of promotional efforts to bring in more traffic.

Q: What is the biggest mistake you made in getting listed with the search engines?

A: I didn't spend enough time creating HTML tags and keywords. In fact, the first time I submitted, I didn't even have these on my Web site!

Online Search Engine Resources

100Hot.com (*www.100hot.com*)

The Hot 100 provides a list of the most popular, or visited, Web sites on the Internet. Although this is a listing of all Web sites—not just portals and search engines, it still provides a good indication of which search engines are the most popular. For instance, Yahoo! was #1 in a recent listing.

HTML Dictionary (*www.htmldictionary.com*)

If you want to learn more about HTML and the different tags, try the HTML Dictionary Web site. Its home page claims that it is the best place to learn how to make a Web page with HTML because: "Every HTML Tag is here.... Everything is written in plain English.... We answer every e-mail question in less than 24 hours."

Metaspy (*voyeur.mckinley.com/cgi-bin/voyeur.cgi*)

This is a fun place to visit on the Magellan Internet Guide (www.*magellan.excite.com*) if you want to see what users are looking for. It provides "12 randomly selected real-time searches that users like you are performing" that are automatically refreshed every 15 seconds.

Search Engine Tactics (v. 2.2) (*www.jayde.com/set/searchen.html*)

This online book covers the various aspects of search engines, including selecting good keywords, META tags, title lines, different types of search engines, automatic submission services, and tracking your rankings.

Search Engine Watch (*www.searchenginewatch.com*)

Search Engine Watch, created and edited by Danny Sullivan, has a lot of good information about search engines, including the "Webmaster's Guide To Search Engines," which covers search engine submission tips, using META tags, improving your placement, and how to submit URLs.

Web Site Positioning Resource Center
(*www.getpositioned.com*)

The Web Site Positioning Resource Center "provides all of the resources needed to get positioned and stay positioned," including software, books, and consulting services.

Yahoo!: Searching the Web
(*dir.yahoo.com/Computers_and_Internet/Internet/ World_Wide_Web/Searching_the_Web/*)

Under its "Computer & Internet" directory listing, Yahoo! provides a wealth of information about searching the Web, including search engine comparisons, search tips, and articles about robots and spiders.

Summary

Marketing your Web site begins with getting listed in a wide variety of search engines and directories. You can either submit your site manually or use an auto-posting service to get listed with portals like Yahoo!, AltaVista, and Excite. Sometimes a combination of manual and auto-posting will give you the best results.

Before you start the listing process, make sure that you have developed a brief description of your site and an appropriate list of keywords. Incorporate these into the META tags on your Web pages to increase your page ranking with search engines. Also, remember that getting your site listed in some of the more popular search engines can take as long as eight weeks; you should build this into your marketing plan.

For more information on this topic, visit our Web site at www.businesstown.com

Promoting Your Online Business

Topics covered in this chapter

- **Developing a press release for nationwide distribution**

- **Starting an e-mail initiative to keep users returning to your Web site**

- **Establishing reciprocal links for a cost-effective marketing approach**

- **Talking up your Web site in newsgroups and discussion lists**

Chapter 14

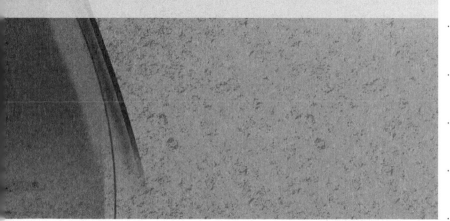

In the words of Mike Valentine (*www.website101.com*), "This isn't the field of dreams kind of 'Build it and they will come' fantasy that so many entrepreneurs believe it is! You've gotta wanna work at it or you might as well be putting a baseball diamond in a corn field!" Mike's point is that just publishing a Web site does not mean that anyone will actually come and visit.

As a Web marketer, your goal is to maximize your response rate using the most cost-effective promotion tools available. For instance, you might set a goal of having 1 out of every 10 visitors to your Web site subscribe to your e-newsletter (a 10 percent response rate); or having 1 out of 100 visitors buy your products and services (a 1 percent response rate). To gauge the cost effectiveness of your promotion efforts, you will need to calculate how much it costs to bring visitors to your Web site. For instance, if you spend $100 on a press release that brings 200 visitors to your site, your cost per visitor is $0.50.

> Consider developing a press release as the first step in your promotional efforts.

Developing a Press Release for Nationwide Distribution

Although there are numerous ways to kick off a publicity campaign for your Web site, you should seriously consider developing a press release as the first step in your promotional efforts. Press releases are a cost-effective way to deliver important information about your business to a broad range of prospective customers. There are many newsworthy reasons why you should issue a press releases, including:

- Launching your Web site
- Announcing a new product or service
- Establishing a business relationship with another business
- Reporting good news or financial results about your company
- Hiring a key executive for your management team
- Releasing important market research information

Formatting Your Press Release

There are a few good reasons why most press releases have a similar structure, or look and feel. First, if you send out a press release that does not look like it was professionally developed, most editors will think the information is not credible and they will simply ignore it. Second, editors and business people are used to reading multiple press releases during the course of the day, and will probably scan the release quickly for selected information. For instance, after reading the headline, these readers may ignore the body of the release and jump right to the bottom for contact information. If this information isn't where they expect it, they may skip it altogether.

It goes without saying that press releases must be error free and contain accurate information. Keep in mind that the editors responsible for deciding whether to publish your press release are trained professionals who can spot typos and grammatical mistakes with a simple glance. Editors are also keenly aware of the types of information that will interest their readers. Therefore, it is pointless to send a press release on new knitting machine technology to the editors of boat enthusiast publications.

It is important to remember that if you are going to send your press release over the Internet, include your company's domain name ("www.yourbiz.com") and your e-mail address ("yourname@yourbiz.com").

One of the best places to find sample press releases, where you can get ideas for layout and content, is on the Internet. If you go to the stock quoting services of any of the major portals such as Yahoo! or Lycos, you will find new press releases appearing almost every minute from companies announcing their latest products, newest Web ventures, or recent financial performance. Simply look up the companies that are most similar to yours, and review the press releases that they have issued over the past few months.

The press release on page 253 was issued by OfficeLinks.com on March 8, 1999, to the Business Wire news service, and appeared as news for many of the publicly traded companies shown in the body of the release. For instance, users of the Yahoo! stock quoting service read this press release under the *Recent News* section for America Online, Excite, and Beyond.com.

> One of the best places to find sample press releases, where you can get ideas for layout and content, is on the Internet.

Carnegie Public Library
202 N. Animas St.
Trinidad, CO 81082-2643

Key Elements in a Press Release

PRESS RELEASE TIPS	DESCRIPTION
Headline	Probably the most important part of your press release is the headline. Like headlines that appear in newspapers, this single statement must capture the attention of your target audience and make them want to read the rest of the story. This is especially true for online press releases, since the body of the press release is usually contained in a separate file that is linked to the headline. Therefore, readers will only see your entire press release if they are interested enough to click on your headline.
First paragraph	The first paragraph of your press release should be no more than two or three sentences in length. Your sentences should be short, to the point, and provide information that builds on your headline. This paragraph should convey to readers why your news is important.
Second and third paragraphs	The next two paragraphs of your press release present the "meat" of your news story, and should include credible facts or references to other experts in the field. You may also want to include in this section the name(s) of people in your company who will back up the story with an appropriate quote. For instance, you might state "According to Ms. Right, the VP of Research and Development, this new product provides the best customer benefits in the marketplace."
Company information	Once you have explained your news and its importance, be sure to include a final paragraph that describes your company and what it does. You may want to describe the products and services that you sell, where you are located, whether you are a public or private company, and when your business was founded.
Contact information	The last part of your press release identifies contact(s) in your company that can answer any relevant questions about the story. You should include a phone number, fax number, e-mail address, and your company URL. Don't be surprised to get called about your story.

Sample Press Release Issued by OfficeLinks

Monday March 8, 9:00 A.M. Eastern Time
Company Press Release
SOURCE: OfficeLinks Corp.
OfficeLinks.com To Be Beyond.com Affiliate

ROCKY HILL, N.J.,—OfficeLinks Corp. announced today that its OfficeLinks.com site will be a Beyond.com Affiliate. Beyond.com (Nasdaq:BYND) is the leading Internet software reseller on the Internet with over 44,000 software titles—5,000 of which are downloadable, from leading vendors such as Microsoft (Nasdaq:MSFT), Adobe (Nasdaq:ADBE), McAfee (Nasdaq:NETA), Intuit (Nasdaq:INTU) and more!

Under the program, OfficeLinks.com will refer users to the Beyond.com site to buy software products. The referral fees that Beyond.com will pay OfficeLinks.com range from 10% on gross sales for downloadable products to 5% on shipped products.

Betsy Goodman, Director of Advertising of OfficeLinks stated, "According to a recent Media Metrix study, Beyond.com's Affiliates, coupled with the company's strategic marketing allies America Online (NYSE:AOL), Excite (Nasdaq:XCIT), Netscape (Nasdaq:NSCP), and Yahoo!(Nasdaq:YHOO), reach a potential audience of more than 80 percent of monthly Internet traffic. We are excited to be in position to offer similar services to our business users."

About OfficeLinks

OfficeLinks, through its flagship portal OfficeLinks.com (http://www.officelinks.com), offers business customers a single source to buy office products and services, including: Books; Computers; Fax and copying machines; Forms; Furniture; Internet service; Office supplies; Pagers and cell phones; Pens and pencils; Phone service; Printers; Promotional items; Software; Stationery; Telephone equipment; and Web hosting services. Additionally, users of OfficeLinks.com can find numerous links to other Web sites that provide advice on business planning, sales, marketing, and finance.

OfficeLinks, Inc., founded in 1999, is a privately held company based in Rocky Hill, New Jersey.

Contact:
Betsy Goodman, (609) 279-9039
Bgoodman@officelinks.com

The OfficeLinks.com press release was very successful and brought nearly seven hundred new visitors to the Web site during the days following its publication. However, you should be aware that one of the things that made this press release so successful was the inclusion of the stock trading (or ticker) symbols for the publicly traded companies. For instance, instead of just stating America Online, the release included (NYSE:AOL), which is the New York Stock Exchange (NYSE) symbol for America Online (AOL). Nevertheless, be aware that some financial news editors frown upon this practice of using stock symbols in press releases.

Distributing Your Press Release

The spontaneous nature of the Internet has generated a whole new variety of services that were previously unavailable in the offline world. Nowhere is this more true than in the distribution of press releases. Previously, in the offline world, you had to print and "snail-mail" your press release to editors who might be interested in your latest news. A tedious process that could take weeks or months before your story was actually printed.

In the online world, you can get your news out almost overnight. You can use an online service such as the Internet News Bureau (*www.newsbureau.com*), which "distributes press releases via e-mail to more than 2,600 journalists throughout the world." Using your credit card and dial-up connection to the Internet, you can distribute a press release in a matter of hours to a nationwide online audience.

If you don't want to pay the Internet News Bureau to distribute your press release, you can still get your message out by e-mailing a formatted press release to a list of editors. The key here is to develop a list of editors that will be interested in your story. For instance, make sure that you include only those publications that cover your industry.

Starting an E-Mail Initiative to Keep Users Returning to Your Web Site

Besides press releases, you can market your online business and attract visitors by sending direct e-mails, publishing an e-newsletter,

> In the online world, you can get your news out almost overnight.

and participating in discussions through newsgroups. The first two methods, direct e-mails and e-newsletters, are discussed in this section, while the more indirect promotional method, participating in newsgroups, is discussed later in this chapter.

Many of the concepts and methods that have been developed in the offline world of direct marketing have been applied successfully in the online world. The most successful include the process of developing an e-mailing list and keeping your users up to date with an e-newsletter.

Promoting Your Web Site with E-Mail

Internet marketers are just beginning to learn that direct e-mailings can produce better results than other forms of online promotion, such as banner advertisements. For instance, you might get a click-through rate in excess of 10 percent for an e-mailing but get a response of less than 1 percent for a banner ad campaign. By understanding the differences between these two types of promotion, you should be able to improve your response rates.

E-mailings should always get a better response than banner ads because of your ability to target prospects more precisely. Targeting means you identify prospects who are more likely to buy your products and services. For instance, an auto parts manufacturer should get a better response by announcing a special tire promotion through e-mail to auto parts purchasing agents, than running a banner advertisement across multiple general interest Web sites.

Although e-mailings will normally generate higher response rates than banner ads, the key is selecting the right target audience or list. If you are trying to find rocket scientists to test your latest jet fuel, your e-mailing should be targeted to engineers in the aerospace industry and not to expectant mothers.

One of the key differences between online and offline direct mailings is your ability to sell products when you deliver the message. In the offline world, direct marketers will tell you to make an offer and include your order form in your mailing package. By using this method, you will get some prospects to buy right away, while others will need more information, such as a follow-up brochure or

> Direct e-mailings can produce better results than other forms of online promotion.

an 800-number to call. For example, the established offline direct marketers, like Lands' End and L. L. Bean, send a catalog of their products with an order form to get you to buy directly over the phone or through the mail.

In the online world, you could include your order form and brochure in your mailing, but e-mail is more effective at warming up prospects (getting them interested in your products and services) and then getting them to visit your Web site to make a sale. There are two reasons for the difference between the online and offline approaches to making a sale: It's impossible, due to differences in browser technology, to create a professional mailing package that everyone will be able to read; and the costs of getting someone to click on a link in your e-mail and visit your Web site are negligible.

Developing Your E-Mailing List

E-mail campaigns start with a list of prospects who will likely be interested in your message or what you have to sell. If you do not already have an e-mailing list, you will either have to develop your own from scratch or buy a list. In fact, even if you have no immediate plans to conduct e-mailing promotions, you should be making every effort to get an e-mail address from everyone who visits your Web site. At some point you will want to use this information to boost your sales.

To develop your own mailing list of your Web site visitors, you can use a service like ListBot (available at *www.linkexchange.com*), or create a form for prospects to fill out. One way to entice users to join your mailing list is to offer them something, preferably for *free*, that they might find valuable. For instance, you can get them to provide their e-mail address by offering them a free subscription to your newsletter. Simply create a link to your registration form that says "Free E-Newsletter." Another way to capture e-mail addresses is to have visitors register before they can view your Web site, or view special information contained within the site. However, keep in mind that many people are reluctant to give their e-mail address to complete strangers, so they may not revisit your site if this is a requirement for entry.

Develop an e-mailing list from your Web site visitors.

Keep in mind that many people are reluctant to give their e-mail address to complete strangers, so they may not revisit your site if this is a requirement for entry.

Sample Invitation to Receive an E-Newsletter

Subject: Free [Industry] newsletter
Dear [Prospect],

Our information shows that you might be interested in receiving our *free monthly newsletter*, called [name of the publication] that specializes in [description and benefit of newsletter].

If you would like to receive a **free** subscription to [name of publication], simply return this e-mail, and your name will be added to our mailing list, or visit our Web site at www.yourbiz.com.

If you would like to be removed from our mailing list, simply send an e-mail to Cancel@yourbiz.com

Thank you for considering [name of publication].
Sincerely,
Director of Public Relations

The other alternative is to buy a mailing list from a third-party provider such as a list broker. However, you should be aware that sending unsolicited e-mail to thousands of prospects can cause a backlash against your online business. (A cautionary word about e-mail "spam" appears later in this chapter.) If you buy a list, or get possible prospects from a list service, make sure to test a few names with your message, and gauge the results. If you don't get any response, or everyone wants you to remove their name from your list, you should evaluate whether your list or message is appropriate.

> You should be aware that sending unsolicited e-mail to thousands of prospects can cause a backlash against your online business.

A Cautionary Word about Spam

Spam, according to the Webopedia (*www.webopedia. internet.com*), is "electronic junk mail or junk newsgroup postings. Some people define spam even more generally as any unsolicited e-mail." Webopedia goes on to say that not all unsolicited e-mail is spam, such as an e-mail sent to a long lost relative, but rather "real

> Be wary of sending out unsolicited junk mail, or "spam."

spam is generally e-mail advertising for some product sent to a mailing list or newsgroup."

In the offline world, sending out unsolicited junk mail is a common form of advertising employed by direct marketers (just check your offline mailbox today). When these offline marketers move online, there is a natural tendency to use this offline method online. After all, you can literally send out thousands of e-mails to individuals, companies, and organizations all over the world in a matter of minutes. Best of all, your incremental expense is minimal because you don't have to pay for additional postage, envelopes, and flyers to get your message delivered. It's free on the Internet (at least in the United States today).

Unfortunately, most people on the Web do not appreciate spam. In fact, many individuals despise receiving spam and have been known to retaliate against spammers in a big way. Keep in mind that it is very easy to organize on the Web. Groups of people can come together in newsgroups and chat rooms almost instantaneously. If you send out 10,000 messages that are considered spam by the majority of your recipients, and they all decide to respond by sending a nasty reply to your inbox, you might be responsible for causing your Internet service provider to overload and crash. Under these extreme circumstances, you will probably be asked to move your e-mail account elsewhere.

Therefore, if you decide to conduct a direct e-mailing campaign, do so judiciously. Test your message and your target audience for any adverse reactions. Ideally, your mailing list will be composed of individuals who have given you permission to send them e-mails on your latest product developments or recent newsworthy events. Also, if you have joined any reputable mailing lists, you will notice that in the first sentence you are usually told: "You are receiving this message because you subscribed to our mailing list.... If you don't want to receive e-mail from us anymore, then... [instructions on how to be removed from the list]."

Creating Effective E-Mailings

Now that you've learned what not to do in an e-mail campaign (sending thousands of unsolicited junk mail messages), here are a

> If you decide to conduct a direct e-mailing campaign, do so judiciously.

few things you can do to get prospects to read your message and even visit your Web site for more information. The key to creating an effective e-mail campaign, besides correctly identifying your target audience, is in the message itself.

Think about the e-mail you receive daily. Which ones do you open for more information and which ones do you skip or delete? You make the open or delete decision based on three pieces of information that are immediately visible when you get e-mail in your in-box: the sender's e-mail address, the subject or tag line, and the date the message was sent. You probably read e-mail from individuals, companies, and organizations when you recognize the sender's address. For instance, if the sender's address is "yourmother@aol.com", there is a good possibility that you will read the message!

If you don't recognize the sender's address, you might open the e-mail if the message captures your interest. For instance, if you were an avid golfer and received an e-mail with a subject line that stated "Free golf newsletter—lower your score," you might at least open the message for more information.

Finally, e-mail dates are important because older e-mails are more likely to be deleted than newer ones. For example, if you don't know the person or company that sent an e-mail, and the subject doesn't grab your interest, you'll probably delete the e-mail just to clear out your in-box.

Once you recognize how you sift through your own e-mail, apply this knowledge to your e-mailing campaign. Your only hope of getting people to read your e-mail is to have a subject line that will interest your target audience. Keep in mind that prospects are looking for benefits: golfers want lower scores, investors want hot stocks, teenagers want the latest super-cool stuff, and parents want a good education for their children.

If you want to start receiving a steady stream of sample e-mail letters, register your e-mail address with other Web sites. Most Web sites that have an active mailing campaign will include a simple text box that states "Enter your e-mail address to be added to our mailing list." A good place to start is with your competitors' Web sites.

> Make sure to stress the benefits of your products and services in your e-mail.

> Once you recognize how you sift through your own e-mail, apply this knowledge to your e-mailing campaign.

E-MAIL TIPS	DESCRIPTION
Sales pitch	The purpose of an e-mailing campaign should be to get prospects to visit your Web site for more information. Give them the capability within the body of your message to click on a link ("www.yourbiz.com") and visit your Web site. Don't use your e-mail campaign to close a sale. Use it to get your prospects interested in your products and services.
Length	In the offline world there is plenty of evidence to suggest that longer letters (containing more information) are better than shorter ones. In the online world there is nothing to suggest that this isn't also true. However, in the online world it is much easier to feed your prospect as much information as they are seeking by providing layered hyperlinks. For instance, you might state in your e-mail "Click here for more information," then once your prospect is transported to your Web site, you can offer them a table of contents on what they would like to look at next (pricing, pictures, order form, etc.).
Layout	As with offline direct mailings, the layout of your e-mail is very important to achieve good results. Begin with a subject line that will capture your prospect's attention. Remember, it's this single line that will determine whether your prospect decides to open the mail or skip it. Once you've gotten your prospect to open the e-mail with your headline, give them an opportunity to visit your Web site in the first couple of sentences (include your Web address here).
Exclusivity	If you are e-mailing to a group of registered users, make sure to tell them that they are the only ones receiving your e-mail or special offer. Prospects and customers will be more interested in exclusive promotions.
Benefits	In addition to mentioning a benefit in your subject line, make sure you repeat it (and any others) in the body of your e-mail message. Let your prospects know the benefits of your products and services. A good way to draw attention to your list of benefits is to use a bullet list of words or phrases.
Instructions	Although you should avoid complicated instructions in your e-mail, make sure to include a phrase like "Click here to learn more ....." next to your hyperlinks. If you have more than one instruction, number them and advise your readers to print them.

Automating Your E-Mailing List and Collecting Market Research Data

At some point you will want to automate your e-mailing list to add and delete registered users. You can do this right from the beginning by creating your own registration form or by using a service like ListBot (available from *www.linkexchange.com*). If you are using Microsoft Frontpage to develop your Web site, you can simply select one of the available templates, such as the Feedback form, and modify it accordingly.

In addition to asking for an e-mail address, there are many pieces of market research data you should consider collecting from your users. For instance, you might ask for some or all of the following pieces of information:

- E-mail address
- User's name
- Postal mailing address
- Phone number
- Age or date of birth
- Occupation
- Gender
- "How did you find our site?"
- Name of business
- Number of employees
- Annual sales

Before you blindly add the preceding list of questions to your registration form, be aware that Internet users are wary of revealing information about themselves. If you ask too many personal questions, users may get turned off and decide not to register on your Web site. Additionally, users don't want to spend a lot of time filling out forms online. If your registration form looks like it's going to take 15 minutes to complete (because there are 50 questions to answer), many users will simply decide that it's not worth registering.

As you create your registration form, ask only questions that will benefit your marketing efforts. If you don't need to know someone's age or gender, don't ask! If you need to know how many employees work in their location, create a drop-down list with ranges. For instance, you might ask:

> **Ask only questions that will benefit your marketing efforts.**

How many employees work in your location? (Choose one.)
- 1 to 5
- 6 to 10
- 11 to 50
- 51 to 100
- 101 to 500
- More than 500

Finally, include a privacy statement on your form (only if it's true) that will reassure users that you are not going to give out their e-mail address to every spammer in the country. You might include something like:

The OfficeLinks.com promise to subscribers:
OfficeLinks.com will not sell, barter, distribute, or transfer any information submitted on this form.

Designing your form and deciding which questions to ask your prospects is the easy part of automating your mailing list. The hard, or time-consuming, part is its administration. You need the capability to add and delete users at their request. As your list begins to grow, you will either have to devote a person to this task or have a system that will perform this function for you.

ListBot and ListBot Gold are two mailing list administration services that are available from LinkExchange (*www.linkexchange.com*). ListBot "provides you with a free way to keep in touch with your Web site visitors by giving you a Web-based e-mail list management system." ListBot according to their product description:

- Collects visitor e-mail addresses automatically
- Sends e-mail to all your visitors with just one click
- Tells you demographics such as age, occupation, etc.
- Manages your mailing lists for you
- Conveniently stores your messages for reuse

Although ListBot is free, you should be aware that it places advertisements in your message every time you send out an e-mail—something that may turn off your subscribers. Additionally, ListBot does not give you the capability to add other e-mail addresses to its database. For instance, if you already have a mailing list, you will not be able to add those names to your ListBot mailing list.

Include a privacy statement on your form (only if it's true) that will reassure users that you are not going to give out their e-mail address to every spammer in the country.

Administering mailing lists can become very time consuming; therefore, you should consider a program to automate the process.

ListBot Gold, a fee-based service, is more robust and eliminates many of the restrictions of ListBot. ListBot Gold benefits, according to their marketing information, are:

- Messages do not include third-party advertisements.
- Existing lists can be imported. Members are automatically added (and assigned passwords if they do not already have one).
- Members-related demographic data can also be imported.
- You may create your own questions to ask list members when they join your list.

Your decision whether to manage your own mailing list program or use a service like ListBot, should be based on how important your mailing list is to your business. If your mailing list is going to be your primary source of revenue, you should consider managing it yourself. On the other hand, if it is only one piece of your marketing mix, consider using a third-party service.

> Your decision whether to manage your own mailing list program or use a service like ListBot, should be based on how important your mailing list is to your business.

Publishing Your Own E-Newsletter

There are two ways you can use e-newsletters to drive traffic to your Web site. You can publish your own e-newsletter, or you can pay a publisher to advertise in their e-newsletter. Publishing your own e-newsletter is significantly easier and less expensive in the online world. Prior to e-mail, newsletter publishers not only had to develop content and manage a mailing list, but they also had to struggle with printing, distribution, and postage costs. Now with e-mail, after the content is complete, a click on your "Send" button gets your message out almost instantaneously and is free of charge.

As for creating content, the offline rules and methods still apply in the online world. In order to create an effective newsletter, you still need to follow many of the guiding principles for this medium.

> Consider publishing an e-newsletter for your online business to enhance customer relationships.

E-NEWSLETTER TIPS	DESCRIPTION
You can say it in words.	Newsletters work best when your message can be expressed with words alone. This is especially true in the online world, where it is still very difficult to include pictures in your mailings.
Common audience and message	Both your audience and your message must be homogeneous. This means your audience must have a common interest and your message addresses that interest. For example, if your newsletter readers are interested in technology stocks, your newsletter must cover financial news about technology stocks.
It is valuable.	Give your readers information that they can act on. If your readers want to know where they can get good deals on antiques, tell them.
Published regularly	Newsletters are published at specified intervals, like every week or month.
Be familiar.	Your goal is to get your readers to think of you much like they would think of a trusted financial advisor or athletic coach. Use your name and provide useful advice that answers their questions.
Be concise.	Everyone wants answers quickly. Make sure that your newsletter gets to the point in a few short sentences or paragraphs.

Before you begin publishing an e-newsletter, research what your competition is doing.

Before you begin publishing an e-newsletter, research what your competition is doing. Subscribe to their newsletters, online and offline, and figure out how your message is going to be different and better. After all, readers don't want the same advice repeated over and over from many different sources. Listed below are a couple of newsletter sources you may want to try:

CMPnet (*www.cmpnet.com/delivery*)
Publishes newsletters in both text and HTML format for the technology industry.

Newsletter Access (*www.newsletteraccess.com*)
On this site you will find a directory of over five thousand newsletters. "Learn what the experts say about everything from how to make money in the stock market to how to pick a fine wine."

Establishing Reciprocal Links for a Cost-Effective Marketing Approach

It is possible to establish reciprocal linking agreements with other Web sites. A reciprocal linking agreement means you will put a link to someone else's Web site on your Web site provided they reciprocate and place a link to your Web site on theirs. This way, visitors to other Web sites will have an opportunity to find yours.

In order to set up these agreements, you will need to find other Web sites that might benefit from being listed on your Web site. For instance, if you provide advice about growing flowers on your Web site, you should approach other sites in the same industry (maybe gardening Web sites, for instance) and see if they would be interested in this type of arrangement.

To get started, make a list of Web sites that will benefit from a reciprocal agreement with your Web site, and try to locate a contact for each site. Look through the prospective sites and see if you can find an e-mail address for the Webmaster, or another appropriate contact. If you can't find one, you can always try sending an e-mail to "webmaster@othersite.com" and hope for a response.

As mentioned in Chapter 13, reciprocal links can also give your site a higher ranking with certain search engines. Some search engine algorithms gauge the popularity of a Web site by counting the number of other Web sites that link to it. Therefore, if 100 other Web sites have links to yours, these search engines will consider your site to be more popular than another site that only has five reciprocal links.

Before you undertake this effort, keep in mind that reciprocal links are free. Therefore, you should not expect a significant amount of traffic from any single link. You will need to have a lot of these agreements to increase your number of visitors from this program alone.

> Reciprocal links can give your site a higher ranking with certain search engines.

Talking Up Your Web Site in Newsgroups and Discussion Lists

Another way to promote your Web site is to do some "stealth" marketing in newsgroups and on discussion lists. The key here is "stealth," since neither of these communities appreciate blatant advertisements for Web sites or products and services. Before you even think about using this medium to promote your Web site, select a few appropriate newsgroups and discussion lists, and follow their message postings for a couple of weeks.

Once you feel comfortable with the other post-ers, you may want to join in the discussions and find some creative ways to mention your Web site. For instance, if at all possible, use an e-mail address associated with your Web site as your identifier when you post a message ("yourname@yourbiz.com"). Most users of these specialized discussions will be able to find "yourbiz" from this address.

Locating Newsgroups and Discussion Lists

NEWSGROUP OR DISCUSSION LIST	WEB ADDRESS	DESCRIPTION
CyberFiber Newsgroups	*www.cyberfiber.com/index.html*	CyberFiber has a complete directory to USENET and alt.Newsgroups.
Deja.com	*www.deja.com*	Deja.com allows you to post comments on a range of subjects, and also to get ratings on a variety of products, services, and people.
Excite Message Boards	*www.boards.excite.com/boards*	Excite has a complete set of online discussions, including Autos, Cars, Computers & Internet, Education, Entertainment, Family, Games, Health, Home & Real Estate, Remodel, Repair, Money & Investing, Politics & News, Relationships, Shopping, Small Business, Sports, and Travel.
Yahoo! Message Boards	*www.messages.yahoo.com/index.html*	You can discuss almost anything on the Yahoo! message boards. Everything from Business & Finance to Sex & Romance.

It should be pointed out that there is an operational difference between message boards and some discussion groups, or mailing lists. On a message board you have the capability of reading every message that has been posted, just like with an offline bulletin board. Some discussion groups, on the other hand, work through a mailing list. In this case (called opt-in), you subscribe to a mailing list and get individual messages sent to your in-box. If you want to send a response, you mail your comments to the entire mailing list.

Promoting OfficeLinks.com to Attract New Visitors

Q: What types of promotional activities have you tried to promote OfficeLinks.com?

A: I have sent press releases, conducted direct e-mailings, created an e-mailing list, published an e-newsletter, and set up reciprocal links.

Q: Of these, what have been the most successful?

A: By far, the press releases that I sent to Business Wire were the most successful.

Q: What made these press releases so successful?

A: A few of these press releases appeared on many of the major portals, like AOL, Yahoo! and Lycos. This gave OfficeLinks wide exposure and brought thousands of unique visitors to my Web site.

Q: Is a high number of unique visitors your definition of success?

A: No. Definitely not. Visitors that do what you want them to do defines success. For instance, if you run a retail site, you want your visitors to buy stuff, not just to visit. In my case, I wanted to generate publicity for my Web site. These press releases generated calls from some big ISPs and a couple of television networks! That's what I call success!

Q: What other promotional tactics have you tried successfully?

A: After the press releases, I would rate direct e-mailing and publishing an e-newsletter about the same. In both instances, I have been able to get prospects to visit my site, or to return for a second time.

Q: Why weren't these as successful as the press releases?

A: Probably the best way to do a comparison is to look at the costs of conducting both efforts. Although I had to spend $100 to get a press release distributed through Business Wire, this was a lot less costly [in terms of time] than writing creative e-mails, editing e-newsletters, and managing an e-mail list.

Q: Have any of your promotional campaigns been failures?

A: Again, it depends on how you define failure. All of my promotional campaigns have attracted new visitors to the Web site. However, generating reciprocal links has been more time consuming than some of my other efforts.

Online Promotion Resources

Electronic Direct Marketing (*www.edmarketing.com*)

EDM specializes in what is called opt-in e-mail marketing "to deliver your offer where it will get the best attention possible." On this site you will find a good directory of online advertising agencies and resources.

EzineSeek (*ezineseek.com/about.shtml*)

EzineSeek is a "searchable directory of e-mail newsletters, containing over 500 listings organized by category. It also contains an extensive collection of resources for e-mail publishers."

Internet Marketing Center (*www.marketingtips.com/main.html*)

At the Internet Marketing Center you will find innovative ideas for marketing your product or service on the Internet, including some tips to participate in e-mail discussions lists and newsgroups.

Internet News Bureau (*www.newsbureau.com*)

The Internet News Bureau "distributes press releases via e-mail to more than 2,600 journalists throughout the world." With a credit card and dial-up connection to the Internet, you can distribute your press release in a matter of hours to a nationwide audience.

WebSite 101 (*www.website101.com*)

WebSite 101 provides many useful tips and links for small business advertisers, including freebies such as banner generator, classified ads, Web resources, weekly Web tips, and daily cartoons.

Wilson Internet (*www.wilsonweb.com/articles/*)

Wilson Internet has a very complete library of articles to help you market your Web site, including informative articles like "The Web Marketing Checklist: 26 Ways to Promote Your Site."

Summary

In this chapter you learned that some low-cost marketing alternatives include sending out a press release, starting an e-mailing list, establishing reciprocal links, and joining online discussion groups. Probably the most effective method to draw immediate attention to your online business is to send out a press release to online and offline publications that might be interested in your new venture.

After your site has gotten some preliminary exposure, you will want to keep visitors returning as often as possible. A direct e-mail newsletter has proven to be one of the most effective online marketing tools at your disposal. Simply collect an e-mail address from your visitors and begin to send them a monthly publication on newsworthy events about your business, the industry, or other subjects that might be of interest.

For more information on this topic, visit our Web site at www.businesstown.com

Advertising Online with Banner Ads and Offline with Traditional Media

Topics covered in this chapter

- Understanding the terminology of online advertising
- Creating a banner ad campaign to attract visitors to your Web site
- Advertising offline to boost your online traffic
- Collecting market research information on your Web site

The goal of marketing is simple: to get more people to buy more stuff.

SERGIO ZYMAN, *THE END OF MARKETING AS WE KNOW IT*

There is a lot of debate about the usefulness of banner advertisements to promote online businesses. Banner ads are those advertisements that seem to appear on almost every Web page these days, either promoting a brand or asking you to click for more information. Since many banner ad campaigns are expensive to run and produce click-through rates that can be less than 1 percent, many online marketers have begun to question their cost effectiveness. However, banner ads still represent one of the most significant ways that you can begin to build brand awareness, or drive traffic to your site, on the Internet. You should view banner ads as another element of your marketing mix, complemented with search engine listings, press releases, and direct mail campaigns.

> The cost of running banner ads ranges from free to thousands of dollars each month.

The cost of running banner ads ranges from free to thousands of dollars each month. In this chapter you'll learn how to create a banner ad using a free service such as Quick Banner (*www.quickbanner.com*), and then display it for free on LinkExchange (*www.linkexchange.com*). If your advertising budget is a little larger, you'll want to explore some of the other online advertising services reviewed in this chapter, like DoubleClick (*www.doubleclick.com*). Finally, you'll also learn why so many online companies are advertising offline to boost their traffic.

> Many online marketers have begun to question the effectiveness of banner ads.

Understanding the Terminology of Online Advertising

While the cost of online advertising hasn't reached the status of Super Bowl commercials, it can still be a fairly significant expense for smaller businesses. Since this expense can outweigh your development and Web hosting costs, you'll need to become familiar with the terminology and types of advertising used in this industry. You must familiarize yourself with terms such as number of hits, unique visitors, click-through rate, cost per impression (CPI), and page views.

A Cautionary Reminder about "Hits"

Once your business goes online, one of the first questions you'll get from colleagues and acquaintances is, "How many hits are you getting?" Although you may be able to impress the unknowing by answering "10,000 hits per month," this measure of Web site activity holds little value for online advertisers.

As mentioned in Chapter 10, a "hit" is recorded every time your Web host's disk drive spins into action and retrieves a file associated with your Web site. If your Web site was simply made up of one page of text, or a single file, the "number of hits" would be a good measure of activity on your Web site. However, since most Web pages display multiple images, each contained in a separate file, you will get multiple hits every time someone looks at an individual page.

It is theoretically possible for you to generate 10,000 hits each minute by placing 9,999 GIF images on your home page. In this case, if someone visited your home page every minute, your Web host would record 10,000 hits per minute. An impressive number of hits during the course of a day, but meaningless in evaluating how many prospects or customers are actually visiting your online business.

> The number of *hits* you receive is not an accurate measure of the visitors to your Web site.

Difference Between Repeat and Unique Visitors

One of the most challenging issues facing Web advertisers is determining how many individuals are visiting a Web site. While it is easy to visualize someone visiting your Web site, it is much more difficult for a computer to capture that information and make it useful for advertisers.

A visitor is someone who types your domain name ("www.yourbiz.com") in their Web browser's address box, or clicks on a link to your Web site, and waits for the Web page to load on their computer. The total number of visitors you have in a day, week, or month includes repeat visitors and unique visitors. For example, if someone visits your Web site five times in one week, and another person visits

> The total number of visitors you have in a day, week, or month includes repeat visitors and unique visitors.

your site once during the same week, you will have had six visits but only two unique visitors.

Taken together, both the total number of visits and unique visitors to your Web site are important measures of activity. Ideally, you want to have a high total number of visits combined with many unique visitors.

Page Views or Page Impressions

A page view, or page impression, happens every time you successfully pull up a Web page in your browser. For instance, if you type "www.yahoo.com" in your Web browser's address box, and the Yahoo! home page appears on your screen, Yahoo! counts that as a page view, or page impression.

From an advertising perspective, a page view is important because it determines how many times your advertisement will be displayed. If you decide to buy some online advertising, you will have to decide how many times you will want your banner shown, or the number of page views (impressions) that you want to buy.

Keep in mind that banner advertisements can appear anywhere on a Web page. This is important because banners can be on a page—and counted as an impression by your advertising service—but never actually seen by the user.

How does this happen? When you look at a Web page, you initially see only the portion of the page that is shown in your Web browser, and its associated ads. However, there may be other advertisements on that page that are not visible until you scroll down the page. Unfortunately, your advertising service has no way of knowing whether a user looked at the entire page or just surfed away after the page was loaded.

Banner Advertisements

Banner ads are the graphic images that appear on most Web sites, usually in rectangular boxes of varying sizes. For many of the larger Web sites such as Yahoo! and America Online, these ads represent a significant source of their revenue (much like commercials on the television networks).

> A page view is important because it determines how many times your advertisement will be displayed.

Banner ads are linked to the advertiser's Web site. For instance, E*Trade might pay Yahoo! millions of dollars to place a banner advertisement on their stock quoting Web pages. If investors viewing stock quotes on Yahoo! click on the E*Trade banner ad, they are transported to the E*Trade Web site. Obviously, E*Trade wants investors to visit their site and open up an online trading account.

Today, the most popular size for banner ads is 468 pixels in width by 60 pixels in height, or 468 screen dots by 60 screen dots. Other popular sizes are shown in the following table:

BANNER WIDTH	X	BANNER HEIGHT
468	x	60
392	x	72
234	x	60
125	x	125
120	x	240
120	x	90
120	x	60
88	x	31

Increasingly, you will notice that banner ads are becoming more sophisticated to entice viewers to actually click on them. It is not unusual to see banner ads that are animated with full motion graphics and sound.

The Importance of Click-Throughs

Online advertising is all about viewers and click-throughs. If you run an online advertising campaign using a banner ad, you will want to know how many viewers saw your banner, and how many clicked on it to visit your Web site. A click-through happens when someone clicks on your banner advertisement (being shown on another Web site) and is transported to your Web site.

An important measurement in banner advertising is the click-through rate, or percentage of prospective customers that respond to

> An important measurement in banner advertising is the click-through rate.

an online advertisement. To calculate this percentage, divide the number of click-throughs by the number of impressions.

Click-through rate = Number of clicks ÷ Number of impressions

For instance, if your banner is shown 5,000 times and is clicked on 50 times, your click-through rate is 1 percent, or 50 divided by 5,000. A higher click-through rate, or percentage, is normally better than a lower rate.

Evaluating Customer Conversions after Click-Throughs

In order to create a successful advertising campaign, you will want to measure your customer conversion rate. To calculate this rate, or percentage, divide the number of customers by the number of click-throughs:

Customer conversion rate = Number of customers ÷ Click-through rate

For instance, if you get 100 click-throughs and make 10 sales, your customer conversion rate is 10 percent, or 10 divided by 100. It is important to compare this measurement with your click-through rate to gauge the effectiveness of your advertising.

If you are getting a lot of prospects (high click-through rate), but only a few buyers (low customer conversion rate), re-evaluate your banner, advertising service, target audience, and even your Web site itself. The ideal scenario for your online business is to get a high click-through rate and a high customer conversion rate.

Creating a Banner Ad Campaign to Attract Visitors to Your Web Site

In order to bring more prospects to your Web site, you should consider a banner advertising campaign. Although large companies might spend millions of dollars to have their banners, or advertisements,

> Customer conversion rate = Number of customers ÷ Click-through rate

displayed prominently on America Online or Yahoo!, there are still many other affordable banner advertising opportunities for your online business. Running a banner advertising campaign involves four steps: designing your banner ad, creating your banner ad, selecting an advertising service to run your ad, and measuring results.

Designing Your Banner Ad

The first step to running a banner ad campaign is to create the actual banner that will be displayed on other Web sites across the Internet. Your banner will need to be professional in appearance and get the attention of your intended audience. Some options for banner ad design include:

- Design a banner yourself using widely available software tools, or
- Use some of the free banner creation services that are available online, or
- Have it professionally designed by an advertising agency.

Before you begin the process of designing your banner, define your goals. Many advertisers will tell you that ultimately your banner should scream "Click on me" to your prospective customers. However, if your only goal was to create a good click-through rate, you could offer FREE MONEY to anyone that clicked on your banner. While this strategy will surely generate a high percentage of click-throughs, it may do little to get people to buy your products and services. Eventually, this strategy would leave you broke.

The goal of your banner advertising campaign should state what you want to happen before and after a prospect clicks on your banner. For instance, your stated goals might include:

> Before you begin the process of designing your banner, define your goals.

- Build brand awareness
- Find new prospects
- Sell products and services
- Obtain newsletter subscribers
- Capture market research information

After you have established goals and objectives for your banner ad campaign, the design and creation process can begin. If your goal is to build brand awareness and gain "mind share" amongst Web users, your banner should prominently display the business name, product name, or logo you want to promote. On the other hand, if you want visitors to come to your Web site so that you can make them an offer, you will want to entice users to click on your banner.

Surprisingly enough, if you want people to click on your banner, you need to tell them to do so. Make sure your banner includes "Click here to find out more" or another phrase that begins "Click here...." Market research has shown that banners inviting users to click get better results (more clicks) than those that don't.

Another consideration is to keep your target audience in mind as you design your banner. Use phrases that are recognizable and will encourage them to click on your banner. For instance, if your target customers are teenagers, the language and tone used will be different than if you are targeting parents of teenagers.

Probably the best and most frequently used word in advertising is the word "FREE." Offering your target audience something for free, like a newsletter or mortgage calculator, is obviously more appealing than offering nothing at all. Keep in mind, though, if you start offering "free money" or even "free mouse pads," it can get very expensive and may not lead to the end result (a sale, for instance) that you had planned.

Asking a question is another way to improve your click-through rate. For example, realtors might ask, "Want to know how much your house is worth?" Or banks might question, "Are you getting the lowest interest rate possible?" These questions would be followed by a "Click here to find out."

Using different banners, or rotating your banners, can also help to maximize your response rate. Changing your message, or design, from one banner to the next can significantly impact your click-throughs. This also will give you an opportunity to test different messages and designs on your target audience, and learn which ones work best.

> If you want people to click on your banner, you need to tell them to do so.

In summary, you will improve your banner advertising results by using the following guidelines:

- Set goals and objectives for your banner ad campaign
- Include the phrase "Click here..." on your banner
- Use phrases that your target audience understands
- Offer something free in your tag line
- Ask a question to get people to click for the answer
- Test different banners to find what works best

Creating Your Banner Ad

Once you have established goals for your banner ad campaign and decided on what type of message you will deliver, it is time to actually create your banner. Banners can be created using software tools or a design service. Again, the most common size banner measures 468 pixels wide by 60 pixels high, and is the one that you will see most often at the top of Web pages. Another popular size is the 88 x 31 banner, since it fits nicely on the sidebar of a Web page and gives advertisers more space to advertise multiple products in the same space as the larger banners.

Banners are graphic images that can be created and edited with a wide variety of off-the-shelf software packages, including Jasc Software Paint Shop Pro, Adobe Photoshop, and Microsoft FrontPage. Using these software tools and a few other applications, such as Java or Shockwave, you have the ability to create very vivid and memorable banner advertisements.

Another way to create a banner ad that is less time consuming is to experiment with some of the free design services available on the Web. Some of these services only require you to choose a format and specify a tagline for your ad, and they will take care of the rest.

> Banners can be created using software tools or a design service.

FREE BANNER DESIGN SERVICE	WEB ADDRESS
Webmaster Resources	*www.ufuweb.com*
Quickbanner	*www.quickbanner.com*
Animation Online	*www.web-animator.com*
Media Builder	*www.mediabuilder.com/abm.html*
Webmosaic	*www.webmosaic.com*

Using LinkExchange to Advertise Your Banner

There two ways you can get your banner shown on other Web sites across the Internet. The first is to join an exchange service like Microsoft LinkExchange (*www.linkexchange.com*) that will show your banner on its member Web sites, provided you agree to display its banners on your Web site. As of this writing, LinkExchange claims to have over 450,000 member sites in 32 languages, and reaches over 40 million viewers on the Web.

Although LinkExchange states that you will get "unlimited free advertising to attract customers," you must display two ads on your site to get your banner shown once on other sites. In other words, if your Web site shows the LinkExchange banner ad 100 times, LinkExchange will show your banner 50 times on other sites.

Since this service is free and easy to use, and will give you a better feel for how banner advertising works, you should definitely test it out. Simply design your banner in the 468 x 60 pixel format and submit it to LinkExchange for approval. Additionally, LinkExchange provides a series of online reports that will show you important traffic statistics, including the number of visits to your Web site, the number of times your banner has been shown on other sites, and your banner's click-through rate. To learn more, go to the LinkExchange home page (*www.linkexchange.com*) and click on the "Banner Network" link.

BANNER EXCHANGE NETWORKS	WEB ADDRESS
Beseen	*www.beseen.com*
Click Taxi	*www.clicktaxi.com*
Excite Affiliates Network	*www.affiliate.excite.com*
LinkExchange	*www.linkexchange.com*

Paying a Service to Advertise Your Banner

The other way to get your banner advertised on the Internet is to pay an advertising service. Advertising on the Web is normally purchased from a service provider on a cost per impression (CPI) basis. However, since the cost per impression is normally so low,

LinkExchange is a service that will advertise your banner for *free*.

LinkExchange provides a series of online reports that will show you important traffic statistics, including the number of visits to your Web site, the number of times your banner has been shown on other sites, and your banner's click-through rate.

advertising rates are quoted as the cost per thousand impressions (or CPM). For instance, you might pay a service $50 for 1,000 impressions, or $0.05 per impression.

Sample Banner Ad Charges—for *Inc.* Magazine Online

CAMPAIGN PERIOD	GUARANTEED IMPRESSIONS	GROSS COST	GROSS CPM (COST PER THOUSAND IMPRESSIONS)	GROSS CPI (COST PER IMPRESSION)
One Month	125,000	$8,500	$68.00	$0.068
Three Months	375,000	$22,500	$60.00	$0.060
Six Months	750,000	$41,250	$55.00	$0.055
Nine Months	1,125,000	$56,250	$50.00	$0.050
Twelve Months	1,500,000	$70,500	$47.00	$0.047

Source: *www.inc.com/online_advertising/banner.html*

As described earlier, an impression occurs whenever someone views a page that contains an advertisement. It's important to remember that banner ads shown at the bottom of a page may not be seen by anyone at all but still be counted as an impression by an advertising service. This is similar to television commercials that are shown in the middle of the night when no one is watching. Therefore, if you are going to buy advertising, it's important to determine where your banner ad will be shown. Advertisements shown at the top of a page ("above the fold"), will always do better than comparable ads shown "below the fold," or toward the bottom of a page.

Besides the design and placement of your banner, the other key to banner advertising is your target audience. Obviously, you want to advertise to viewers that will be interested in what you have to say or sell. You want to advertise on Web sites that can get your message to appropriate demographic segments. For instance, if you are selling baby items, you will want to find sites that cater to young parents or grandparents.

The following table lists some of the larger advertising services and their associated CPMs (cost per thousand impressions). Note that CPMs tend to increase as your target audience becomes more defined. For instance, the $10 CPM is usually for a "run of the network," while the higher rates are for specific target groups, such as "Technology buyers."

> Banner ads shown at the bottom of a page may not be seen by anyone at all.

COMPANY NAME	WEB ADDRESS	CPM*
24/7 Media	*www.247media.com*	$10–$40
Ad Smart	*www.adsmart.net*	$15–$70
DoubleClick	*www.doubleclick.net*	$12–$70
Flycast	*www.flycast.com/*	N/A
Real Media	*www.realmedia.com*	$35–$50

*Note: Rates vary by content and may change over time.

DoubleClick allows you to target specific content sites with your banner ad in the following categories: Automotive, Business & Finance, Career, College, E-Commerce, Entertainment, Health, ISPs, News & Culture, Search, Yellow Pages, Sports, Technology, Travel, and Women & Family. Each of these categories has a different CPM that varies by their popularity. To learn more, simply visit the sites listed in the previous table and click on the "Rate Card" or "Advertiser" tabs.

Finally, if you are going to run a banner ad campaign using a service provider, keep in mind that most of the rates quoted are "Gross" as opposed to "Net" rates. Recognized advertising agencies will usually get a 15 percent discount off the "Gross" rates when making a purchase for their clients. Additionally, all of the rates quoted are negotiable for larger volume purchases and other special circumstances.

Cost of Banner Advertising

In the preceding section you learned how much it will cost to show your banner, or get an impression, on other Web sites. However, you'll get a better idea of your actual costs by estimating your click-through rate in conjunction with the CPM. For instance, if you expect to get a click-through rate of 0.5 percent, and you spend $1,000 for 20,000 impressions ($50/CPM), your cost per click-through would be $10:

Cost per click-through = $10, or $1,000 \div (20,000 \times 0.005)$

In the offline world, a direct marketer will tell you that $10 per lead (click-through in the online world) is comparable. Consider a

> You'll get a better idea of your actual costs by estimating your click-through rate in conjunction with the CPM.

direct mailing program that gets you a 10 percent response rate and costs you $1 for every letter, or flyer, you mail. If you spent $1,000, or mailed 1,000 letters, your cost per response would also be $10:

$$\text{Cost per response} = \$10, \text{ or } 1,000 \div (1,000 \times 0.10)$$

Keep in mind that no one can, or should, predict click-through rates for your banner advertising campaign. In the preceding example, if your click-through rate turned out to be 1 percent rather than 0.5 percent, your cost per click-through would drop to $5. Only your experience will help you to estimate click-through rates and their associated costs. There is no doubt that advertising offline is as good or better than advertising online, which explains why so many online companies are advertising offline (on television and radio) to attract visitors to their Web sites.

Other Banner Advertising Considerations

As you begin to explore your banner advertising alternatives, you might come across an offer from an advertising service in which you only pay for click-throughs. In this case, instead of paying for impressions, you only pay when someone clicks on your banner ad. Hypothetically, this is a much better alternative, because the advertiser is guaranteeing to deliver visitors to your Web site. This is analogous to you setting up an affiliate program for your Web site. You will only pay when someone comes to your site from an affiliate site and makes a purchase on your site.

Along the same lines, an advertising service may be willing to place your banner advertisement on their site(s) for a percentage of the sales you get through referrals, or click-throughs, they deliver. For instance, you will often read that some of the larger portals, such as Yahoo! or AOL, have reached an advertising agreement with other large companies that includes a percentage of the sales made through their relationship. In this case, the portals believe that the fees for generating sales will be larger than strictly negotiating a CPM rate.

If you get to the point where your Web site is starting to get more than twenty-five thousand unique visitors per month, you should begin thinking about some of these more specialized

> There is no doubt that advertising offline is as good or better than advertising online.

relationships with advertising companies. At some point, if you run a very popular Web site, these companies will be willing to entertain a wide variety of marketing relationships with your business, including paying you to be a member of their network.

Advertising Offline to Boost Your Online Traffic

Probably the most important piece of advice about advertising your online business in the offline world is to include your Web address on all of your promotional materials. That means that "www.your-biz.com" should be displayed on everything that you mail, fax, or give to customers, including business cards, letterhead, order forms, brochures, flyers, and promotional items.

A more difficult question to answer is whether you should run an offline advertising campaign specifically to bring prospects to your online business. For instance, you may be considering an advertising campaign using traditional offline media such as:

- Direct mail
- Magazines
- Newspapers
- Radio
- Television

The answer to this question depends on your type of business and your advertising budget. First, if your online business is your only form of business (meaning you don't already have a bricks and mortar operation), you might consider some offline advertising if you can afford it. However, in this case, your priority should be to use online advertising to bring prospects to your online business. Once you get this working, then look at your offline advertising alternatives.

Many of the larger pure online businesses like Amazon.com and Yahoo! do a lot of offline advertising to get prospects to visit their Web sites. However, much of this advertising is directed at building brand awareness, rather than trying to sell specific products. For instance, you don't see Amazon.com advertising specific books on

> Probably the most important piece of advice about advertising your online business in the offline world is to include your Web address on all of your promotional materials.

> Many of the large online companies use offline advertising to build brand awareness.

television, you see Amazon.com advertising how much space they need to sell all of their books. Additionally, these online businesses have big enough advertising budgets that they not only blanket the Internet with advertising but have enough left over to run print, radio, and television campaigns.

On the other hand, if you already have an offline business, you may be considering an offline advertising campaign to drive traffic to your online business. In this case you will be sacrificing some of your offline advertising dollars to promote your online business. This is a difficult tradeoff because you may force prospects that would normally buy from your offline business, to buy online. In a sense you are cannibalizing your offline business.

The best approach for an existing offline business is to expand its channels of distribution by finding a new segment of customers online. For instance, if your offline patrons visit your store during normal business hours (9:00 A.M. to 5:00 P.M.), you may want to create an advertising campaign that appeals to customers who can't get to your store during those hours. Another alternative is to expand your geographic reach by identifying prospects who live too far away from your offline business, and targeting them with offline advertisements.

> The best approach for an existing offline business is to expand its channels of distribution by finding a new segment of customers online.

Advertising Alternatives

TYPE OF BUSINESS	OFFLINE ADVERTISING	ONLINE ADVERTISING
Existing offline (bricks and mortar) business	Keep offline prospects returning to your offline business; include Web address in your offline advertising.	Expand your channels of distribution by identifying potential online buyers.
Pure online business	Expand your channels of distribution by building brand awareness among offline prospects.	Keep online prospects returning to your online business.

Since the offline and online worlds are relatively different places, attracting different sets of customers with different sets of needs, you should first concentrate on using online advertising to attract online customers. Once you have saturated the online advertising possibilities and feel that your incremental ad dollars might go further with traditional media, then you should create an offline advertising campaign.

If you would like to learn more about offline advertising, visit Business Owner's Toolkit (*www.toolkit.cch.com/text/P03_7000.asp*) or the Small Business Administration (*www.sba.gov*).

Collecting Market Research Information on Your Web Site

At some point you will want to know more about your visitors than simply their e-mail addresses. You will want to capture some demographic information, like age, gender, and geographic location. Once you have collected this data, you can begin to develop more targeted advertising campaigns to increase your click-through and customer conversion rates. For instance, if your online business provides financial analysis about the stock market for individual investors, you might want to know the average income, sex, and age of your visitors. You could then use this information to create targeted advertising programs to groups of individuals with similar characteristics.

Unfortunately, if you ask your visitors too many questions or request information that is too personal, there is a good possibility that they will simply "surf" away from your Web site and go somewhere else. Therefore, only ask questions that you absolutely need to know, and try to keep them as general as possible. As mentioned earlier, if you create a list of questions that looks like it's going to take 15 minutes to answer, many users will simply decide that it's not worth it. If you ask too many personal questions, your visitors might also turn away because they feel like you are invading their privacy.

While there are many questions that market researchers want to ask prospects and customers, some of the most common are some or all of the following pieces of information:

- E-mail address
- User's name
- Postal mailing address
- Phone number
- Age or date of birth
- Occupation
- Gender
- "How did you find our site?"
- Name of business
- Number of employees
- Annual sales

If you ask your visitors too many questions or request information that is too personal, there is a good possibility that they will simply "surf" away from your Web site and go somewhere else.

Use a form on your Web site to capture important market research information.

One of the best approaches to get your prospects, or Web site visitors, to answer questions about themselves is to provide an incentive. For instance, you could offer a free e-newsletter or a market research report in exchange for their answers. To do this, simply create an online registration form, or survey, that says something like, "In order to receive our free monthly newsletter, please complete the following survey form."

Again, as you create your registration form, ask only questions that will benefit your marketing efforts. If you don't need to know someone's age or gender, don't ask! If you need to know about their annual income, create a drop-down list with ranges. For instance, you might ask:

What is your annual household income? (Choose one.)

- Less than $25,000
- Between $25,000 and $75,000
- Between $75,000 and $150,000
- More than $150,000

And don't forget to include a privacy statement on your form (only if it's true) that will reassure users that you are not going to share this information with anyone else. For instance, a survey on the StrikingItRich.com (*www.strikingitrich.com*) Web site, includes the following privacy statement:

> All sign-up information is confidential and will not be sold, bartered or otherwise serviced.

> Ask only questions that will benefit your marketing efforts.

MARKET RESEARCH TIPS AND TECHNIQUES	WEB ADDRESS
Lodestone Research	*www.lodestone.com*
SalesDoctors	*www.salesdoctors.com/patients/1survey.htm*
The Business Research Lab	*www.busreslab.com*

Advertising OfficeLinks.com with Banner Ads

Q: Do you run any banner advertising campaigns for OfficeLinks.com?

A: Yes. I use two services available from LinkExchange (*www.linkexchange.com*). I participate in their banner exchange program and I also buy additional impressions from their AdStore.

Q: What is the LinkExchange banner exchange program?

A: I get to show my OfficeLinks.com banner on the LinkExchange network [currently has over 400,000 Web sites] in exchange for showing the banners of other network members on my Web site. The best part about this service is that it is free.

Q: How does this banner exchange program work?

A: Basically, I have to include some special HTML code on OfficeLinks.com that displays different LinkExchange banners every time someone visits my site. I also had to create a banner and submit it to LinkExchange so that it could be shown on their network.

Q: Did you create your own banner?

A: Yes. I designed it myself with the image editor that was included in Microsoft FrontPage.

Q: You said you also buy additional impressions from AdStore. Why?

A: I do this to supplement the impressions that I get from the free banner exchange program with LinkExchange. This gives OfficeLinks.com greater exposure on the LinkExchange network.

Q: How successful have these banner ads been for OfficeLinks.com?

A: It depends how you define success. The click-through rate for OfficeLinks.com on LinkExchange has averaged between 0.5% and 1.0%, which turns out to be about $1 per visitor.

Q: Isn't $1 a visitor pretty expensive?

A: It is, but advertising is expensive. This seems to be about right based on my experiences using direct mail in the offline world.

Q: What advice would you give to others who were considering banner ads?

A: The most important thing is to pick the right target audience. I noticed that my click-through rates were significantly higher when I use the targeting options on LinkExchange, rather than just choosing the "run-of-the-network" alternative. It costs more per impression, but the click-through rate is significantly higher.

Q: Do you use any offline advertising for OfficeLinks.com?

A: The only thing I have done so far is to get some business cards that prominently display the business name and offer a brief description of the Web site.

Q: Are you planning to do any more offline advertising?

A: In the future I might. But right now there are enough online advertising opportunities that I don't feel it's necessary. Obviously, if I had a bigger budget, I would definitely use offline advertising to build some brand awareness.

Online Advertising Resources

Adbility's Web Publishers' Advertising Guide (*www.adbility.com*)

This is Mark Welch's guide to online advertising, and includes numerous resources that you will find useful if you are planning to run a banner ad campaign, including comprehensive "how to" information and a list of service providers.

Ad Resource (*www.adresource.com*)

According to their About page, "Ad Resource is a listing of resources for Web advertising and marketing community. Web marketers can use the site to do research, build contacts, and keep up to date on the latest happenings in Internet advertising."

FreeLinks (*www.freelinks.org*)

As its name implies, FreeLinks.org has a wide variety of free products and services you can obtain on the Web. If you need some help designing a banner advertisement, FreeLinks has at least a dozen links to Web sites where you can create a professional-looking banner for free.

Quickbanner (*www.quickbanner.com*)

Quickbanner is "an easy to use, free tool which allows you to create professional-looking banners and icons quickly and easily."

WebSite 101 (*www.website101.com*)

WebSite 101 provides many useful tips and links for small business advertisers, including freebies such as banner generator, classified ads, Web resources, weekly Web tips, and daily cartoons.

Wilson Internet (*www.wilsonweb.com*)

Wilson Internet has a very complete library of articles to help you market your Web site, including a section devoted to "Banner Ad Design Tips."

Summary

Your key takeaway from this chapter should be that while banner advertising is more expensive than some of the other promotion methods outlined in earlier chapters, it is still an effective way to build or maintain traffic to your Web site. The other important thing to remember about banner advertising campaigns is that you can get them up and running much more quickly than their offline print counterparts.

Before you begin a banner ad campaign make sure you define your objectives. Decide whether you want to build brand name recognition or simply to get surfers to click and visit your Web site. These decisions will impact the message that is displayed on your banner ad. Finally, remember to add the words "click here . . . " to your banner, since research has shown that this will increase your click-through rate.

For more information on this topic, visit our Web site at www.businesstown.com

Making Your Web Site Pay for Itself Through Affiliate Programs

Topics covered in this chapter

- **Understanding how affiliate programs work**
- **Joining affiliate programs**
- **Creating affiliate links to post on your site**
- **Establishing your own affiliate program**

> If 1998 was the Year of the Portal in electronic commerce,
> 1999 may be the Year of the Affiliate.
>
> BOB TEDESCHI, THE *NEW YORK TIMES E-COMMERCE REPORT*

Affiliate programs provide another source of income for your online business.

Description of the LinkShare Affiliate Program (*www.linkshare.com*)

Affiliates choose to partner with merchants with whom they can be successful. The partnerships work like this: the affiliate puts links from the merchant on its site. These links market the merchant's goods or services on the affiliate's site. Site visitors who click through on the link are sent to a specified page of the merchant's site. It the visitor completes the action desired by the merchant (clicks on the link, fills out a form, buys something, etc.), the affiliate is compensated. LinkShare facilitates all aspects of the partnership and tracks all elements of the transaction.

An affiliate program is a way for you to begin generating additional revenue for your online business. These programs pay participants a percentage of sales, or a flat fee, for sales that originate on its Web site. For instance, if you joined the Dell Computer affiliate program, you would receive a percentage of sales that originate on your Web site. The sales process begins, or originates, when a visitor to your Web site clicks on a special hyperlink that transfers them to the Dell Computer Web site (or host site). If that visitor buys something from Dell Computer, like a PC, then you would receive a percentage of the sale.

One of the more challenging aspects of joining affiliate programs is creating and maintaining the hyperlinks between your Web site the host site. These links contain a special code that identifies you as a participant in the program, and are used to track the impressions, click-throughs, and sales you make for the host site. Although companies like LinkShare (*www.linkshare.com*) completely automate the "link-making" process, you still need to get this HTML code onto your Web pages. Additionally, because the hosting companies can change links or cancel their programs, you will have to spend some time maintaining these links.

The *New York Times* article that opened this chapter was really written from the perspective of companies that are thinking about creating their own affiliate programs. In the article, Bob Tedeschi says, "The biggest draw of affiliate programs is that merchants do not have to spend marketing dollars to acquire a customer until a purchase is actually made." If you were to create your own affiliate program, you could enlist other online businesses to help you sell your products and services. In this instance, you would pay affiliates a percentage of sales, or a flat fee, for every sale they made for your online business.

Understanding How Affiliate Programs Work

To review, an affiliate program establishes a business relationship between your business and another business, for which you will receive a percentage commission, or a fee, for the sales that you generate for the other business. In a sense, by joining an affiliate program you become an agent for another business and get a commission every time you sell something for that business. For instance, let's say that you joined an affiliate program that paid a 15-percent commission on every sale that you made. If you sell an item worth $100, you would receive a $15 commission from the affiliate program.

On the Web, affiliate programs work in much the same way. Your business would join an affiliate program being hosted by another business, or Web site, and you would receive a payment for every sale that could be attributed to your business, or Web site.

Affiliate programs can either be administered directly by a merchant, like Amazon.com, or be run through a third party, like LinkShare. For instance, if you wanted to join the Amazon.com affiliate program, you can go directly to the Amazon.com Web site and fill out their registration form. On the other hand, if you wanted to become a Dell Computer affiliate, you would sign up with LinkShare (*www.linkshare.com*) on their home page, since they run the Dell Computer affiliate program.

Affiliate Linking Arrangements

In order for your online business to participate in an affiliate program, you must place special hot-links or banners on your Web site that connect it with the other merchant's, or host's, Web site. Embedded within these links is a special code that identifies your business. This way, when someone clicks on the link on your Web site, the host can tell which Web site originated, or referred, the visitor.

> An affiliate program establishes a business relationship between your business and another business.

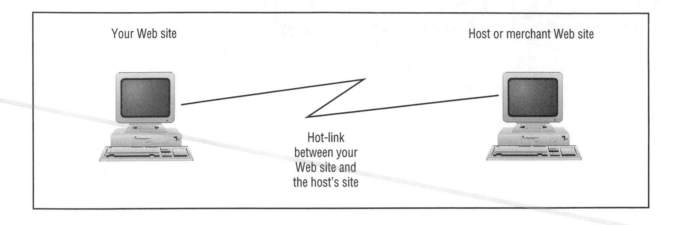

Your Web site

Host or merchant Web site

Hot-link
between your
Web site and
the host's site

> Affiliate links normally include text, e-mail, storefronts, individual products, and banners.

It is not unusual for a host to have thousands of affiliates, each of which refers visitors to its Web site. By using these special coded hot-links, the host can keep track of which Web site generated the referral, the number of impressions, the number of click-throughs, and the actual sales made by its individual affiliate members.

Affiliate programs normally have a few ways that participant sites can link back to the host site, including text, e-mail, storefronts, individual products, and banners.

TYPES OF LINKSHARE LINKS	DESCRIPTION
Textual/E-mail	Get maximum sales from these proven-to-be-effective and easy-to-use links.
Storefront	Easy-to-use links to a prefabricated page of hot products.
Individual Product	Recommend specific products to your visitors by linking directly to a particular product.
Banners/Images	Less effective but highly colorful graphical links.

Source: *www.linkshare.com*

According to LinkShare, textual and e-mail links to affiliate programs are more effective than the "highly colorful graphical links" used for banners and images.

Affiliate Program Commissions

The biggest benefit of joining affiliate programs is that it gives you the opportunity to generate additional revenue, or commission payments, from your Web site. The size of these payments varies from affiliate program to affiliate program, so you should take the time to understand how the individual programs work.

The following list is a sampling of the different types of commission structures offered by some of the affiliate programs available through LinkShare (*www.linkshare.com*). You will notice that both the fee structure and amount of payment differs significantly between affiliate programs.

From the list you can see that there are three types of commission structures: percent commission for items sold, flat fee for items sold, and a fee for simply generating click-throughs, or referrals. However, you cannot evaluate what your potential payments might be without comparing the different items (and their associated prices) offered under these affiliate commission structures. For instance, a plan that pays a 25-percent commission on a $10 item will generate a $2.50 ($10 x 0.25) commission payment. On the other

Sample affiliate commissions

- 25% commission
- 20% commission on selected goods
- 12% commission
- 7–10% commission
- 5% commission
- $10 flat fee on selected goods
- $5 flat fee
- $1 flat fee
- $0.10 per click-through

Sample Affiliate Agreement for Sparks.com (Paper Greeting Cards)

We are offering you a $1 flat fee on items purchased by visitors who are referred to us from your site.

Once you are approved for our program, you can use the code we supply to generate links from your site to ours. We offer you a variety of links and link types. Use your creativity and your knowledge of the people who come to your site to choose the types of links that will be most appealing and most likely to invite clicks. The more your links lead to sales on our site, the more money your site will earn.

You may create links to our site in the form of banners, textual, individual product, search box and store front. You may choose to use one or many of the links we provide, or you may create your own links. However, we will need to authorize any links that you create independently.

www.sparks.com

hand, an affiliate program that pays a 5-percent commission on a $100 item will generate a $5 ($100 x 0.05) commission payment. In this instance, the 5-percent commission is worth 100 percent more than the 25-percent commission!

Affiliate Program Terms and Conditions

In addition to understanding the commission structures for affiliate programs, you should also be aware of their legal terms and conditions. Most of these programs require that you "accept" their terms and conditions prior to joining. For instance, most companies include the following about "Web site suitability" in their terms and conditions.

Therefore, if your site promotes sexually explicit materials or violence, BizBuyer.com will not accept you into their affiliate program.

In addition to the terms and conditions that cover the content of your Web site, affiliate programs also dictate certain responsibilities that affiliates must adhere to. For instance, you will be required

> In addition to understanding the commission structures for affiliate programs, you should also be aware of their legal terms and conditions.

Sample of BizBuyer.com "Web site Content" Terms and Conditions

Unsuitable sites include, but are not limited to, those that:

- Promote sexually explicit materials
- Promote violence
- Promote discrimination based on race, sex, religion, nationality, disability, sexual orientation, or age
- Promote illegal activities
- Include "BizBuyer.com" or variations or misspellings thereof in their domain names
- Otherwise violate intellectual property rights; or
- Otherwise are considered inappropriate, unacceptable or offensive at BizBuyer.com's discretion.

Source: LinkShare (*www.linkshare.com*)

to use the format of their links as generated by the company or through a third party like LinkShare.

You might be asking yourself why a company does not want you to modify their links before you place them on your Web site. As mentioned earlier, some links created by affiliate companies are dynamic in nature, and actually generate impressions on their Web site, or the third party's site, when someone views your Web site. Unfortunately, these links can cause your Web pages to load very slowly. Therefore, some Web masters modify these links so that the only activity seen by the affiliate host Web site occurs when someone clicks on the links.

The other important area covered by affiliate program terms and conditions concerns commission payments. Normally these terms and conditions cover the "when" and "minimum" aspects of commission payments. For instance, the BizBuyer.com affiliate program states that you will only receive your eligible commission payments every quarter, and only then if your commission payments are in excess of $50.

> Many affiliate links on a single page in your Web site can slow performance.

Sample of BizBuyer.com "Responsibilities" Terms and Conditions

Affiliate's Responsibilities

- Affiliate will not alter or modify any link, graphic or banner ad of BizBuyer.com provided by BizBuyer.com or obtained through The LinkShare Network. Affiliate may post as many such links, graphics or banner ads as it likes on Affiliate's site.

- Affiliate will not generate false or dishonest memberships on BizBuyer.com. Only valid Qualifying Links will be tracked for purposes of determining referral fees that you may be eligible to receive.

- Affiliate agrees not to make any representations, warranties or other statements concerning BizBuyer.com, BizBuyer.com's site, any of BizBuyer.com's products or services, or BizBuyer.com's site policies, except as expressly authorized by this Agreement.

- Affiliate is responsible for notifying BizBuyer.com and The LinkShare Network of any malfunctioning of the supplied links, graphics and logos or other problems with Affiliate's participation in the performance of this Agreement. BizBuyer.com will respond promptly to all concerns upon notification by Affiliate.

Source: LinkShare (*www.linkshare.com*)

Sample of BizBuyer.com "Commission" Terms and Conditions

Commissions

- BizBuyer.com agrees to pay Affiliate the commission specified in this Agreement. To be eligible to earn a referral fee for a new BizBuyer.com member acquisition, the Customer must have accessed BizBuyer.com's site and registered as a new member via a Qualifying Link from the Affiliate's site to our site.

- A "Qualifying Link" is a link from Affiliate's site to BizBuyer.com's using one of the links, graphics and logos or any other URL provided by BizBuyer.com for use in The LinkShare Network if it is the last link to the BizBuyer.com's site that the Customer uses during a Session where the Customer becomes a registered member of BizBuyer.com. A "Session" is the period of time beginning from a Customer's initial contact with BizBuyer.com's site via a link from the Affiliate's site and terminating when the Customer returns to the BizBuyer.com's site via a link from a site other than Affiliate's site, the term of this Agreement expires or this Agreement is terminated.

- BizBuyer.com shall have the sole right and responsibility for processing new memberships made by Customers. Affiliate acknowledges that all agreements relating to services delivered to Customers shall be between BizBuyer.com and the Customer.

- All determinations of Qualifying Links and whether a commission is payable will be made by The LinkShare Network and will be final and binding on both BizBuyer.com and Affiliate.

- Unless otherwise stated in an Offer Addendum, we will pay you referral fees on a quarterly basis (a "quarter" is calculated on a calendar year basis for purposes of this Agreement). Approximately thirty (30) days following the end of each calendar quarter, we (or our designee, The LinkShare Network) will send you a check for the referral fees earned on our sales of Qualifying Products that were shipped during that quarter, less any taxes, shipping, returns and canceled orders. However, if the referral fees payable to you for any calendar quarter are less than $50.00, we will hold those referral fees until the total amount due is at least $50.00 or (if earlier) until this Agreement is terminated.

- If you become an Affiliate less than thirty (30) days prior to the end of a quarter, then any and all referral fees generated during that initial period shall be included in the next quarter for purposes of payment of those fees by BizBuyer.com.

Source: LinkShare
(*www.linkshare.com*)

If you are unsure whether your Web site meets the terms and conditions of an affiliate program, consult with an attorney. You definitely want to avoid any activities that might hold up your commission payments, or involve a legal battle.

Joining Affiliate Programs

There are essentially two ways to join an affiliate program: directly through a company, like Amazon.com, or through a third-party provider, like the LinkShare Network. The differences between these two methods include the way you will create links for your Web site and access to management reports. Although each method has its own benefits, it is generally easier to manage your affiliate memberships through a third-party provider than through individual companies.

In order to join affiliate programs, either directly or through a third party, your first requirement will be to complete an application form. Most of these applications will require some or all of the following information:

- Web site domain name ("www.yourbiz.com")
- Contact person
- Mailing address
- Phone and fax numbers
- Classification of site, such as small business or entertainment
- Taxpayer identification number

Note that you will be required to provide a taxpayer identification number when you join an affiliate program. This can either be your social security number or an employer identification number (EIN) issued by the federal government. The affiliate program will use this for tax reporting purposes whenever they issue you a commission check.

There are literally thousands of affiliate programs that you can join, each offering different types of products and services that you can sell for a commission.

> It is generally easier to manage your affiliate memberships through a third-party provider than through individual companies.

Sample Categories of Products and Services on LinkShare

Auto	Gift & Flowers
Business & Career	Health & Beauty
Clothing & Accessories	Hobbies & Collectibles
Computer & Electronics	Home & Living
Department Store	Internet & Online
Entertainment	Mature/Adult
Family	Office
Financial Services	Sports & Fitness
Food & Drink	Telecommunications
Games & Toys	Travel

> Third-party providers make it easier for you to join multiple affiliate programs.

Within each of these LinkShare categories there are a number of individual company affiliate programs that you can join. For instance, if you were thinking about joining affiliate programs that specialize in Games & Toys, you could offer products and earn commissions from companies such as Disney, CD Universe, iBaby, and Sandbox.net.

Joining Affiliate Programs Through Third-Party Providers

Some companies use a third party, such as LinkShare, to administer their affiliate programs. They do this to avoid the additional expenses associated with running their own affiliate program, and, especially for smaller companies, it gives their affiliate program greater exposure than it would normally get if they had to promote it themselves.

> After joining your first program and learning how to create the links, the process will essentially be the same for all programs that you join through the same third-party provider.

Third-party providers also give you two benefits. First, you don't have to learn how to create individual linking arrangements every time you join a new affiliate program. After joining your first program and learning how to create the links, the process will essentially be the same for all programs that you join through the same third-party provider. For instance, if you join the Dell Computer affiliate program through LinkShare and learn how to create the links to

Dell Computer, the process for joining other affiliate programs through LinkShare, such as Disney, is basically the same.

The other benefit of third-party providers is their ability to consolidate affiliate activity, such as impressions, click-throughs, and sales, into a single easy-to-use report. For instance, if you join five affiliate programs through LinkShare, you can see your Web site activity for all five of these affiliate programs in a single report. This is much easier than having to log into five separate affiliate programs, on five different Web sites, run by five different companies, and retrieve five individual reports.

> A benefit of third-party providers is their ability to consolidate affiliate activity, such as impressions, click-throughs, and sales, into a single easy-to-use report.

Popular Third-Party Providers of Affiliate Programs

THIRD-PARTY PROVIDER	WEB ADDRESS
Associate-It	*www.associate-it.com*
Be Free!	*www.befree.com*
LinkShare	*www.linkshare.com*
Refer-It	*www.refer-it.com*
Reporting.net (part of Be Free!)	*www.reporting.net*
RevenueAvenue (LinkExchange.com)	*www.linkexchange.com*
Webworker Top 10 List	*www.webworker.com/affiliates/top10w.html*

As you begin your search for appropriate affiliate programs to join, you will probably have to use more than one third-party provider, and even a few individual programs that have opted not to join these networks. For instance, you might join Barnes and Noble through Be Free!, Dell Computer through LinkShare, and Amazon.com through its self-administered program.

Joining Affiliate Programs That Are Self-Administered

At this point, many individual companies have not joined a third-party provider, like LinkShare, and still continue to administer their own affiliate programs. There is little difference between the way you join these self-administered programs and those run by third-party providers, other than you must sign up for each one individually.

Additionally, since there are no standards for creating affiliate linking arrangements, you will have to learn a separate process for every individual affiliate program you join.

Amazon.com is credited with being the pioneer of affiliate programs, and still runs its own program. However, you can now join the Amazon.com affiliate program through RevenueAvenue, which is part of LinkExchange (*www.linkexchange.com*). Probably for every affiliate program that is administered through a third party, there are three or four others that are self-administered. Your challenge is to locate self-administered programs that will produce commissions for your online business.

Begin your search for self-administered programs by visiting some of the following Web sites. Most of these sites provide a comprehensive directory of self-administered affiliate programs.

> Amazon.com is credited with being the pioneer of affiliate programs, and still runs its own program.

DIRECTORIES OF AFFILIATE PROGRAMS	WEB ADDRESS
AffiliateWorld Directory	*www.affiliateworld.com*
CashPile.com	*www.cashpile.com*
HowToWeb Affiliate Programs	*www.howtoweb.com*
New Concepts Marketing	*www.freeaffiliateprograms.com*
Referral Madness	*www.referralmadness.com*
ReveNews.com Affiliate Program Guide	*www.revenews.com/guide/*
Webworker Top 10 Affiliate Programs	*www.webworker.com/affiliates/top10.html*

The other way to locate self-administered programs is to simply search individual sites and look for something like "Click here to join our Affiliate program." You can also contact the site's Web master or marketing director to see if they currently offer, or plan to offer, an affiliate program.

Creating Affiliate Links to Post on Your Site

Once you have joined an affiliate program, you will need to create special links from your Web site to the host, or merchant, site. For example, if you wanted to become a Dell Computer affiliate, the first thing you would do is go to LinkShare and complete their application form. Once you become a member of LinkShare, you can apply for any of the affiliate programs that they manage, such as Dell Computer or Outpost.com.

Although the process for creating links between your site and a merchant's site varies from company to company, and from third-party provider to third-party provider, the general methodology is very similar. Essentially, you create a link from a page within your Web site to a page within a merchant's site. The link on your page is designed to entice visitors to click on it and buy the product or service shown on the merchant's page. You can visualize this linking arrangement as shown in the following diagram:

> The link on your page is designed to entice visitors to click on it and buy the product or service shown on the merchant's page.

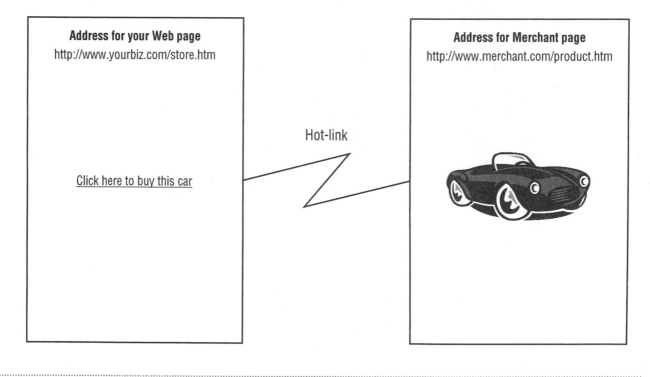

Your Web site

Merchant Web Site

Address for your Web page	Address for Merchant page
http://www.yourbiz.com/store.htm	http://www.merchant.com/product.htm

Click here to buy this car

Hot-link

The format of the "hot-link" between your Web site and the merchant's must include an identification number for your site. The format of these links varies greatly from one affiliate program to the next, but in the preceding example it might look something like this:

http://www.merchant.com/product/car/**yourbiz**

By including an identification number in the hot-link, the merchant knows who transported the visitor to their Web site. You should keep in mind that the merchant might have hundreds of links to the same page within their site from hundreds of different affiliates. This special identification number is used by the merchant to keep track of all affiliate activity.

The formats for these linking arrangements differ from company to company. For instance, when you join an affiliate program managed directly by the host company, such as Amazon.com, you will be assigned an affiliate identification number that must be included in your links back to Amazon.com.

In the example link between OfficeLinks.com and Amazon.com, there are two key pieces of information. The first piece identifies the page, or product, that is being linked to within the Amazon.com Web site (http://www.amazon.com/exec/obidos/ASIN/1564143694/). In this instance, OfficeLinks.com has a link to the book *Online Business Planning* within the Amazon.com site. The second piece of information is the OfficeLinks.com affiliate ID (officelinks) which is shown at the end of the product identifier.

This entire link is used by Amazon.com to track the affiliate activity of OfficeLinks.com. Every time a visitor to the OfficeLinks.com Web site clicks on this link, Amazon.com can tell where the visitor came from and what they bought on the Amazon.com site. It should be pointed out that even if the visitor that came from OfficeLinks.com decides not to buy *Online Business Planning*, but does buy other items on Amazon.com during the same session, OfficeLinks.com will still get a commission on the other items that the visitor buys from Amazon.com.

When you join an affiliate program that is managed by a third party such as LinkShare, the links are different from those used in the Amazon.com affiliate program. Below is an affiliate link between

---

The special affiliate links are used to track activity and sales from your Web site.

When you join an affiliate program managed directly by the host company, such as Amazon.com, you will be assigned an affiliate identification number that must be included in your links back to Amazon.com.

Sample of OfficeLinks.com Affiliate Link to Amazon.com

http://www.amazon.com/exec/obidos/ASIN/1564143694/officelinks

OfficeLinks.com and Dell Computer that was created through LinkShare.

The example link between OfficeLinks.com and Dell Computer, created through LinkShare, is different from the link to Amazon.com for a couple of reasons. First, the affiliate identification number (DpEqZt0MuZs) is completely different from the Amazon.com ID (officelinks), because LinkShare generates this ID automatically. Second, this link is more dynamic than the Amazon.com link, because the LinkShare link is activated every time someone visits the OfficeLinks.com Web page that contains the link. By using this dynamic linking arrangement, LinkShare is able track not only click-throughs, but also the number of impressions, or page views, generated by OfficeLinks.com.

At this point, if you are not familiar with affiliate linking arrangements, you may be thinking that these links are too complicated for you to implement on your Web site. However, in the case of Amazon.com, you simply need to locate the books, or other products, that you want to link to and add your affiliate ID to create the links. For LinkShare, the link generation process is completely automated and you only need to copy the HTML code from the LinkShare site to your Web page.

Most company-managed (Amazon.com) and third-party (LinkShare) affiliate programs provide plenty of advice and "how-to" information for their affiliates. You simply need to register for the programs that will benefit your Web site and test them out. In no time you will become an expert at creating these linking arrangements.

> **Sample of OfficeLinks.com Affiliate Link to Dell Computer (through LinkShare)**
>
> <a href="http://click.linksynergy.com/fs-in/stat?id=DpEqZt0MuZs&offerid=6548.27& subid=0"> <IMG border=0 alt="Be Direct 120" src="http://ad.linksynergy.com/fs-bin/show?id = DpEqZt0MuZs &bids= 6548.27&subid=0"></a>

> By creating your own affiliate program, you could enlist other online businesses to help you sell your products and services.

Establishing Your Own Affiliate Program

By creating your own affiliate program, you could enlist other online businesses to help you sell your products and services. ClickTrade, a third-party, service-provided LinkExchange (*www.linkexchange.com*) that helps you to create and manage your own affiliate program, states that "an affiliate program can increase your site traffic, create qualified leads or generate sales."

Before you can set up an affiliate program, you must decide whether you will run the program by yourself or use a third-party provider, how you are going to pay affiliates for sending prospects to your Web site, and what type of Web sites you will allow to participate in your affiliate program.

Using a Third-Party Provider or Running Your Own Affiliate Program

There is a lot of evidence to suggest that using a third-party provider, like ClickTrade or LinkShare, to create and manage your affiliate program is a better alternative than running your own affiliate program. For example, large companies, like Dell Computer and Avon products, with multimillion dollar marketing budgets, have opted to use a third party to manage their affiliate programs. Additionally, other companies, like OfficeMax, that initially ran their own affiliate programs have since handed their affiliate programs over to a third-party provider.

It is easy to imagine why these companies have decided to let someone else manage their affiliate programs. Creating special linking arrangements, commission payments, and activity reports for thousands of affiliates is a very time-consuming process. Also, if you run your own program, you will have to promote it (spend money on advertising) to get affiliates to join. The disadvantages of running your own affiliate program are normally outweighed by the fact that you can get an affiliate program up and running quickly and inexpensively with a third-party provider.

That being said, some of the real Internet innovators, like Amazon.com, still continue to run their own affiliate programs. By running your own affiliate program, you will have complete control over the linking arrangements, commission payments, and affiliates that participate in your program. Therefore, you should carefully evaluate the tradeoffs between third-party services that offer ease-of-use with the flexibility provided in running your own affiliate program.

> Creating special linking arrangements, commission payments, and activity reports for thousands of affiliates is a very time-consuming process.

Companies That Will Create and Manage Affiliate Programs

AFFILIATE PROGRAM THIRD-PARTY PROVIDERS	WEB ADDRESS
Be Free!	*www.befree.com*
ClickTrade (part of LinkExchange)	*www.clicktrade.linkexchange.com*
LinkShare	*www.linkshare.com*
Refer-It	*www.refer-it.com*

Before making a final decision on whether to use a third-party provider to create and manage your affiliate program, or running it yourself, you should consider the number of affiliates you are planning to sign up. If the answer is "as many as possible," a third-party provider is probably your best alternative. However, if you are only going to use a few highly targeted affiliates, you may want to run the program yourself.

Paying Your Affiliates

Your purpose for creating an affiliate program is to have affiliates help you sell the products and services on your Web site. In order to entice affiliates to join your program and help you with your marketing, you will need to pay them.

Each of these payment methods have their own advantages and disadvantages. From an affiliate perspective, the advantage of a "pay per click" payment method is that they will get paid for simply placing a link to your Web site on their Web site (assuming prospects actually click on it). Unfortunately for you, having someone click on a link to your site does not mean that you will get more sales. If an unscrupulous affiliate decides to heavily promote your link, you might have to pay mightily for thousands of unqualified prospects!

A better alternative for you is to pay only for qualified leads. By using the "pay per lead" program, you only have to pay affiliates when one of their prospects completes your application form or actually buys your products and services. Alternatively, you can view this method as the "flat fee" method.

One of the most popular payment methods employed by online retailers is the "pay per sale." By using this method you pay affiliates a percentage of the selling price. This entices affiliates to not only help you make sales, but also helps you sell higher ticket items. For instance, if you pay 10 percent of the selling price on a $500 item, an affiliate will get a $50 commission ($500 x 0.10 = $50).

Creating Terms and Conditions for Your Affiliates

After you decide on the method for paying your affiliates, you should turn your attention to any special terms and

Sample of ClickTrade Affiliate Payment Methods

- Pay per click: For driving traffic to your site. Ideal for advertising sponsored sites.

- Pay per lead: For developing prospects that you will later close either online or offline.

- Pay per sale: For generating revenues directly from your site.

Source: *www.clicktrade. linkexchange.com/ mpricing.htm*

One of the most popular payment methods employed by online retailers is the "pay per sale."

conditions that will be required for your affiliate program. You should decide what types of affiliates you want, and whether any types of affiliates (or Web sites) should be excluded from your affiliate program. If you use a third-party provider, like ClickTrade or LinkShare, some of these terms and conditions will already be predetermined.

Deciding on the types of affiliates you want and don't want is relatively straightforward. For instance, you might want to consider some form of exclusivity from your affiliate Web sites. For example, if you are going to sell flowers online, you may decide to only accept affiliates into your program that promise not join other "flower" affiliate programs, like FTD.com. Or you might be less exclusive and demand that on any page where your "flowers" link is displayed, there cannot be any other links to online "flower" merchants. Keep in mind that the more exclusive you make your affiliate program terms and conditions, the less likely you will have multiple participants.

> Instead of exclusivity, your main concern may be in the overall content of your affiliate Web sites.

Instead of exclusivity, your main concern may be in the overall content of your affiliate Web sites. Will you allow other Web sites that promote pornographic material or violence to be a part of your affiliate program? If you don't want these types of sites, or any others, make sure that your terms and conditions adequately reflect these restrictions.

Your terms and conditions should also reflect when and how often you will pay affiliates. Are you going to pay commissions on a monthly or quarterly basis? Are you going to include a minimum threshold that affiliates must meet before they will get paid? For instance, many programs require that affiliates earn at least $25 in commissions or fees before they will get paid.

Finally, before you hire an attorney to develop a list of terms and conditions for your affiliate program, review what your competitors are doing. Visit their online affiliate programs and review their terms and conditions. Additionally, if you are going to use a third-party service, review the terms and conditions they place on affiliates. For instance, some third-party services will not allow "adult" sites, even if you are catering to this market.

Establishing Affiliate Relationships for OfficeLinks.com

Q: Do you participate in any affiliate programs?

A: Yes. Many of the hot-links on the OfficeLinks.com home page are affiliate links to different companies, like Dell Computer, Beyond.com, and OfficeMax.

Q: How did you create these affiliate links?

A: First of all I joined LinkShare. Then I registered OfficeLinks.com with some of the affiliate programs that participate in their network. After that, once the site had been approved, I just followed their directions to create the links.

Q: Was it difficult to create these links?

A: Creating the affiliate links with LinkShare is simple. You just select the type of link you want, like text or a banner, and LinkShare creates the links automatically. The hard part, at least the first time I tried it, was getting the links onto my Web site.

Q: How come it was so difficult to get these links onto your Web site?

A: LinkShare creates HTML links that you need to copy from their site onto your site. So the copying and pasting part is very straightforward, but the actual placement on my Web pages was a little trickier. Since I didn't know HTML, I wasn't exactly sure how to get them into my Web using Microsoft FrontPage 98.

Q: Did you ever figure it out?

A: Finally, after a little experimentation, I did. FrontPage uses an editor that basically helps you to create Web pages—without learning HTML. You actually need to bypass this editor and work with your pages in HTML. Once you can view the HTML code, you simply paste the LinkShare code right into that page.

Q: Besides the affiliate programs you joined through LinkShare, have you tried any others?

A: Absolutely. In fact, I was a member of the Amazon.com affiliate program before I even knew about LinkShare. I've also joined a few other individual company programs, like iPrint.

Q: What's the main difference between LinkShare and the individual affiliate programs?

A: LinkShare makes it much easier to manage a bunch of these programs all at once. You only need to log into LinkShare once, and you can see the activity for all of the affiliate programs at once. Also, you don't have to remember any special formatting to create the links, since LinkShare takes care of that for you.

Q: Have you generated any commissions from your affiliations?

A: Yes. But I've only gone above the minimum so far in one program—meaning I haven't generated enough commissions to get above the quarterly threshold for the other programs. In the next few months or so I should get commission checks from other companies.

Q: It sounds like you're not getting rich from affiliate programs?

A: That's true. But as its been said before, "every little bit counts."

Online Affiliate Marketing Program Resources

ClickTrade (*www.clicktrade.linkexchange.com*)
ClickTrade, part of Microsoft LinkExchange (*www.linkexchange.com*), is "a Web-based service for advertisers and direct marketers who want to set up an affiliate program for their Web site and for site owners who want to earn cash by joining affiliate programs." Their home page also states that you can sign up as a ClickTrade member and create an affiliate program in "about five minutes."

LinkShare (*www.linkshare.com*)
LinkShare describes itself as "the worldwide leader in affiliate marketing programs for companies doing business on the Web," and boasts such members as Dell Computer, Disney, Avon, and Outpost.com. You can use LinkShare to join affiliate programs and to help you create and manage your own program.

Make Money Without Inventory (*www.techweb.com/smallbiz/howto990226intro.html*)
This guide, published by CMPnet, has a seven-step description of affiliate marketing programs that includes Understand Affiliate Programs, Build an Ad-Friendly Site, Join a Book Program, Join the LinkShare System, Find Other Programs, Create the Ads, Conclusion.

New Concepts Marketing: Affiliate Program Directory (*www.freeaffiliateprograms.com*)
On this site you will find a comprehensive guide to affiliate programs that are categorized as follows: Art & Media, Business, Electronic, Fashion, Gifts/Specialty, Health/Beauty, Toys/Games, Automotive, Computers, Entertainment, Food/Drink, Home/Family, Sports, and Travel.

Refer-It.com (*www.refer-it.com*)

Refer-it.com is "the definitive directory of affiliate and referral programs on the Internet." On their home page you can search through more than 1,000 affiliate programs in categories ranging from Accessories to Women. Additionally, the Refer-it.com database provides a brief description of affiliate programs and commission rates.

Webworker Top 100 Affiliates Directory (*www.webworker.com/affiliates/directory.html*)

Webworker provides numerous directories on its Web site, including a few specifically related to affiliate programs, like the "Top 100 Affiliates Directory." You can access their listing by three major categories (Merchandise, Food and Drink, and Services), and by sub-category from A to Z.

Summary

This final chapter was written to show you how you can supplement your online income. Through affiliate programs, you can earn commissions by selling the goods and services of other online merchants. Most large business-to-consumer Web sites, like Amazon.com and Disney, have affiliate programs that will pay you a commission whenever you refer a customer to their respective Web sites.

You can also set up your own affiliate program to get other online merchants to help you with your sales. No matter whether you join affiliate programs or set up your own, it is usually easier to work through third-party providers than trying to do it all yourself. Third-party providers have standardized many of the process, reporting, and payment methods to make it easier for you to work with multiple programs at once.

For more information on this topic, visit our Web site at www.businesstown.com

Glossary

ActiveX

ActiveX, developed by Microsoft, gives you the capability to add controls to your Web site, like scroll bars, drop down menus, and radio buttons.

Once you add these controls to your Web pages, then they can be downloaded and used by Web browsing software.

Affiliate Program

An affiliate program offers you a way to make money for your online business by advertising for another online business. In their simplest form, affiliate programs establish a business relationship between your business and another business, where you will receive a percentage, or a fee, for the sales that you generate for the other business. In a sense, by joining an affiliate program, you become an agent for another business and get a commission every time you sell something for that business.

Announce Sites

Announce sites were created to let surfers know about new Web sites being added to the Internet, and also gave marketers another way to promote their sites. Announce sites are a hybrid of press releases, and list new Web sites, fresh articles, and online developments in general.

Auto-Posting Service

An auto-posting service automatically notifies multiple search engines and directories simultaneously that you have created a new Web site on the Internet.

Bandwidth

Bandwidth is the measure of bits that a connection to the Internet can carry in a certain amount of time. Think of bandwidth as being similar to the size of a water pipe. The larger the water pipe, the more water it can carry in a specific period of time. Common measurements for bandwidth are bits per second (bps) and megabits per second (Mbps).

Banner Advertisement

Banner ads are the graphic images that appear on many Web pages, usually in rectangular boxes of varying sizes, and are designed to promote specific products and services.

Bit (or BInary digiT)

Every computer uses an instruction set that is composed of a series of "bits" or "on-off" signals that are usually represented by a "1" or a "0." A bit can be thought of as a single instruction that tells a computer processor whether it is "on" or "off." Think of this like the relationship between a light bulb and a light switch—when the switch is up, the light is on, and when it is down, the light is off. A computer language combines a series of "bits" into "bytes" and provides an instruction set that tells a computer processor what to do.

Business Plan

A business plan is a document that describes for investors how your proposed venture is going to make money. The U.S. Small Business Administration recommends that the body of your business plan be divided into four distinct sections, including the description of the business, the marketing plan, the financial management plan, and the management plan.

Byte (or 8 bits)

A byte is composed of 8 bits or "on-off" signals. You can think of a byte as being the computer representation for a letter, like "A," a number like "7," or an instruction to multiply two numbers, like "3 x 6."

Cable Modem

A cable modem is a device that connects your computer to the Internet through the cable television network infrastructure, or over the cable lines. Once this service becomes widely available, you will be able to establish a high speed 2Mbps (Million bits per second) connection to the Internet for about the same price as your dial-up service.

Click-Through

A click-through happens when someone clicks on your banner advertisement (being shown on another Web site) and is transported to your Web site.

Click-Through Rate

The click-through rate measures the percentage of prospective customers that respond to an online banner advertisement. To calculate this percentage, divide the number of click-throughs by the number of impressions.

Common Gateway Interface (CGI)

CGI specifies how information is transferred between a server on the World Wide Web and a computer program. If a Web host provides CGI capability, it will be able to "talk" to any computer program that conforms to the CGI specification.

Content

Content consists of the text, sound, and pictures that visitors read, hear, and see on a Web site.

Control Panel

The control panel provided by your Web hosting service gives you the capability to view the activity on your Web site, change e-mail information, set up autoresponders, and set passwords.

Demographic Variables

Demographic variables define a human population by their age, geographic location, gender, race, education, occupation, or other common characteristics.

Dial-Up Access

Dial-up access connects your computer to an Internet service provider (ISP), like America Online, through a modem and a telephone line. Since dial-up connections to the Internet use regular phone lines, the quality and data speeds are limited. Typical speeds for this type of connection range between 9.2Kbps (Kilobits per second) to a maximum of 56Kbps (Kilobits per second).

Digital Subscriber Line (DSL)

A service provided by your local phone company or ISP that connects you to the Internet. Like dial-up access and ISDN, DSL is provided over copper phone lines, but it is much faster. DSL can download data into your home or office at speeds up to 32Mbps (Million bits per second), and take uploads in excess of 1Mbps. DSL is also more expensive than dial-up service and requires special equipment to be installed in your home or office.

Domain Mail Forwarding

Domain mail forwarding gives you the capability to have e-mail addressed to your Web site domain forwarded to another e-mail address, like your dial-up e-mail account.

Domain Name

Your domain name, or "www.yourbiz.com," is your Internet Web address. By using your domain name, anyone in the world connected to the Internet can come and visit your online business and purchase your products and services.

DS1

DS1 service, also known as T-1 Carrier, is another offering from your local phone company or ISP that can give you a faster connection to the Internet. A DS1 combines 24 individual channels, each at 64Kbps (Kilobits per second), to provide a data speed of 1.544Mbps (Million bits per second).

E-Commerce

E-commerce describes the way business is conducted over the Internet. Although e-commerce is normally associated with credit card processing online, e-commerce is more general and provides for a multitude of online business functions, such as customer service, order processing, and auction technologies.

Electronic Wallets

Electronic wallets store encrypted credit card numbers on a customer's computer that only need to be entered once. When a customer makes a purchase from a participating seller's Web site, the encrypted credit card information is transferred from the customer to the seller, and then from seller to a bank.

File Transfer Protocol (FTP)

FTP is a protocol that is used to send files over the Internet.

Frequently Asked Questions (FAQs)

FAQs are a common set of questions that are normally asked by different visitors to your Web site. Depending on your business model, these might concern warranties, registration profiles, returning merchandise, or directions to your offline business. These Frequently Asked Questions (FAQs), and their associated answers, should be placed on a separate page in your Web site.

Gigabits per Second (Gbps)

Gigabits per second are a measure of the bandwidth, or data transfer rate, for a connection to the Internet. A gigabit is equivalent to one trillion bits.

Gigabytes (GB)

A Gigabyte is equal to one trillion bytes of electronic information.

Graphic Interchange Format (GIF)

Developed by CompuServe, GIF images are very popular for displaying simple images, cartoons, text graphics, and logos. GIFs use a special compression technology that makes them smaller and load faster.

Hit

A hit is recorded every time your Web host's disk drive spins into action and retrieves a file associated with your Web site.

Home Page

A home page is the first page in your Web site, and the one that is displayed when a user enters your domain name in their Web browser.

Hyper Text Markup Language (HTML)

HTML is the computer language used to create Web pages on the Internet. This language uses a special set of "tags" to create Web pages that can be read by Web browsers like Microsoft Internet Explorer and Netscape Navigator.

Image File Format

These file formats specify how images are displayed on Web pages, and include GIF, JPEG, and PNG.

Impressions

A page impression, or page view, happens every time you successfully pull up a Web page in your browser.

Integrated Services Digital Network (ISDN)

ISDN is a service provided by your local phone company or ISP that allows you to connect to the Internet. The "Integrated" in ISDN means that this service has the capability to combine voice, video, and data over the copper phone lines running into your home or office. ISDN is normally set up to provide a data speed of 64K but can be configured to run at twice that speed, or 128K per second.

Internet

The Internet is the largest network of computers in the world.

Internet Service Provider (ISP)

An ISP provides you with virtually unlimited access to the Internet by connecting your PC to their network through ordinary copper phone lines.

InterNIC

A database managed by Network Solutions that contains all the domain names within the dot-com, dot-org, and dot-net extensions.

Joint Photographic Experts Group (JPEG)

JPEG is an image file format that is best when you want to display photographs on your site, or other images that have many color and tone variations.

Keywords

Keywords provide single word descriptive information about your Web site. They are used by search engines and directories to index your site in their database.

Kilobits per Second (Kbps)

Kilobits per second are a measure of the bandwidth, or data transfer rate, for a connection to the Internet. A Kilobit is equivalent to 1,000 bits.

Kilobyte (KB)

A Kilobyte is equal to 1,000 bytes of electronic information.

Market Segmentation

Market segmentation is the process of dividing larger markets into smaller, and more manageable, groups of prospects and customers.

Megabits per Second (Mbps)

Megabits per second are a measure of the bandwidth, or data transfer rate, for a connection to the Internet. A Megabit is equivalent to one million bits.

Megabyte (MB)

A Megabyte is equal to one million bytes of electronic information.

Merchant Account

A merchant account is a special type of account that allows you to accept credit cards. A merchant account acts as the intermediary between your business bank account and your customer's credit card account. Think of it as a clearinghouse for credit card transactions. Money is transferred from your customer's credit card account, to the merchant account, and then finally to your business bank account.

Merchant Account Provider (MAP)

A MAP is a financial institution that offers merchant account services.

Message Board

A message board allows your visitors to post messages, queries, and comments on your Web site.

META Tags

META tags are part of the HTML instruction set, and allow you to include a description and keywords about your Web site. META tags are often used by search engines to index your site in their database.

Niche Marketing

Niche marketing, or target marketing, is the process of identifying a similar set of prospects through demographic or psychographic variables and then creating specific marketing programs to meet their needs.

Page View

A page view, or page impression, happens every time you successfully pull up a Web page in your browser.

Paid Subscription Sites

A paid subscription site requires that you pay a fee in order to view the contents on the Web site. It is analogous to a magazine subscription in the offline world.

POP E-Mail

POP e-mail accounts receive e-mail on your Web host's server, as opposed to your dial-up account. E-mail sent to the POP would stay there until you read it.

Portable Network Graphics (PNG)

PNG is an image file format that combines some of the best qualities of GIFs and JPEGs, but cannot be viewed by older browser versions. At some point they should replace the GIF format.

Portal Web Site

A portal Web site is a gateway, or directory, to other Web sites on the Internet. Yahoo! and AltaVista are Internet portals.

Post Office Protocol (POP)

Post Office Protocol defines how e-mail is retrieved from an e-mail server. There are two versions of this protocol: the newer POP3, which does not require SMTP to send messages; and the older POP2, which does require SMTP to send messages.

Practical Extraction and Report Language (Perl)

Perl is a very popular text programming language developed by Larry Wall that is often used for writing CGI scripts.

Psychographic Variables

Psychographics identify groups of consumers in terms of their needs, or motives, and are not usually as widely available as consumer demographic variables.

Reciprocal Links

A reciprocal linking agreement means that you will put a link to someone else's Web site on your Web site, if they reciprocate, and place a link to your Web site on theirs.

Search Engine

A search engine allows you to search millions of Web pages by particular keywords or phrases. Yahoo! and AltaVista are two popular search engines.

Secure Sockets Layer (SSL)

SSL was developed by Netscape and is a protocol for transmitting encrypted documents over the Internet. SSL establishes a secure connection been your customer's computer and your Web host's server, so that all information transmitted over the connection is secure.

Shopping Cart

A shopping cart system gives your customers a convenient way to buy multiple items from your online store during the same session. It is better than the traditional "grocery cart" system because it updates the shopping list and total price every time something is placed in the cart.

Spam

Spam is unsolicited e-mail. In the offline world it is equivalent to junk mail.

T-1 Carrier

T-1 Carrier, also known as DS1 service, is another offering from your local phone company or ISP that can give you a faster connection to the Internet. A T-1 combines 24 individual channels, each at 64Kbps (Kilobits per second), to provide a data speed of 1.544Mbps (Million bits per second).

Target Marketing

Target marketing, or niche marketing, is the process of identifying a similar set of prospects through demographic or psychographic variables and then creating specific marketing programs to meet their needs.

Theme

A theme provides every page in your Web site with a similar "look and feel."

Top-Level Domain

Top-level domains include dot-com, dot-net, and dot-org.

Unique Visitors

A unique visitor is a single individual who views at least one page on your Web site.

Web Hosting

Web hosting is a computer server that houses, or hosts, your Web site on the Internet.

Web Site

A Web site consists of multiple Web pages that fall under the same domain name and that can be accessed from the home page.

What You See Is What You Get (WYSIWYG)

WYSIWYG is a term used to describe computer software applications that produce on-screen representations of what the finished product will look like.

Index

About OfficeLinks.com

I just wanted to let you know that I thought your site [OfficeLinks.com] was very useful and sent a link to it to my 100 novice website owner clients.
    Good Information!

–BLAKE E. DOWEN, THEDOTCOMBIZ WEB DESIGN
HTTP://WWW.THEDOTCOMBIZ.COM

OfficeLinks.com (*your small business network for success*) is a Web site for small business owners and entrepreneurs that I created early in 1999 over the course of thirty days. Although the site has grown significantly since that time, I would like you to know that I still maintain it myself using commonly available software tools and services.

OfficeLinks.com has plenty of information to help individuals like you to create and market successful online businesses. For instance, you can find information and resources that will show you how to:

- Create an online business plan
- Select a great domain name
- Set-up a *free* e-commerce site (online store)
- Advertise to a worldwide audience
- Design banner ads for higher click-through rates
- Find easy-to-use software tools
- Get listed in popular search engines and directories
- Join affiliate programs to make a little extra money

As you embark on your mission to establish an online business and identity of your own, I would like to impart the following guiding principle that I've learned since creating OfficeLinks.com and writing this book:

Although the Internet is constantly changing, as new Web sites and technologies emerge daily, the basic principles of business and marketing still apply–you will only make money by providing information, products, and services that are useful for your target audience.

Bob Gorman
RTGorman@officelinks.com

Also available from Adams Media

STREETWISE BOOKS

Learn step-by-step how to build customer loyalty into your Web site strategy!

**Relationship Marketing
on the Internet**

$17.95, ISBN 1-58062-255-0

Repeat customers are your most profitable customers. But how do you create and implement a customer-focused strategy for the Web? *Streetwise Relationship Marketing on the Internet* is filled with creative, low-cost ideas to turn browsers into loyal customers.

Whether you have an existing Web business or are considering starting one, this book will give you the tools you need to:

◆ Increase traffic to your site
◆ Create a positive customer service experience
◆ Develop a site that customers will return to again and again

Also available in this series:

**Motivating & Rewarding
Employees**
$17.95
ISBN 1-58062-130-9

Small Business Start-Up
$17.95
ISBN 1-55850-581-4

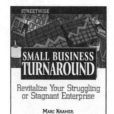

Do-It-Yourself Advertising
$17.95
ISBN 1-55850-727-2

**Small Business
Turnaround**
$17.95
ISBN 1-58062-195-3

Independent Consulting
$17.95
ISBN 1-55850-728-0

Available wherever books are sold.

For more information, or to order, call 800-872-5627
or visit www.adamsmedia.com

Adams Media Corporation, 260 Center Street, Holbrook, MA 02343

FIND MORE ON THIS TOPIC BY VISITING
BusinessTown.com
The Web's big site for growing businesses!

☑ **Separate channels on all aspects of starting and running a business**

☑ **Lots of info on how to do business online**

☑ **1,000+ pages of savvy business advice**

☑ **Complete web guide to thousands of useful business sites**

☑ **Free e-mail newsletter**

☑ **Question and answer forums, and more!**

businesstown.com